WALKING SWITZERLAND THE SWISS WAY

Walking
SWITZERLAND
the
Swiss Way

FROM

Vacation Apartments, Hotels, Mountain Inns, and Huts

MARCIA and PHILIP LIEBERMAN

THE MOUNTAINEERS/SEATTLE

The Mountaineers: Organized 1906 "... to explore, study, preserve, and enjoy the natural beauty of the Northwest."

7   6   5   4   3
8   7   6   5   4

Published by The Mountaineers
1011 S.W. Klickitat Way, Suite 107, Seattle, WA 98134

Published simultaneously:
    In Canada by Douglas & McIntyre Ltd.
        1615 Venables Street
        Vancouver, B.C. V5L 2H1
    In the United Kingdom
        by Cordee, 3a DeMontfort St.
        Leicester, England LE1 7HD

Manufactured in the United States of America

Edited by Connie Bourassa-Shaw
Designed by Shawn Lewis
Cover design by Elizabeth Watson
Maps by Harry Mourachian
Photos by Philip Lieberman

Library of Congress Cataloging in Publication Data

Lieberman, Marcia, 1936-
        Walking Switzerland--the Swiss way.

        Includes index.
        1. Hiking--Switzerland--Alps, Swiss--Guide-books.
    2. Tourist camps, hotels, etc.--Switzerland--Alps,
    Swiss--Guide-books. 3. Switzerland--Description and
    travel--1945-   --Guide books.   I. Lieberman, Philip.
    II. Title.
    GV199.44.S9L53   1987   914.94'70473   87-12350
    ISBN 0-89886-137-3 (pbk.)

Cover photo: The Unterer Theodul Gletscher flows from between the Breithorn (left) and Klein Matterhorn (right) in this view from the Gornergrat.

Frontispiece: Trail to Schynige Platte, 500 meters from the Weber Hütte Gast Stübli

To Benjamin and Daniel Lieberman, *for the happiest summers of our lives.*

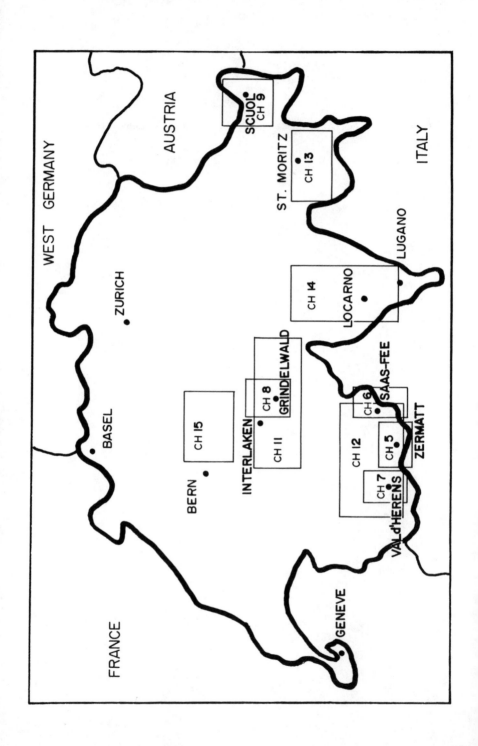

Contents

Overleaf: Sgraffito (folk art house design) in the Lower Engadine village of Ardez

Acknowledgments

We are grateful to a number of people who helped us with this book. Lois Atwood read early drafts and provided some invaluable suggestions and insights. Luther and Sara Hill generously shared with us their incomparable knowledge of Swiss walking routes. Barbara Ginzburg helped us with German translations. Our Swiss friends Kurt Raaflaub and Theo Meyer patiently answered many questions, and we owe special thanks to Erika Faisst for her helpful information. We also wish to thank our editors, Ann Cleeland and Connie Bourassa-Shaw. Finally, we are deeply grateful to our friends in Zermatt, Rony and Stephanie Inderbinen and Edmund and Trudi Biner, for many years of warm friendship. We are particularly indebted to Rony Inderbinen, Bergführer, for his patience as a teacher and his skill as a guide.

Farmer's daughter at a high alp in the Bernese Oberland

Introduction

The Furggtal is a wild, beautiful, deserted valley in the Swiss Alps. Narrow and long, the valley is scooped from curving rock walls descending from the Furggen Glacier. Below the rock are meadows and a clear stream flows through green banks. At the head of the valley stands a little farm; after that, there's nothing but rock and grass and water for 7 kilometers as the valley floor rises to the Antrona Pass and the Italian border. If you chance to notice them or know where to look, some of the stones look different: upright in the ground and closely set, like cobbling. These are the only remaining traces of the medieval road from the time when the Antrona Pass was a primary route for the import of salt from Italy. You can spend the day rambling in this wild valley or climb to the pass, and then walk down to the town of Saas-Fee for fondue or raclette, a bottle of Fendant—the dry white wine of the region—and a slice of apfel kuchen.

In a neighboring valley, from a mountain shoulder called Höhbalmen, you can sit in a meadow and see a vast region of ice, snow, and rock, of forest and meadow: fifteen mountains (including the Matterhorn) each over 4,000 meters, three massive glaciers and a dozen small ones. You don't need to trek in for three days to get to Höhbalmen; you don't need a mule or a 50-pound backpack. It's a 3 hour 30 minute climb with a 1000-meter ascent from Zermatt.

All the alpine splendor of Switzerland is accessible to hikers. Moreover, a walking vacation in Switzerland is within the physical capability of most people. In this book, we explain how you can tailor a walking vacation to your own abilities and make your holiday as strenuous or as gentle as you wish. This is the Swiss way.

You can rent a vacation apartment by the week and use it as a base for day trips. This is an excellent way to hike with children. These apartments are quite inexpensive, and the fact that you can prepare meals at home makes this an economical way to spend a family vacation. On a walking tour, you move on each day to a new place or spend a couple of nights at one village or mountain inn and explore the region for a few days. The excellent Swiss transportation system enables you to link "base camps" together without having to walk every portion of the route. We explain how to find and rent such an apartment, and we suggest numerous walking tours and day trips in various parts of Switzerland, including ones that are quite unknown to most Americans.

There are advantages to walking Switzerland the Swiss way with your family or friends rather than signing up with a hiking tour group. With a tour group, not only does the leader select the itinerary, but he or she also sets the pace, which can be an uncomfortable, relentless one. Moreover, you can arrange your vacation yourself for one-third the cost. The purpose of our book is to give you the information and confidence to plan your own trip.

Switzerland is a matchless center for walking. The variety of scenery ranges from the great Alps to the lower foothills to gentle, rolling farmland. Every canton (state) is laced with marked trails. More than any other country in the world, Switzerland is developed for walking. And its temperate climate makes the country ideal for walking (it's less rainy than the British Isles, Austria, or Scandinavia, cooler than Spain or Greece).

A transportation network of buses, trains, and lifts makes every district, every village easily accessible to walkers of varying ages and levels of energy. And it isn't hard to find reasonably priced hotels and simple inns. If you're actually looking for luxury, there are also elegant country hotels. If you like walking but don't care for camping, you can find hotels, mountain inns, huts and farms that can provide overnight shelter along the routes.

For cultural variety Switzerland offers visitors four linguistic and ethnic sectors—German, French, Italian, and Romansch—and cities such as Bern, Lucerne, and Lugano can easily be visited during walking tours.

Every country has its own approach—its ethos—for hiking, based on cultural as well as physical conditions. The Swiss approach is pragmatic: a clear reflection of the Swiss style and character. The Swiss hike and climb for the beauty of the mountains and the love of the exercise. To the Swiss, a vacation is a vacation, not a test of your will or a ritual of purification. The key to the Swiss approach is to make sensible use of all available options. Cable cars, buses, funiculars, and trains can help you gain altitude and distance and enable families with young children and older people to walk portions of some of the grandest routes. For each route in this book we give precise information about where you can find cable cars or buses to make the trip less strenuous or to save time; conversely, we provide those who prefer a more rigorous hike with the walking instructions for those segments.

One of the striking aspects of hiking in Switzerland—if you can tear your eyes away from the mountains—is the age range of the hikers you see.

*The campanile (bell tower) of a village church on
the Strada Alta Leventina near Calonico*

Men and women in their sixties, seventies, and even eighties are out
hiking on alpine trails. There are also families with children, the little
ones sometimes held on leads fastened around their waists or to small chest
harnesses. Descending from the Corvatsch in the Upper Engadine, we
once encountered a blind man hiking with his dog and a sighted friend.
Another time, on a trail about an hour above Zermatt we came upon a
one-legged man, resting on two crutches, chatting and laughing with another hiker. After their first hiking trip in Switzerland, some older friends
told us happily, "One of the things we loved was that there was always
someone older—and fatter—than us on the trail!"

Another distinctive feature of the Swiss approach is that the Swiss
don't camp at night. When hiking through the Alps they sleep at a hut,
inn, or hotel, where they get their evening meal and breakfast. This
means that you never have to carry a heavy pack with sleeping and cooking paraphernalia. It also protects the fragile alpine environment from the
campers who would be strewn about the country with numerous tents and
cooking sites. (Campgrounds are available in many towns, but these are
used by motor tourists, not hikers on walking tours.) A day's walk will al-

ways bring you to a village, and there are numerous huts and mountain inns along these routes, so you can often divide your walking tour into sections. For each route, we indicate where you can stop for the night.

The superb Swiss transportation network and the small size of the country present hikers with still other choices not available in North America. Train and bus routes cover the country, and service—astonishing to the American visitor—is frequent. You can spend most of your time in the mountains and keep your passage through cities to a minimum. But if you wish, you can combine mountain walking with city visits, using the train and bus routes that cover the country. One year, for example, we walked from Grindelwald over a rather wild, relatively unused mountain pass to Brienz, where we caught a train to Bern. The contrast was extraordinary: during the day we roamed over a high, virtually deserted plateau set among great towers of rock, then descended to meadows and farms, and in the evening dined in a restaurant in the arcades of Bern.

You can easily plan a trip with alternating visits to cities and alpine regions. The rail and bus network is so efficient that if bad weather settles in, you can—usually within a few hours—go to a town, visit a museum, perhaps hear a concert. You will be welcome at good hotels in Bern and Zurich in your hiking boots and pack because of the Swiss social approval of hiking.

There are historical reasons for the wide availability of mountain inns, village hotels, and lifts. Switzerland is an old country and was for a long time a poor one, a farming country, so the Swiss actually live on the slopes of their mountains. For longer than anyone knows, the Swiss have grazed their cattle and driven their sheep as high as the grass will grow. As a result, there are villages and summer farming communities—the word alp actually means a summer farm or pasture—clustered at the foot of the great mountains. Some of the most beautiful walking trails follow the ancient routes and passes that once connected one village, one valley, with another. A few of these places are now virtually abandoned, and these empty valleys have a special, haunting beauty. The famous mountain chains—the area of the Matterhorn and Monte Rosa, of the Eiger, Mönch, and Jungfrau, and numerous other areas—have very old villages clustered at their bases. And wherever there's a village, there's an inn.

In this book, we suggest two ways to go hiking in Switzerland: (1) using a vacation apartment as a base for day trips and (2) walking from point to point on an extended tour. If you have time, you can combine these two ways of walking in Switzerland. Rent an apartment for one or two weeks, get accustomed to the country and get into condition. Then, feeling fit and also more adventurous, go off for a few days, a week or longer on a walking tour.

How to Use This Book

This book is organized into three parts. Part I, Switzerland for Walkers, gives practical advice and information on conditions and customs in Switzerland. Chapter 1, Travel Basics, provides information about hotel accommodations, the Swiss transportation system, Swiss languages, the weather, and other general topics. Chapter 2, Walking Tips, gives advice about how to condition yourself for alpine hiking, what pace to take, and what to pack. It also offers tips on buying food and supplies, an explanation of the Swiss trail sign system, and a review of safety rules and suggestions. Chapter 3, The Alpine Environment, gives a brief background of Swiss environmental law and concerns and points out what the hiker needs to know about Swiss law and customs, as they pertain to the alpine region.

Part II, Day Hikes from a Vacation Apartment, explains how to find and rent a vacation apartment in an alpine village and offers descriptions of five villages or alpine centers: Zermatt, Saas-Fee, the Val d'Hérens, Grindelwald, and the Lower Engadine. We then list a full range of day hikes that can be taken from each of these five alpine centers.

Part III, Walking Tours between Hotels, Mountain Inns, and Huts, presents a selection of routes for extended point-to-point tours, on which you stay in a different village hotel, mountain inn, or hut every night. Sometimes, however, you may spend more than one night in the same place in order to hike side trips in the area, and then move on. We describe extended tours in the Bernese Oberland, the Valais, the Upper Engadine, and the Ticino. We have also included a chapter on the Emmental, a pastoral region of family farms where you can walk from village to village and from farm to farm.

Walk Headings

For each walk in this book we provide a brief list of basic information to give you the difficulty, distance, elevation, and time measures of that particular route.

Rating code. Each route is rated in terms of how technically difficult and how physically demanding it is. Though none of the routes we describe are considered technical climbs, some involve such conditions as descent on scree (loose rock), traverse on snow, or walking on narrow paths with great exposure ("exposure" means simply a sharp vertical drop below you). An *easy route* is a short, well-graded trail with little ascent—about 1 to 2 hours of walking and 300 meters of ascent. A *moderate* route has a medium length and ascent—about 3 to 4 hours of walking and a 600–700 meter ascent. A *strenuous* route is long, with a considerable ascent, steep sections, and the possibility of exposed sections of narrow trail, scree, snow traverses, etc. These are typically 6 to 8 hour walks involving ascents of 1000 meters or more. A *very strenuous* route involves long distances with some difficulties that approach a technical climb.

These ratings are based on normal conditions for the route, but in bad conditions such as fog, snow, or ice, the ratings should be upgraded. A strenuous route might well become very strenuous or should be avoided altogether.

Distance and type of walk. The walk heading then characterizes the type of hike for the route and gives the distance in kilometers. In this book we describe three types of hikes. A *one way* trip starts in one place and ends in another. A *round trip* starts and ends at the same place, and you return from the destination by retracing your route. We indicate the total distance out and back for such walks. A *loop trip* goes to its destination by one route and returns by a different route, and we indicate the total distance.

Altitude. The *high point* gives the altitude in meters of the highest point on the route. *Ascent/descent* gives the total amount of ascent or descent of the route in meters. Alpine walks do not necessarily just rise in one direction and descend in the other, but may jog up and down along the way. Therefore the ascent or descent may be more than the distance between the high point and the starting point. For round trip walks the ascent and descent must be the same, so we use the term *total climb* to indicate the vertical distance that you must ascend and descend.

Time. The number of hours given for a route indicates the walking time from the starting point, unless otherwise noted.

Recommended and optional transportation. *Recommended transportation* indicates that we recommend you use a lift, bus, or cog railway available at the start or end of a walk, and we usually make these recommendations because the walking route parallels a busy highway or because it is unexceptional or lengthy. If you prefer to walk all the way, we also describe the walking routes to the destination. *Optional transportation* indicates that optional lifts, bus, or cog railway are available for part of a route. The distance, ascent/descent, and walking time listed in the walk headings do *not* include the distance covered by recommended transportation; the distance and time by which optional mechanical aids shorten the walk are given in the text.

Maps. Each walk in this book is shown on a sketch map, and each information block indicates the page on which the map appears in the book. The keys to trail maps indicate when you are walking on a jeep road or mule path, a wide path, a distinct trail, or a blazed route. A few walks involve short segments on paved roads, which are also shown. The maps indicate lifts, cog railroads, restaurants, and overnight accommodations, as well as prominent features such as glaciers, lakes, rivers, and major peaks.

Some of the places named on Swiss maps might lead you to believe that they must be villages, hamlets, or at least clusters of farms. Often, however, there is literally nothing there. A hiker may find a signpost planted on some empty meadow or slope, bearing a place name and the altitude, though there isn't a single house in sight. This is because the Swiss often name their meadows or grazing areas; in some cases, there may once have been an alp (a summer farm) on a site, but there is no longer any trace of it. These place names are now used as markers on maps and on signposts and are useful in helping hikers keep track of their progress on a route.

The spelling and even the name of a Swiss place name may vary on different maps and on signposts. The notch between the Unter and Oberrothorns above Zermatt, for example, appears on some maps and signposts as Furggsattel, on other maps as Furggji. (What counts here is the word root, Furgg, which means saddle or pass.) The Reichenbach valley near Meiringen is also spelled Rychen Bach. For the most part, we have used the spellings that you'll see on trail signs, and you can assume that phonetically similar names in one locality refer to the same place.

Most of the maps in this book are based on the 1:25000 "Landeskarte der Schweiz" series. We strongly recommend that you also purchase the topographic maps that we cite for each walk. Many of the other "tourist maps" that we recommend, on which hiking trails are marked in red or blue, can be obtained only in the region they describe. You can buy them at bookstores, newsstands, sport shops, grocery or general stores, train stations, or the local tourist office.

PART I

SWITZERLAND

FOR

WALKERS

1

Travel Basics

Accommodations

The Swiss Hotel Association publishes an annual paperback guide called the Swiss Hotel Guide (Schweizer Hotelführer, Guide Suisse des Hotels) listing most of the hotels and inns in the entire country, with addresses, telephone numbers, facilities, prices, and other information. You can obtain a copy from the Swiss National Tourist Office in the United States, Canada, or Great Britain for a small fee. A few establishments are not included: some of the mountain inns (Berghotels) and a small number of places that don't want to pay for membership. Once you are in Switzerland, you can look up hotels in the phone books. Telephone directories for the whole country are found in Post and Telephone-Telex offices, in railroad and bus stations, and in some large hotels.

You can generally get a hotel room upon arrival in a Swiss city through the tourist information office at the railroad station. The only difficult periods are during large conventions, which are infrequent and generally held in the larger towns. During the last week of August, for example, a convention of antique dealers takes nearly every available room in Zurich. But because Switzerland is so small, you can take a room in Bern if one is unavailable in Zurich—even if your flight home leaves the next morning. From Bern you can get to the Zurich airport in about two hours.

The period from July 1 to August 15, when Swiss children go back to school, is considered high season in the summer, but winter is now the big

Bridge in Lucerne at dusk

tourist season in the Alps, and towns have built hotels and apartments to handle the winter influx. Towns like Zermatt and Saas-Fee are therefore overbuilt for their summer trade. There are nearly always rooms and apartments available in the summer at the last minute. You can walk into any town and get a room; however, if you want to stay at a particular hotel (especially in high season), you should probably telephone in advance. There is usually someone around who speaks English.

Village Accommodations

Most villages have an assortment of hotels, and, depending on the village, some hotels may be very modern. In less-frequented villages, most hotels will be simple and old-fashioned. Besides "hotel," they may also be called "Gasthof," "Gasthaus," "Pension" or "Garni" (the latter means a hotel without restaurant or where meals are optional). All but the smallest villages have tourist offices that can also provide you with a "Hotelliste" or "Liste des Hotels." Simple hotels and pensions often have dormitory (Matratzenlager) accommodations as well as rooms; inquire for these at the village tourist office. You can also check the local telephone book for hotels. In the smallest villages and hamlets, establishments that offer rooms may be listed in the telephone book under the heading "cafés" or "restaurants."

Mountain Accommodations

There are two types of mountain accommodations: mountain inns, which are privately owned, and Swiss Alpine Club (SAC) huts. In general, these mountain lodgings provide shelter, a dry place to sleep, and hot meals. Period. Do not expect baths or showers, hot running water, or gourmet food.

You will, however, find that a stay in a mountain inn is one of the best ways to get to know the Swiss. Though they are courteous and careful of each other's rights, the Swiss are not reserved, formal, or stiff; they like to enjoy life. Sitting over a bottle of wine on a Saturday night at an inn, they're merry but not boisterous. The Swiss neither whisper in a dining room nor roar in a public drinking place.

Mountain inns. In this book, mountain inns refer to what the Swiss call Berghotels. These simple old hotels are a sort of Swiss institution. In America, they would have been shut down or rebuilt 40 years ago, but in Switzerland, they're a beloved tradition. Perhaps it doesn't pay to renovate them, as their season is short; like the Swiss Alpine Club huts, they are open only from late June to the end of September or early October. Or perhaps the Swiss love them as they are—they're part of the mountain experience.

In decor the mountain inns vary widely: some have old carved furniture and gingham curtains, others look more rough and plain. Many can be reached only by foot (and are provisioned by mule or helicopter). They are often found in splendid locations, and most are nearly a hundred years old. In terms of comfort and facilities, they're usually just a step or two up from Alpine Club huts. Indoor toilets are the rule, but hot water is rare and the bathing facilities run to Victorian pitchers and basins. The inns generally offer both private rooms and dormitory accommodations (Matratzenlager).

The real center of a mountain inn is the dining room, for social rather than culinary reasons. Meals are simple and hearty. Some offer the basic type of menu you find at Alpine Club huts; others provide a little more, such as salad or pastry. After dinner everyone remains in the dining room, playing cards, reading, talking, enjoying an after-dinner drink, and, as at the Alpine Club huts, new friendships are easily made.

Mountain inns are the one exception to the general easy availability of accommodations in the summer: for a room or a space on a weekend you should phone ahead, especially if you want a private room. Inns are favorite spots for group outings; social organizations, sports clubs, town choral societies, and the like will meet at an inn for a weekend of hiking and conviviality. Saturday nights are particularly joyful—the groups sing favorite old songs, dance if there's any space, refresh themselves with wine and such concoctions as tea laced with schnapps, and look even happier when the other guests join in. If the inn is booked for the weekend, you'll want to know about it before you arrive, footsore and weary, in the late afternoon.

In addition to offering private rooms, mountain inns have dormitories and bunk rooms (Matratzenlager, Massenlager, Touristenlager, dortoirs). These accommodations usually consist of sleeping shelves or platforms, with mattresses laid out, on which people sleep side by side. Occasionally inns may also have bunkbeds. You will be provided with a thin mattress, a pillow and as many blankets as you'll need, but you won't have sheets. These bunk rooms are often shared by both sexes and by families with children. The code of behavior is decorous and discreet. People are quiet in the Matratzenlager; any singing in an inn is confined to the dining room. In the morning you're expected to fold up the blankets and place them neatly at the foot of your mattress.

Swiss Alpine Club huts. Though erected to serve climbers, Swiss Alpine Club huts (SAC or, in French, CAS) are also available to hikers. Many people have heard talk of "walking from hut to hut," but this applies to countries such as Austria and Norway. In those countries, the hut system was designed primarily for hikers, and huts are therefore placed conveniently along a route. Swiss huts, however, are positioned for particular climbs. On a walking tour, you might stay at a hut one night and at a mountain inn or in a village hotel the next.

The huts are very simple: dining room, kitchen (closed to the public), and Matratzenlager. The toilet may be indoors or out. No showers, and no hot water. Meals are simple but filling. They have to be: the caloric expenditure of climbers is prodigious. (For that matter, your own caloric output will be pretty high. A walking tour in the Alps may be the surest method of dieting ever devised.) The kitchens always serve soup, potatoes, noodles or spaghetti, sausages, and sometimes eggs, cutlets, and canned vegetables. In some huts, the hutkeeper makes one meal and serves everyone together. These dinners generally consist of soup, stew or a platter of schnitzel, noodles or potatoes, canned vegetables, and canned fruit or pudding. Some climbers bring their own food, which the hutkeeper cooks for them for a small fee. Soft drinks, wine, and beer are always available. Breakfast is comparatively small: bread, jam and butter, and bowls of tea or coffee. Alpine climbers start on a light stomach, rather than with big bacon and eggs or pancake breakfasts.

Climbers go to bed early, and most everyone else turns in by 21 or 22 hours. The bunk rooms may or may not have a dim electric light. As in all Swiss Matratzenlager, both sexes share the rooms and although no one brings a bathrobe, people are quiet and discreet. Boots must be parked in the entryway. (A few easily accessible huts get a lot of day hikers at lunchtime and in these, boots are allowed in the dining room.)

On summer weekends, especially during a spell of fine weather, the huts may be crowded, especially ones that are reasonably accessible and that serve popular climbs. You can telephone a hut (they have radio telephones) and reserve a place. Otherwise, hikers are assigned sleeping places in the order in which they arrive; after the Matratzenlager are filled, everyone else gets to sleep in the dining room. Unlike privately owned mountain inns, SAC huts provide shelter to everyone who comes. This is necessary because some huts are in remote and high places, and to send someone away in late afternoon might force that person to undertake a long and possibly tricky descent in the dark, perhaps in bad weather.

The huts are so popular with hikers because they almost invariably occupy locations that range from splendid to breathtaking. An evening at a hut has a special appeal. After the four hours that it took you to get there, you will eat whatever the hut serves with relish, and the camaraderie is often incomparable.

Farm Accommodations

The isolated alps or summer farms that you pass on trails sometimes sell simple refreshments: milk and cheese from the alp, hot chocolate, coffee or tea. And occasionally they offer the simplest kind of accommodations, Matratzenlager, in the barn or hayloft. These may be called "Nachtlager," and are generally announced by a sign, but sometimes you'll have to ask the farmer if Nachtlager are available.

Accommodation Prices $SFl = \$.70$

A Swiss franc is presently (1987) valued at US $0.60, although its exact value fluctuates. In this book, we note the accommodations available in towns and villages and give a general indication of their prices—based on figures that will cover room, dinner, and breakfast for two people. Inexpensive accommodations cost SFr. 60–100; moderate, SFr. 101–150; and expensive, SFr. 151 and up.

A night at an SAC hut is in the inexpensive range, although meals are more expensive. Prices are high because the huts are provisioned by helicopter.

1.337   Transportation

The word "excellent" doesn't begin to describe the Swiss rail and bus system. Swiss public transportation is extensive, efficient, intelligent, and convenient. The Zurich airport, for example, is linked by rail to the city's main railway station. Not only are luggage carts plentiful at the terminal, but you can load your cart onto specially designed escalators that take you from air terminal to train platform. When you disembark from the train, you'll find more carts available, which you can take right up to the taxi line outside. The transportation network is so comprehensive that every village is accessible by train or bus. Service is frequent, and stations, trains, and buses are clean.

At railroad stations, large white posters indicate arriving trains (Ankunft, Arrivée), and yellow posters show departing trains (Abfahrt, Départ). Little pocket-sized timetables called Regionalfahrplan (or horaire régional) and showing the rail or bus service in the immediate area and important connecting trains, are available free at ticket windows. When you ask for a schedule at a ticket window or information office (indicated by the letter "I"), the staff will not only tell you your connections but write them for you on a slip of paper. The complete timetable for every train and bus route in the country is listed in the Kursbuch or Indicateur Officiel, which you can sometimes consult yourself in railway or bus stations. The Kursbuch is also often available at hotels, and is on sale at rail stations.

The national bus system is run by the Swiss Post Office, the PTT or Poste-Telephone-Telegraphe. A curving post horn is the emblem of these

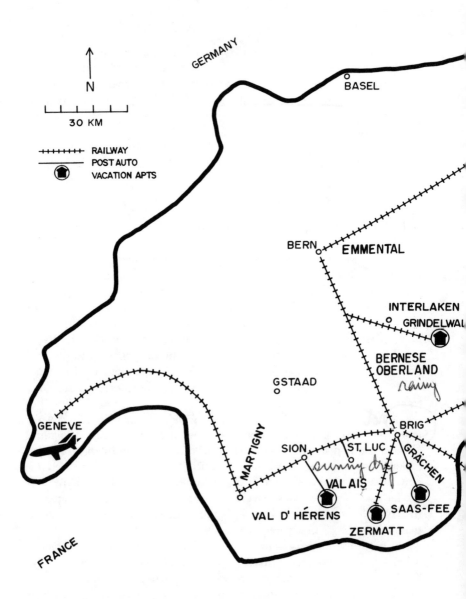

MAJOR TRANSPORTATION ROUTES

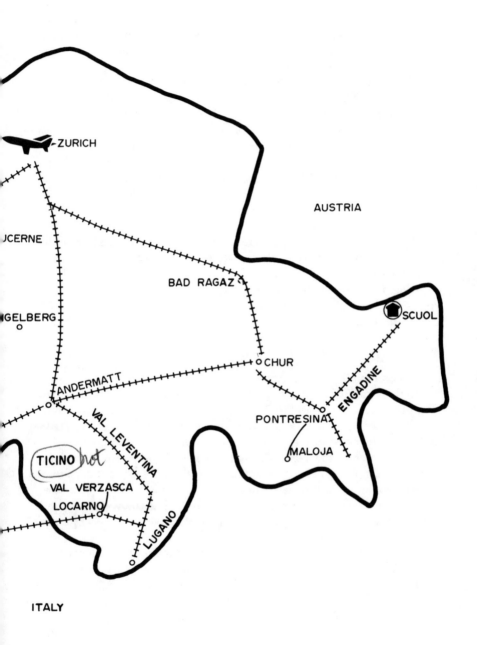

red and yellow buses (Postautos, Autobus, cars postales). Buses have the right of way on highways and roads because they also deliver the mail. Upon hearing the unforgettable three notes of the PTT horn, car drivers are supposed to stop. Those who continue and meet the bus face on must then back up or pull off the road somehow to let the Postauto pass—to the merriment of the passengers.

In country districts, bus schedules are often posted on a little card at the bus stop, which is very helpful if you've just stepped down from a mountain trail and want to know if and when you can catch a bus to town. Infrequently, reservations may be required. Passengers must sometimes deposit their luggage or rucksacks in a little cart pulled behind the bus.

One invaluable aid to traveling in Switzerland is the Gepäck (baggages) system. You can take your luggage to any rail or bus station, pay a small fixed charge per item, and ship it off to any other station. Your suitcase will arrive within a day or two and is held until you arrive. This enables hikers to send a suitcase with city clothes, film, extra maps, books, or whatever to a point they intend to reach later, and to hike carrying only a light rucksack. We have never lost a piece of luggage through this system. You can insure your baggage if you wish. When you arrive to claim your luggage, you may have to pay SFr. 1 per day for storage; this fee is sometimes levied, sometimes not.

With a new system called Fly-Gepäck, you can check luggage from any point in Switzerland onto your flight from the Zurich, Geneva, or Basel airports and collect it again at your destination abroad.

Swiss Holiday Cards. Anyone with a permanent residence outside Switzerland can purchase a Swiss Holiday Card from the Swiss National Tourist Office in New York, Chicago, San Francisco, Toronto, or London. (See the list of addresses in the Appendix.) With the card you will have unlimited free travel on Swiss trains, PTT buses, and on the lake steamers. To order the card, you must supply your passport number, but not a passport picture. Holiday Cards are available for 4, 8, or 15 days, or a month—for either first- or second-class travel. (For a stay of more than a month, you would have to purchase two cards.) A month's second-class card costs about $130; second class is quite comfortable and is used by most Swiss travelers. There are only a few privately owned bus lines in the country that will not accept the card in lieu of a fare. Eurailpasses cost much more than the cards and are not valid on buses or the mountain railroads that serve mountain resorts such as Zermatt and Grindelwald.

When you arrive in Switzerland take your card to the railroad desk in the airport terminal, where the personnel will enter the dates of validity and stamp your card—but remember that you cannot buy Swiss Holiday Cards in Switzerland.

The cards are available at a discount to groups of 10 or more people. You can also buy half-fare travel cards from the Swiss National Tourist Offices in North America. With these cards, you can purchase half-fare tickets in Switzerland for railroads, postal buses, and steamers. Special senior citizen half-fare travel cards are available to men over 65 and women over 62. In addition to half-fare travel, this card entitles senior citizens to reduced hotel accommodations at participating hotels. Holders of half-fare and senior citizen half-fare travel cards can also buy supplemental travel cards that entitle them to unlimited travel on the days of their choice on lines indicated on a special map. These supplemental cards can be purchased only in Switzerland.

If you plan to stay in one Swiss region or town, you might also consider a regional holiday season ticket, which provides free days and large discounts on all transportation, including lift tickets. Inquire about these tickets at the Swiss National Tourist Offices in the United States, Canada, and Great Britain.

Weather

Although temperatures during a Swiss summer are generally pleasant, you may encounter either very warm or cold temperatures, rain or dry weather, during any part of the summer. You should therefore bring clothing for warm and cool weather, as well as for rain. During what counts as a heat wave in Switzerland, temperatures in the mountains can reach 25 to 27 degrees C. (80 to 85 degrees F.), and 32 degrees C. (90 degrees F.) in the lowlands. It will be dry heat, and evenings in the mountains are always cool. A "heat wave" can last for a week or two. Or you may have an extended period of cool or wet weather. The daily weather forecast always tells the "Schneefalle" or "Null grad Grenze," the lowest altitude at which snow will fall and the freezing point will occur. The "Föhn" is the warm, dry wind that brings extremely clear skies, followed by rain.

The weather also varies from place to place within Switzerland. The Bernese Oberland gets much more rain than the Valais, which is relatively sunny and dry. The Ticino is more likely to be hot in midsummer than any other region. In planning your vacation, note that there may be a good deal of snow left until mid- to late-June, so if you go before July, your hiking may be restricted. Most SAC huts and mountain inns don't open till the end of June. Good weather occurs about equally in July and in August. We know people who prefer to hike at the end of August or in September, as there are fewer tourists then, much less snow on the passes, and (some say) better weather. On the other hand, the alpine flowers are best in July and early August. The hiking season ends by late September or early October.

You can dial 162 on a telephone anywhere in Switzerland and get weather forecasts in the language of the region. Forecasts are also broadcast on the radio—and are listened to intently after dinner in SAC huts. In the glossary at the end of the book, we list a few key terms that will enable you to understand the gist of the forecast.

Languages

Switzerland has four official languages: German, French, Italian, and Romansch. Standard German, however, is regarded as a foreign language. The native language of the Swiss-Germans is Schwyzer Dütsch, a dialect that differs from German in spelling, vocabulary, pronunciation, and even grammar. The Swiss use High German as a formal language, and all Swiss in the German-speaking regions learn it in school. It's the language they use for formal speeches, international relations, teaching, and literature. It's the language you'll hear when the news is read on Swiss radio or television. Therefore, if you speak German, you'll be able to use it in Switzerland. But the Swiss, who do not regard themselves as Germans, are proud of their own language, and Schwyzer Dütsch is increasingly seen on billboards and in magazine advertisements.

On the other hand, Swiss French is almost identical to the French spoken in France, though rural villages in the French-speaking region use a patois or dialect as well. Italian is spoken in the Ticino, and Romansch, the native language of the Engadine, is used in the canton called Graubunden (Grisons or Grischun).

Many people in Switzerland, especially those who work with tourists (hotel and restaurant personnel, railway conductors, climbing guides), speak English. If you ask for someone who speaks English when you go into a shop or restaurant or when you phone a hotel, someone on the staff who does can usually be found. If you have a little high school or college French or German, you might brush it up, but don't hesitate to travel across Switzerland—even on a walking tour between remote villages— with only English. Among the other guests at a mountain inn or hut there are bound to be people who speak English: students, Dutch people (nearly all of them speak English), teachers, business people. And it's a good way to make friends. A request for a brief translation on a train or at an inn often leads to a pleasant conversation for the rest of the journey or the evening.

Telephones

Telephone calls can be made from the coin boxes found in most hotels and restaurants, as well as at PTT offices. (There are also special Telephone-Telex offices that handle only telephone and telex calls.) Direct-dial calls to the United States can be made by following the instructions that are printed in English in every telephone directory.

Currency

Travelers' checks are universally accepted by banks, where foreign exchange rates are always posted (the current exchange rate is SFr. 1 for $0.68 U.S.). Most hotels, stores, and restaurants (but not SAC huts or mountain inns) will accept major U.S. credit cards. You can often exchange currency at railway stations outside of banking hours.

As crime is almost unknown in Switzerland, you can safely carry more cash with you than you're accustomed to carrying in the U.S.

Business Hours

The Swiss use the European timetable, based on a 24-hour clock. Shop hours are generally 8 to 12:00 and 13:30 or 14:00 to 18:30. Banking hours are generally 8:30 to 16:30. Post offices are closed from 12 to 13:45 and then reopen until 18:30. In large cities, department stores may stay open during the noon recess. Most stores of all kinds close at 16:00 on Saturdays. In some cities, stores remain closed on Monday mornings, and a few shops may be closed all day Monday. Shops are closed on Sundays, though in some alpine resort towns one or more bakeries and perhaps a grocery store may be open part of the day, but this depends on the custom of each town.

2

WALKING TIPS

Alpine Walking

Conditioning. It helps to be in good condition before you start an alpine vacation. Various forms of aerobic exercise, including walking, can provide this kind of conditioning.

Sometimes the obvious needs to be said. For your first day in the Alps, select a route with only a moderate ascent. We provide information on the ascent (in meters) for every route listed. If there are any hills near your home, walk in them a few days before you leave. If you live in a flat region, count on taking a few days in Switzerland to get your thigh and calf muscles into condition. If you build up gradually, this won't take long. The soles of your feet will also be less sore and tender after a couple of days of climbing.

Pace. Setting the proper pace is crucial in the mountains. It can mean the difference between arriving at your destination comfortably or in a state of exhaustion. Mountains, even low ones, look high. This makes people think that if they don't move quickly, they won't get to the top. Consequently, the pace that some inexperienced hikers take would wear out anyone but an Olympic long-distance runner. After several minutes of rapid ascent these hikers fall to the side of the trail, panting, then as soon as they recover their breath, they start up again as fast as possible. All-out rushes alternate with short and ever-less satisfactory periods of rest, and they arrive at the top ready to collapse.

A nineteenth-century English traveler described his disappointment

Looking toward the Gornergletscher between Gagihaupt and the Riffelsee near Zermatt

at watching the Swiss in motion. Instead of gracefully bounding up like chamois, he complained, they plod like peasants. But what he saw was the right pace—the only way to handle these mountains or any others. On one of our first trips to Switzerland, we were resting by the side of a steep trail when we saw two figures approaching: young men with full packs topped with ropes, ice axes and crampons, obviously heading for an Alpine Club hut and some serious climbs. They moved upward so slowly that they appeared to be taking baby steps. We watched in fascination as they slowly but steadily mounted. They passed us, although our packs were light compared with theirs, and we never caught up with them. This is the way Swiss guides teach novices to ascend a trail.

When walking uphill, move slowly, steadily, and regularly. Though your objective looks high above you, the vertical distances are less than you might think. Plodding methodically upward can give you an ascent of 300 meters (about 1000 feet) an hour. On a moderate slope, this pace might translate into about 55 or 60 fairly short steps a minute; on a steep slope, about 45 steps a minute. When the trail starts to rise, slow down. With the proper pace, even elderly people in good health can hike in the mountains, and in Switzerland they do.

Altitude acclimatization. Unless you already live at a high altitude, you will need to acclimatize to it. High altitude produces various effects on the human body, chiefly because of the reduced amount of oxygen in the air. Yet the body adapts, generally within two to three days, to these new conditions. Respiration increases in volume and depth, and your blood vessels open up, allowing oxygen to be more efficiently absorbed and larger amounts of oxygen to be carried to body tissues. This adjustment process occurs faster for some people than for others. People do not acclimatize well to elevations over 18,000 to 20,000 feet, but this is considerably higher than what you'll encounter in the Swiss Alps; even the great alpine summits are lower than this.

You acclimatize to higher altitude mainly by going up and staying there. This adjustment is a silent process involving the sort of physiological changes referred to above, but you need to give it a few days. During the first day, your physical activity should be fairly light. Just as you condition your leg muscles for mountain walking, you must also condition yourself for altitude. Upon your arrival in Switzerland, even if you think your leg muscles are ready for anything, do not attempt any climbs that take you up a considerable distance (1000 meters or more) before you are at least conditioned to the altitude of the town you're starting from. Altitude sickness, ranging from mild to acute, can occur if you try to rush the process. The symptoms of mild altitude sickness include shortness of breath and mild insomnia. In Switzerland, acute symptoms are likely only among people who attempt a major climb (4000 meters or higher) within a few days after their arrival. They may also occur occasionally in people who sleep in the few Alpine Club huts that are over 3500 meters high (none of these huts are listed in this book). Acute symptoms of altitude sickness include severe headache, dizziness, weakness, chills, nausea, and vomiting. These acute effects are not common at the lower altitudes of alpine hiking trails.

For some reason not yet fully understood, teenagers run a greater risk of altitude sickness than older people—although you cannot predict who will be affected. At the first sign of nausea, dizziness, or breathing difficulties during a climb, descend to a lower altitude at once.

Even after you get conditioned to the altitude of a town like Zermatt or Saas-Fee, you will feel the effects of the higher altitude if you take one of the longer cable cars or funiculars. After you use one of these long lifts as a boost for a hike, start climbing slowly; in a few minutes you should adjust to the higher altitude. If you do a small climb, you will certainly feel the altitude at 3000 meters (about 10,000 feet). Though there's always a temptation to rush to the top once you see the summit, go slowly!

(Note: you should consult your doctor before undertaking an alpine walking holiday if you are middle-aged or older, sedentary, out of condition, overweight, a smoker, or have any cardiac or respiratory problem, high blood pressure, diabetes, or any other chronic health problem.)

Clothing and Equipment

Boots and socks. If you don't have hiking boots, buy a pair at home and break them in before you get to Switzerland. Wear them on as many walks as possible, even if you're just clumping along the sidewalk. Count on at least 15 to 20 good walks before your boots are broken in.

Look for hiking boots with Vibram soles; they're sturdy and have the best grip. We recommend a medium-weight leather boot with a three-quarter length steel shank. The problem with lightweight boots is that they don't give enough support on rubble and scree (loose rock), and the soles are too flexible to protect your feet from rocks. Moreover, the new lightweight boots of leather and laminated cloth are not waterproof and won't keep your feet dry in snow, which you may encounter because the Swiss summer is unpredictable. If you're thinking of trying some of the mountain pass routes or the routes with permanent snow (the Britanniahütte above Saas-Fee or Zermatt's Mettelhorn), a medium-weight leather boot will serve you.

Whether you're being fitted in a store or measuring your own foot for a catalog order, wear a couple of pairs of socks. Many hikers use a thin inner liner sock and a heavier outer sock—a wool or thick wick-dry sock.

The Swiss, who usually hike in knickers, wear a knee-high sock that they roll down in warm weather and a short sock underneath. Various insole pads now on the market provide wonderful cushioning, if you have a little extra room in your boot.

It's a good idea to apply a seal treatment to leather boots: you can have relatively waterproof boots this way. In fact, take your seal with you to Switzerland because if conditions are wet or snowy, you should repeat the treatment often.

A special note for beginners: if your feet hurt on the trail, relace your boots. You may not be aware that you have put a little too much pressure over your toes and arches, yet this can cause pain. Lace your boots fairly loosely near the toes and instep, and tighten only at the ankle, where your foot flexes. When going downhill, however, tighten the lacing slightly along your instep and toes if your foot is sliding forward and your toes are hitting the front of your boot. If you tie the top too tightly, you may later feel a sort of burn around your leg.

Packs. The most useful pack for a trip that will include day hikes and a walking tour is a medium-capacity pack, with a volume between 35 and 50 liters (2000 to 3000 cubic inches). The current trend in America is toward large internal frame packs with elaborate suspension systems, but these packs are heavy, expensive, and unnecessary—unless you intend to carry 50-pound loads. We recommend a simple top-loading pack that weighs between two and three and a half pounds. It will be more comfortable to wear if it has an internal frame of light aluminum or fiberglass-reinforced "stays" that conform to the shape of your back. A load-bearing waist belt is a useful feature because it allows you to shift the weight you're carrying from time to time during a long hike.

Packs are sized to different back lengths, and you should look for one that is long enough for your back. Short men, many women, and children will be more comfortable with a pack that has shoulder straps set closer together. Lightweight, smaller, internal frame packs are available in the U.K.; if you have difficulty finding one in the U.S., you can easily buy one in any city or alpine town in Switzerland.

No pack is waterproof. Since they all leak in a downpour, you should pack the items you want to keep dry in lightweight plastic bags.

Clothing. The traditional Swiss hiking pants are knickers, in either lightweight gabardine or a wool and polyester blend. The advantage of knickers is that you can roll down your knee socks if it gets hot, but you're snug and warm when it's cold. Proponents also claim that knickers give you freer knee movement. The lightweight wool blend knickers available in Switzerland are ideal for conditions there—they're warmer than corduroy or cotton knickers, but are much more comfortable for summer hiking than 100 percent wool ones. Otherwise, comfortable, loose-fitting long pants are all you need. Cotton pants will be fine in warm weather but a synthetic-wool blend is better for cold, wet weather. A pair of shorts will greatly enhance your comfort should the weather turn warm, which it often does. At higher altitudes there's a lot of radiant energy, and it can occasionally get uncomfortably hot.

Take both long- and short-sleeved shirts. A tank-top is nice in hot weather—the only disadvantage is the added risk of sunburn. And take at least one warm garment, such as a Shetland type of wool sweater, as it can get too cold for cotton sweaters or sweatshirts.

You'll also need a full rain suit. The new "breathable" rain gear provides protection from wind and rain. Even if it's not raining, the rain pants worn over your pants or knickers can give you extra warmth in freezing weather, and you can also wear them over your shorts on a sultry day while hiking in the rain. If you have old rain clothes, check them before you leave home and seal the seams if necessary.

A sun hat is a must. The Swiss use little ones with tiny brims. These may fold into a pocket but they don't shade your face, so if you have a lightweight cotton hat with a good brim, take that. A bandana can shade your neck. Take a wool cap and a pair of gloves or mittens for cold days.

Gaiters—waterproof leggings that fit over boots—are useful for keeping snow and water out of your boots. You can buy knee-high ones or short gaiters that extend just above the ankle. The latter weigh much less and work very well.

Other equipment, preparations, and gear. Sunglasses are essential. Don't go out onto a glacier or take an extended snow walk without good sunglasses—you could get temporary snowblindness. Consider taking glacier goggles if your plans include snow trips. If you wear eyeglasses, you can buy lightweight glacier goggles that fit over your glasses. You can even wear them over your sunglasses for extra protection.

At high altitudes, wear a sunblock or a good sunscreen and use one on your lips as well. For glacier travel use glacier cream on all exposed skin and a total sunblock on your lips. You can buy these items in Switzerland, though sunblock is almost twice its U.S. price.

You can make your own medicine kit in a self-sealing plastic bag. Include aspirin, a small bottle of disinfectant, adhesive bandages, a few large sterile wound dressings, a roll of stretch adhesive tape for bandages and sprained ankles, moleskin for blisters and irritations, tweezers for removing splinters, plus any sort of medication you need. (You can get practically any standard medication in Switzerland.)

Take a compass, which is essential if you have to find the route. An altimeter is also useful but not essential. Swiss maps, particularly the 1:25,000 scale series, have detailed, accurate altitude data for points along the trail, and an accurate altimeter enables you to find your location. Pack a whistle, in case you need to call someone.

A water bottle is also essential and should hold at least three-quarters of a liter (24 ounces). Screwtop plastic bottles are light and odor-resistant. In Switzerland you can get ceramic-coated, light metal bottles that are easier to drink from but are slightly heavier. The blade of the traditional Swiss Army knife is a little short for slicing bread. We find a three-inch folding "lockblade" a useful size. Also take a small flashlight.

An ice ax is usually unnecessary, although it is a useful safety measure on walks where steep snow-covered slopes are traversed. You can simply avoid the routes where snow is always found on a slope. If the season is unusually snowy, you may want to take an ice ax on the mountain pass routes. You can rent an ice ax in most alpine centers, but remember that simply renting an ice ax isn't enough—you have to know how to use it.

Photographic equipment should be simple, rugged, and light. Don't take equipment that you will want to get rid of after ascending the first 500 meters. We usually carry photographic equipment in a small army surplus canvas bag lined with waterproof ripstop nylon and padded with ensolite foam. In heavy rain we keep lenses and cameras in small waterproof nylon bags within the camera case. As for film, Kodachrome still has the greatest color stability, both before and after processing. High-quality black and white photographs that match the resolution of large-format tripod-mounted view cameras can be taken using Kodak Technical Pan or TMAX-100 film. Kodachrome and TMAX film can be purchased in Switzerland at about the standard prices; Technical Pan film can be obtained only in Bern, Zurich, Lugano, and Geneva. Keep the weight of film in mind on a walking tour. A roll of 35 mm film, which you should take out of its cardboard box, weighs 1 ounce. You can store a reserve supply of film in your Gepäck suitcase while you're hiking from point to point. If you'll be flying home from Switzerland, pack some lead-lined film protection bags in your suitcase. Hand inspection of film is *not* possible; *all* carry-on and some checked luggage will be x-rayed by airport security.

The walking tour pack. When you walk from point to point, you must carry everything you need, but the primary thing to remember is weight. If you plan to walk over mountain passes, you may be hauling your wardrobe up a few thousand feet. Experienced alpine walkers consider the weight of every toilet article, every item of clothing.

In addition to the items mentioned above, you should carry a spare pair of outer socks and one or two extra pairs of liner socks. You should also bring some very light footwear because boots are not allowed inside Alpine Club huts. The SAC (Swiss Alpine Club) provides everyone with scuffs or clogs, which are usually enormous. (You will see dozens of them in the entryway; select two that are least likely to fall off your feet.) Mountain inns usually don't provide clogs, and hotels in towns never do, though the proprietors usually ask that you remove your boots inside. Some hikers bring a pair of lightweight slippers or slipper socks. Our preference is to bring the most lightweight pair of canvas shoes that we can find. They double as slippers in a hut, and if we spend an evening in a town we can wear them out in the street. But if the weight seems too much, bring slippers instead.

Always carry food, including a small reserve supply of high-energy food. A little supply of plastic bags is handy to wrap your lunch in, and a plastic spoon or fork can come in handy. Remember when you spend the night in a village or town to stock up on lunch foods, flashlight batteries, etc., for the days that you will spend at an SAC hut or mountain inn.

If you want to shave, consider a plastic, disposable razor, and a small amount of brushless shaving cream in an empty plastic 35mm film can. You can also carry a week's supply of skin conditioner, face cream, or a dollop of shampoo in one of these tiny cans. You can take all this and keep your pack light. Be inventive! One fellow we met in a hut gleefully showed us his toothbrush, which he had sawed in half. He had also milled flutes into the remaining handle to reduce the weight a little more.

A brief note about what you don't need: all Swiss huts and mountain inns provide blankets, so you don't need a sleeping bag. Swiss hikers don't take sheet sacks (sleeping bags made of sheets) either.

Food

You can buy provisions at reasonable prices anywhere, though prices are lowest at the two supermarket chains, Migros and Coop. Swiss bakeries are a delight; they often sell five or six different kinds of bread. Whole grain bread is usually called Vollkorn, Funfkorn or Siebenkorn (or however many types of grain it contains) Brot, or "Fitness" Brot (Blé complet), or Graham. Bran is "Weizenkleie." The most common bread is "Halbweiss," which is like our rye bread, but without the seeds. Their rye bread or Roggenbrot is darker and heavier. The round loaves of Walliser Brot (Pain Valaisanne) is rather dark and very dense. In the old days, when the Valais was one of the poorest and most remote regions of Switzerland, and wheat was difficult to obtain, the inhabitants made bread only once or twice a year, but they made it in this form so it would last them through the season. Outsiders tend either to like it very much or not at all. All bread is sold either by the loaf or by weight. You can ask for a "halb kilo," for example. If all they have left at a bakery are big loaves of bread, they will cut a loaf in half if you request "ein halb."

Peanuts (Erdnussen, cacahuètes), raisins, and dried fruit are widely available, and you can replenish your own trail mix every time you get to a village or town.

Most hikers will buy sliced meat or cheese for lunch. Another possibility is Bundnerfleisch or Trockenfleisch, thin slices of air-dried meat that are a Swiss specialty. Canned sardines and tuna won't spoil and are therefore handy. Peanut butter is virtually unknown.

Switzerland has an old vegetarian tradition, predating the American health food movement. Cities have vegetarian restaurants, and natural food stores (Reformhaus) are found in many middle-sized towns. A pharmacy or any shop with the word "Reform" in its title sells organic or natural foods, cosmetics or drugs. One useful item for trail lunches is a vegetarian pâté that comes in tubes, available at every Reformhaus. Some supermarkets sell a tofu spread in tubes. You can generally get mint tea (Pfefferminze, Thé de Menthe) for breakfast at hotels, and you can buy mint and many sorts of herbal tea bags in ordinary pharmacies, as well as at most food shops. Pharmacies also stock bran cereals and baby foods. Yogurt is popular, and the nonfat or skim-milk kind carries the word "Mager" or "Écrémé" in its title.

What should the hiker drink? Is stream water safe? Since there may be animals grazing above you it would be impossible to guarantee the safety of stream water. And because glacier-fed streams carry silt, you should make it a habit to fill your water bottle at the inn or hut—or your apartment—before you start out in the morning.

Trail Signs

Trail signs are standardized throughout most of Switzerland. Walking routes are marked by yellow metal signs on signposts, rather like street signs. The signs give the walking time but not the distance. For example, a sign may read, "Furggtal 3 Std. 15 Min."—Std. is the abbreviation for Stunde, or hour. Or the sign may read, "Furggtal 3.15." The tip of the sign ends in an arrow, pointing you in the direction that Furggtal lies. Often there's a white metal tag in the center of the signpost with the name of its location and altitude.

The Swiss distinguish two kinds of routes. A Wanderweg or chemin pédestre is a relatively easy, graded trail through hills or lower mountain slopes. Wanderweg signs are entirely yellow. A Bergweg (mountain path) or chemin de montagne is a rougher trail through more difficult terrain. Bergweg signs have a yellow body, but are marked at their arrow tip with a white-red-white blaze (the Swiss national colors). A small yellow or white and red metal plate fastened to a tree or rock is an intermediary sign, showing that you are still on the route.

In the absence of signs, mountain trails or routes are blazed with white-red-white paint on rocks, although in a few regions you may see older blazes in blue, yellow, or some other color. If the blaze is painted with a right angle bend, the trail turns in the direction of the bend. A yellow or white and red diamond-shaped blaze or metal indicator is usually placed on the route after a turn to show that you're still on the route.

Maps

In addition to the sketch maps in this book, the topographic maps listed in the text are absolutely essential to the hiker, and we strongly recommend that you purchase the relevant map for each region. The walk descriptions in this book are keyed to the topographic maps, which show mountains and other features that are off the scale of the sketch maps. Though practically all the major geographic features in each region are indicated on the sketch maps, the limited scale of these maps cannot include everything you will see on the route, and possession of the topographic map will enhance the interest of each walk. Moreover, should a hiker lose the route, a topographic map with its fine detail would be extremely useful.

Safety

Hiking in the mountains entails unavoidable risks that every hiker assumes and must be aware of and respect. The fact that a route or area is described in this book, for example, is not a representation that it will be a safe one for you or for your party. In our route descriptions we use a grading code to indicate the degree of difficulty of each route. But this code can provide only a rough guide; within each category, trails obviously vary greatly in difficulty and in the degree of physical conditioning and agility you need to enjoy them safely.

Trail conditions and routes may have changed or deteriorated since these descriptions were written. Winter storms and avalanches can produce rock slides that cover a section of trail, and spring torrents can wash out small bridges. Also, trail conditions can change from day to day—a trail that is safe on a dry day may be dangerous in rain, snow, or fog. A trail that is safe for a well-conditioned, properly equipped hiker may be too difficult for someone else.

Thousands of people enjoy safe and satisfying hikes every year. But while Switzerland is not a wilderness, a certain amount of risk is always present. Exercising your good judgment and common sense will help. You can minimize many risks by being well prepared, alert, and knowledgeable. Be aware of your own limitations and of the conditions when and where you are hiking. If conditions are dangerous or if you or anyone in your party is unwell or exhausted, stay in for the day or turn back if you have already started.

Switzerland has long been a safe and peaceful country. But political conditions may add to the risk of travel in Europe in ways that no one can predict. When you travel, you assume this risk too and should keep informed of political developments that may make travel difficult or impossible.

Climbers distinguish between two sorts of dangers: objective and subjective. Objective dangers stem from external factors, such as the greater likelihood of rock slides and avalanches in the afternoon; subjective ones arise from your own bad judgment, inexperience, poor condition, or lack of equipment.

Weather hazards. Use common sense: don't start a long route if the morning looks ominous or if the forecast calls for threatening weather. If you're out on a trail and the sky gets heavy and dark, turn around if that is still possible. You should always carry warm and waterproof clothes in your pack, and some food for energy. Because lightning is most likely to strike high, exposed points and ridgelines, you should descend at once if a thunderstorm approaches. Most storms occur in the afternoon, so if you get an early start you should be down from exposed places by then.

Rockfall. Occasionally, signs are posted warning of falling stones (Steinschlag or chute de pierres). If you're passing under or close to a slope, you should both watch and listen. Animals grazing above you can knock over stones, and so can climbers or hikers. If you knock over a stone yourself, shout a warning in case anyone is below you. Likewise, watch out if you hear a shout ("watch out" is "Achtung" in German, "attention" in French). Never sit down for lunch directly under a cliff or steep slope littered with loose rock.

Avalanches. Avalanches are not a hazard on hiking trails in the summer hiking season; they are a danger only on certain technical climbing routes in the summer. But avalanches can occur at lower altitudes in the spring skiing season, so anyone planning to snowshoe (or ski) on hiking routes in the spring should consult the local guides' office about avalanche conditions.

Travel on rock or scree. Some of the more difficult trails may involve a descent or traverse on loose talus or scree. You can descend these slopes by coming down first with the heel of your boot. Since there may be great exposure as well, you should avoid these routes if you're doubtful of your

Below the Oberhornsee in the Bernese Oberland

ability. (In the vocabulary of alpinism, "exposure" means simply a great vertical drop below you.) Remember that rain can make a route on firm rock difficult and snow can turn a walking trail into a technical climb.

Travel on snow and ice. You should always be careful on a steep snow-covered trail, and traversing a snow slope can be dangerous. Remember that snow stays longer on northern slopes. If you have to make such a traverse across a steep slope and you are not equipped with an ice ax, pick up a long pointed stone and hold it ready to jam into the snow should you fall. A hiker's main use of an ice ax is for self-arrest. If you rent an ice ax for a particular route, ask the shopkeeper to demonstrate how to use it. Basically, you carry it in the hand that's on the uphill side, pick end forward. If you start to fall, jam the pick into the snow with all your force.

Glaciers are always dangerous. When a glacier is covered with snow, crevasses are invisible. Even uncovered glaciers, however, can be dangerous. Stay off them, unless you are roped and led by a guide or trained person. There are only a handful of glacier crossings that are considered safe for unequipped hikers; the local guides' or tourist bureau can always advise you.

Travel on steep grassy slopes. Wet grass is slippery, and people have slid off meadows with steep slopes. The alpine fatality lists include such cases among the climbing statistics.

Swiss Military Ordnance. The Swiss military practices maneuvers in remote areas. They try assiduously to remove all expended materiel, but if you see any metal objects lying about that look like shells or parts of them, do not touch them, and inform someone when you get to the next town.

Lakes. On a hot afternoon, a clear alpine lake can look inviting. But the glacier-fed water is icy cold. Whatever others are doing, play it safe.

Electrified fences. Some of the fences used to pen livestock are electrified. You can always tell because these have insulators along the wire—they look like little brightly colored plastic spools. You can also hear a low, rhythmic clicking from the charging unit. Electrified fences are always equipped with a safe-passage gate. To pass through, grasp the plastic handgrip and unhook the wire. There's no real risk here—Swiss farmers and their children use these gates all the time.

Animals and plants. Poisonous snakes exist in the Alps but they're rare. There are no bears left in the Swiss Alps, and, though you'll probably walk past dozens of cows, Swiss farmers do not send bulls out to graze in open pastures.

Rabies (Tollwut, la rage or hydrophobie) is found in parts of Europe, including Switzerland, and warning signs are sometimes posted. Beware of wild animals that appear ill or unnaturally friendly.

Poison ivy, poison oak, and poison sumac don't exist in Europe.

Near the First lift station above Grindelwald

There is one plant, however, that is a nuisance: stinging nettle. Its touch causes a stinging pain and the affected area may turn red. Fortunately, the effects don't last long, and if you're near a stream, a splash of cold water helps a great deal. Look out for tallish plants with notched, pointy leaves. The nettles have little sprays of dusty, gray-green or purplish tiny flowers, especially near the top of the plant. The stalk is reddish-green.

Emergencies. The Alpine S.O.S. is a series of six signals evenly spaced within one minute, and then a repetition of six more after a minute's pause. The signals may be six whistle blasts, six light flashes, etc. Standing upright with both arms stretched above your head signals a request for a helicopter rescue; holding only one arm up, with the other arm held down at your side, indicates that helicopter rescue is not needed.

The helicopter is the ambulance of the Alps. Should you fall ill at a hut, you can be evacuated by helicopter directly to a hospital within minutes after a call for help is transmitted (all SAC huts have radio telephones). Evacuation after a climbing injury or illness on a trail is also rapid, once a call for help is received.

3

THE ALPINE ENVIRONMENT

The Swiss have long been committed to environmental protection and conservation. Theirs was a relatively poor European nation until recently, and they never had the illusion of unlimited natural resources. A quarter of their total land surface is agriculturally useless—an alpine desert. The qualities that were once necessary for their survival—thrift, conservation of limited resources—are engrained into Swiss culture.

Swiss national policy aims to protect the land and conserve natural resources, and to preserve the Swiss agricultural base and rural population. In North America, preservation of the wilderness is an important environmental objective for obvious historical and cultural reasons. The preservation of the Swiss agricultural base stands in the same relation to the Swiss heritage as preservation of our wilderness does to ours.

During the two World Wars, Switzerland—small, neutral, and landlocked—had to feed itself. Since the food shortages of the 1940s, the Swiss have viewed food production as a component of national security and self-defense. Moreover, the Swiss agricultural system is a historic part of Swiss culture. Centuries ago, the mountain people devised a system to enable them to farm their difficult terrain. Herds and flocks are led up to special high pastures in the summer, and meadows are mowed—up to three times in a summer—to provide winter fodder. Today, hikers still pass among grazing sheep and cows in the high country, and you'll see intensive mowing and haymaking throughout rural Switzerland. In the very high country, you may pass large, communal dairy barns and tiny, one-family summer farms on which a group or a single family will pass the summer,

Two brothers at the alp that has belonged to their family for 500 years

herding, milking, and making cheese. Alpine meadows also form part of the Swiss concept of natural beauty and the Swiss wish to preserve the character of this land.

To stem the movement of Swiss farmers to the cities (in 1900, 40 percent of the population was engaged in agriculture; in 1975, only 7 per cent), the Swiss government spends a substantial portion of their federal budget to subsidize mountain farmers. Agricultural price guarantees enable Swiss farmers to earn considerably more than the average farm income in the European Economic Community—which the Swiss have avoided joining because the adoption of EEC agricultural policies would accelerate the decline of the rural population.

Perhaps the two greatest threats to the alpine environment are acid rain and the overwhelming popularity of winter downhill skiing. The effects of acid rain are highly visible; in some regions, you can see large stands of dead and dying trees, and the Swiss are deeply concerned about the issue. In 1985 the Swiss federal government approved gasoline emission standards that will be tougher than those of any other European country, and that will equal those of the United States. But much of the problem is outside Swiss control, the result of pollution and industrial emissions from the factories of neighboring countries.

As for downhill skiing, which has brought so much prosperity to the Swiss, it has intensified environmental problems. Every winter a huge influx of skiers pours into the Alps, and, to accommodate them, new highways have been built, towns and villages expanded, and ski lifts erected.

In addition to its physical effects on the environment, downhill skiing has had social and cultural consequences. Though the Swiss looked to tourism for profit and as a means to stem the movement from rural areas to the cities, they have become aware that tourism can have a contrary effect. Villages such as Les Haudères, which is not geographically suited to skiing, retain their traditional appearance and customs far more so than most ski resort towns.

Summer tourism, which concerns most hikers, is not a serious environmental threat. Unrestricted camping, which would be damaging to the fragile alpine terrain, is not allowed. Hikers and climbers stay overnight at huts, mountain inns, or village hotels, and overnight use is thus concentrated within a relatively small area.

Fauna. The wild animal most commonly seen, or heard, is the marmot (murmultier), a plump, furry rodent about the size of a woodchuck. The short, shrill whistle you often hear in the high country is a marmot call. Those that live near a lift station may be semi-tame—the marmots of Saas-Fee are a favorite tourist attraction. You may also see deer, chamois (Gemse), and an occasional Steinbock (bouquetin), a mammal that is larger than a deer. You can also see ermine, foxes, and eagles.

Flora. It would be impossible for us to name all the wildflowers that grow in the meadows and on the high slopes of the Alps. Their profusion, variety, and color are dazzling. (Edelweiss, the Swiss national flower, is rather rare.) If you want to learn the names of the dozens of flowers that you'll see, buy the flower guides sold in Swiss bookstores.

Alpine Etiquette and Environmental Laws

There are some unwritten rules as well as specific environmental laws that hikers must observe.

Fences. You should close any gate you have to open. Often there are signs posted reading, "Bitte die Tür Schlossen," or "fermez la porte, s.v.p.," which mean please close the gate! Although many of the fences that you'll pass through enclose areas of private property, you can walk across these areas freely and know that you are welcome to do so.

Fire. Anyone who causes a fire, whether on purpose, through negligence, or by accident, is responsible for the damage and can be made to pay for it. Starting a fire—even for a picnic—in an area where signs forbid the making of fires is punishable by law, even if no damage results from the fire.

Garbage. The deposit of garbage in the woods is punishable by law in all of Switzerland. Some cantons—the Valais, for example—impose fines for leaving garbage anywhere. Polluting rivers by dumping garbage in them is a federal crime and punishable by imprisonment. When you're hiking you should pack out your personal trash.

Personal matters. The local protocol for toileting between huts, lift stations, and mountain restaurants is to be discreet and leave nothing in sight. Climbers, for example, when taken by surprise on a glacier, are not expected to endure lengthy discomfort, but generally use their ice axes as shovels. Spare sandwich bags are useful for waste paper. Take care not to foul streams.

Protected plants. Many flower species are protected, and posters are widely displayed with pictures of protected species. It is illegal to gather protected flowers. Usually, offenders first receive a warning, then a fine, and in more severe cases (if the offender, for example, gathers many flowers and attempts to sell them), imprisonment is possible.

Gathering mushrooms is allowed on certain days. Wild mushrooms must be presented for inspection for safety reasons, since some species are poisonous. Every community has an individual appointed to inspect mushrooms.

PART II

DAY HIKES

FROM A

VACATION APARTMENT

4

VACATION APARTMENTS

Most Swiss rent vacation apartments for their alpine holidays, summer and winter. There's no more economical way to take a hiking holiday, and because the apartment serves as a base to which you return every day, it's an excellent way to hike with a family. Another delightful advantage is that you can hike with a light pack, taking only what's needed for the day.

Many of the best trails in Switzerland can and traditionally have been done as day hikes: that is, trips in which one returns in the evening to a base. The walks to the Schönbielhütte and to Höhbalmen in Zermatt, to Schynige Platte from Grindelwald, to Grächen from Saas-Fee, to Pas de Chèvres in Arolla, and many others described in this book, are among the finest, most scenic routes in Switzerland, and all can be done as day trips.

The alpine resorts and villages that we feature here are (with the exception of Scuol) set at the foot of high mountains. You can walk out of Zermatt, for example, in 10 minutes and be in fields and meadows; in another 15 minutes, you're well on your way up a mountain slope. And the lifts near most of these villages can give you a quick boost into alpine terrain—another advantage for families hiking with children.

The extraordinary thing about hiking in Switzerland is that you can take a vigorous hike into the Alps and return in the evening to the comfort of your own apartment, where you have more room and more privacy than in a hotel, and where you can prepare your own meals. This is a delightful way to get to know a region: you will see the mountains in different conditions of light and weather, watch the life of the village, and make friends with neighbors, your landlord, or local merchants.

A house in the old town of Bern

An Engadine house with sgraffito (house design) in Ardez

Every Swiss town and village has holiday apartments for rent. Such an apartment is a "Ferienwohnung" in German, "une appartement de vacances" in French. These apartments are built solely for rental purposes—they do not serve as the owner's residence. Holiday apartments are fully furnished and equipped with bed linen, warm coverings (down comforters or featherbeds), pillows, towels, dishes, silverware, and cooking utensils. Some have radios, but televisions are rare. Many apartments have small balconies and deck chairs. These apartments are comfortable, generally attractive, and always spotlessly clean. They range from small studios that will accommodate one or two people to large apartments suitable for a family or several couples. They are listed according to the number of beds, but the information listings also report the number of rooms in the apartment.

It is not necessary or customary to use an agent to find an apartment. You can do it yourself, like the thousands of Swiss, Germans, Dutch, Belgians, and others who rent them every year. People write their own personal inquiries and rent directly from the owner.

Most local tourist offices say that you can get an apartment for summer use if you write one to two months in advance, but to ensure that you rent your apartment in time, you should probably start the process about three or four months in advance. For the ski season, you would need to write earlier. The turn-around time on airmail correspondence from the United States to Switzerland takes at least two weeks or more, so you should write as early as possible. It is also a good idea to request a reply by airmail and to enclose two international postal coupons, obtainable at all U.S. post offices, to cover the cost of an airmail reply.

Because Alpine towns have built apartments to accommodate the winter season, when the greatest number of visitors travel to Switzerland, apartments are often available for summer use at the last minute. You can probably walk into a place like Zermatt or Saas-Fee in the summer and get an apartment on the spot, though it may not have a view of the Matterhorn or the Mischabel range. Rather than be disappointed, however, write in advance.

In order to find an apartment, write to the tourist office—the Verkehrsbüro or office du tourisme—of the town or village in which you are interested. A few of the big alpine centers have recently computerized their apartment listings and will handle requests in English as well as German or French. For Zermatt, Saas-Fee, and Grindelwald, for instance, you should write to the tourist office (see the Appendix, page 261, for the addresses), informing them of the number of beds you'll require and the dates of your proposed stay. The office will then check its computer files and send you a list of 10 or 12 available apartments of the size and for the dates you desire, along with the name, address, and telephone number of each owner and the name of the house (often, the name of a house serves as its address). Some tourist offices will send you a little map of the town, with the houses marked on it, so you can see where the apartments are located. The tourist office will also send a printed card for you to return, with statements in German, French, and English. You then select one apartment from the list, fill out the printed card with the dates you want and the number of persons in your party, and send the card directly to the owner.

The initial listing of apartments that you receive from the tourist office may not indicate the prices. The owner's response to your inquiry, however, will quote the price and tell you how much of a deposit is expected.

You can write to the apartment owner in English. If you receive a reply in German or French, inquire in your community for translators—

often someone at a local school or college will be glad to help translate a letter. Your reply can be in English: the landlord will find a translator. The fact that you receive a letter in German does not necessarily mean that the landlord cannot speak English. We had an excellent landlord in Zermatt who spoke English quite well, but could not write it.

Vacation apartments are generally rented on a weekly basis, from Saturday to Saturday. Other arrangements can be made in the off-season (before July 1 and after August 15), but weekly rentals keyed to Saturdays are usual. The cost of an apartment is always computed in terms of the number of people who will be staying there. In 1987, apartments cost between SFr. 10 and 35 per person per day, with the average rate about SFr. 20 per day. In some regions, a weekly rate is quoted for the entire apartment rather than a daily rate per person. A typical rate is SFr. 300 or 750 per week for apartments for two or four people, respectively. Rates may decrease for longer rental periods: in Les Haudères, for example, a studio apartment for two people rents for SFr. 800 to 1,000 per month. The customary deposit is about SFr. 500, and you can send an American bank check. You can usually obtain an apartment that has five beds at the four-person rate if four people will actually occupy the apartment. Some minor charges are often added to the rate: for example, a local "Kurtaxe" of about SFr. 1 per person per day (half that for children under 14). You should include the ages of your children when sending your inquiry to the tourist office, since that information will help them select apartments that are most suitable for you.

Your landlord or landlady will provide changes of bed linen, bathtowels, dishtowels, and tablecloths, usually once a week. You will probably have your own mailbox or mail cubby hole; it's up to you to write your name on a strip of paper and put it into the empty slot in the mailbox that corresponds to the number of your apartment. Apartments usually have no telephones. You will have to bag and carry out your own trash—your landlord will show you where to leave it. Plastic garbage bags are sold in all supermarkets and grocery stores.

Your apartment will be equipped with a small refrigerator, a stove, and all the utensils you'll need for cooking and serving. The pantry, however, will be bare. Occasionally we've found a small amount of toilet paper still on the roller in the bathroom, a pinch of salt in the saltshaker, or a small amount of soap or detergent, but you can't count on that. Most Swiss arrive with such staples as salt, pepper, sugar, toilet paper, and whatever else they can cram into their car. Just remember to put staple items on your shopping list when you go out to buy your first provisions.

If you arrive at your apartment late on Saturday afternoon, do your shopping as soon as possible. Generally, shops are closed on Sunday—

though in some resort towns they may be open for part of the day. Usually, shop hours are 8 a.m. to noon and 14–18:30. Generally, there's a little card on the front door marked Offnungszeiten or heures d'ouverture and listing the hours, European style: 14–18:30 means 2–6:30 p.m. Geschlossen or fermé means closed. And if you arrive on Saturday, check the sign on the door of your village bakery. If it says "Sontag Geschlossen" or "Dimanche fermée," stock up on bread and goodies for the weekend.

The prices of food in supermarkets or small shops are comparable to prices in the United States. In general, meat is more expensive, quality fruit and vegetables are less costly, and most staples are about the same. Beer and wine are less expensive, whiskey and brandy are more so. If you have access to one of the large supermarket chains, you can save quite a bit.

In Part II, we feature five places that would each make a good center for a week or two of hiking, using a vacation apartment as a base, and we describe the major trails accessible from these villages. At the beginning of each chapter, we offer a brief description of the village or area. If you have never been to Switzerland or if you have visited it only briefly, we hope this will help you decide where you'd want to stay for a week or two. As every alpine village in Switzerland has vacation apartments, our list of five places is necessarily limited, but we made our selection on the basis of the most outstanding scenery and the greatest number of hiking routes. We've also tried to give you an assortment of villages in different geographical and linguistic regions of Switzerland.

5

ZERMATT WALKS

The alpine scenery above Zermatt is perhaps the most breathtaking in Switzerland. There are more 4000-meter peaks clustered around Zermatt than around any other village in the Alps. The Matterhorn looms over Zermatt, but from a viewpoint on the Gornergrat or Höhbalmen, the well-known peak becomes just part of the grand chain of great mountains that loops around the Zermatt valley. Zermatt also has the greatest number and the finest collection of walks of any place in the Alps: you could stay there for two weeks and take a different walk every day.

The Matterhorn is not the highest mountain above Zermatt, nor even (by the normal route) the most difficult to climb, but this is the mountain that has become the emblem of Zermatt, its silhouette reproduced on everything from ski badges to cookies. Among mountains, its shape is unique and magnificent and its history has a tragic glamor. Numerous efforts having failed, it once seemed unconquerable. In 1865 it was the only great Alpine peak still unclimbed. In that year, 25-year-old Edward Whymper led a party of seven to the summit, racing another party climbing from the Italian side. As they descended in triumph, their rope broke and four of the party fell to their deaths.

The Matterhorn remains an attraction and a lure unlike any other peak in the Alps. People flock to Zermatt from all over Europe, the Americas and Japan to climb the legend. And there is no summer in Zermatt that does not bring new deaths on the mountain.

Zermatt has its drawbacks as well. The Matterhorn, the Gornergrat cog railway, and its superb skiing (in summer as well as winter) have made

North wall of the Matterhorn from Höhbalmen

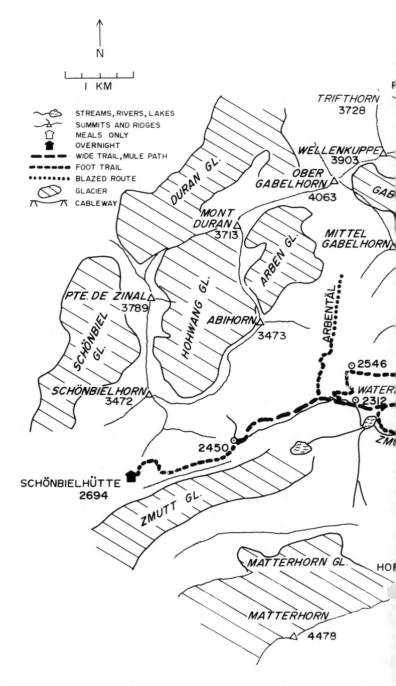

ZERMATT WALKS 1 THROUGH 8

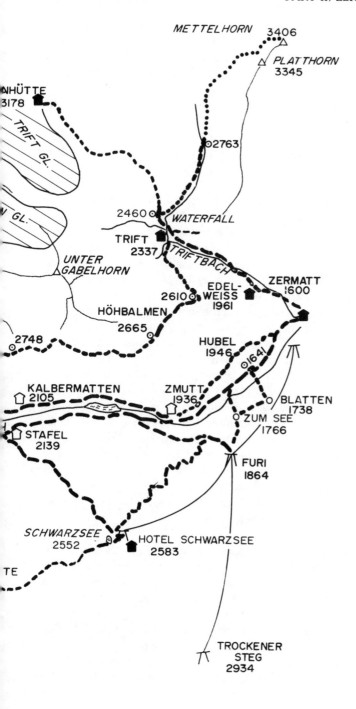

Zermatt an international tourist attraction. If climbers and hikers are plentiful, tourists are more so. Large numbers come in on the narrow-gauge Brig-Visp-Zermatt railroad to spend the day, to ride the cog railway up to the Gornergrat or take the new Kleine Matterhorn lift, the highest in Europe. Fortunately, hikers can be in open country in 5 or 10 minutes, leaving the crowds behind. Most of the tourists who ride up to the Gornergrat or take the Matterhorn lift never set foot on a walking trail.

Because tourists flock here from around the world, and because Zermatt was once almost the province of the great first generation of British climbers, many people here speak English, perhaps more so than in other major Swiss alpine centers.

Once a simple mountain village, Zermatt is now a popular resort with a good deal of chic. You can buy a thousand-dollar watch at several establishments on the main street; there are boutiques with fashionable clothing, a fancy photo store. Yet these are jumbled among other shops selling toy ice axes and Matterhorn pennants. The main street gets crowded and noisy in the afternoon and after dinner, when people turn out to stroll and window-shop. Zermatt is also a popular center for summer skiing, and the well-to-do American youths who attend the summer ski camps often hang out in the evening at the couple of bars on the main street. Zermatt is not as built up or as opulent as St. Moritz, but if you want a place where there's no luxury hotel, where gold bracelets don't flash in shop windows, where you'll never see a crowd, choose one of the other towns described in this book. On the other hand, if you like to look at a variety of people and shops, if you like a large choice of restaurants, you will enjoy Zermatt. And there are things to do here on a rainy day: visit the little alpine museum, the English church dating from the Victorian era, or the cemetery, which is filled with the graves of climbers of all nations, as well as those of the villagers. Some of the headstones are cut in the shapes of the mountains on which the climbers perished. And buried here are the four members of Whymper's party who fell when the rope broke: the Rev. Charles Hudson, Douglas Hadow, Michel Auguste Croz, and Lord Francis Douglas.

Zermatt has allowed almost unlimited growth, and there are now many concrete chalets showing just enough exterior wood trim to give them a "chalet" appearance. The main areas of new growth are on what were once the edges of the village (which is now almost a small town). Fortunately, many old wooden chalets still exist in the little narrow streets in the center of Zermatt and are scattered elsewhere as well. The tour groups and the shops are clustered on the main street; once you leave that, Zermatt is neither crowded nor noisy. And it has not been paved over. The people of Zermatt still cultivate potatoes, enormous Bibb lettuces, rhubarb, and strawberries in their gardens, and every little plot of grass is scythed for hay.

No automobile traffic whatsoever is allowed in Zermatt. Tourists must park their cars elsewhere (usually at Täsch, the village just down the valley) and take the train into Zermatt. In Zermatt, goods are delivered by electric carts, and both horse-drawn carriages and little electric cars serve as taxis. The electric cars and carts run almost noiselessly—you often don't hear one until it's almost upon you.

Zermatt is a little spoiled, but the scenery around the village is matchless, and because of Zermatt's topography, the walks are numerous and superb—the best set of walks from any one village in the Alps. Zermatt lies at the confluence of three large glaciers at the southern end of the Mattertal. In addition to these three glacier valleys, two narrow valleys topped with high glaciers also enter the Mattertal. From Zermatt, therefore, you can walk in five directions, and in each direction there are several different routes available.

The best-known view of the Matterhorn is seen from the meadows above Findeln (page 80). The walk to Gagenhaupt (page 90) offers closer, excellent views of the northeast ridge and, as you proceed toward Rotenboden and Gornergrat, views of the mountain's east face. The walks to the Schönbielhütte (page 67) and Höhbalmen (page 74) provide superb views of the north wall of the Matterhorn.

The recommended topographic map for all Zermatt walks is ZERMATT-TÄSCH-CERVINIA (BREUIL), Landeskarte der Schweiz (2515) mit Überdruck, 1:25000. Edition of Air Zermatt and WE WE Verlag: St. Gallen. 1982.

ZMUTT REGION

The Zmutt walks take you along the north bank of the Zmutt glacier and its stream, the Zmuttbach, and offer views of the north wall of the Matterhorn.

There are no mechanical aids available for these walks.

1. ZMUTT HAMLET, THE LOW ROUTE

Rating: easy
Distance round trip: 5 km
High point: 1936 m

Total climb: 320 m
Time: 50 minutes up, 40 minutes down
Map: pages 62–63

This is an easy, short walk to a pretty hamlet set in an appealing location among meadows. It also has a notable view of the northeast ridge of the Matterhorn.

From the village church, continue south along the main street toward the Matterhorn. A signpost at the end of town points you toward Zmutt, Stafelalp, Kalbermatten, and Schönbiel. Ascend a very gentle grade on a mule path that leads through woods, then climbs up to the Zmutt meadows, which give their name to the famous Matterhorn (in Valaisian dialect, the meadow-horn). In this valley where nearly all the land slopes, often steeply, this long, narrow shelf of level meadow is an unusual sight. Before the grass is cut, there's a beautiful profusion of several dozen varieties of wildflowers. After 40 minutes you reach a simple little restaurant (which serves drinks and sandwiches) in a wooden farmhouse and, 5 minutes beyond that, Zmutt (1936 meters). The hamlet consists of a few old, slate-roofed wooden houses and barns, a tiny white chapel, and several simple restaurants. The view of the hamlet from above is a very pretty one—the houses are clustered tightly together amid the green meadows. Across the river gorge stands the Matterhorn: from Zmutt you see the northeast ridge and the beginning of the broad north face. You will encounter more people walking on this easy path than on any other Zermatt walk. If you continue past Zmutt, however, the numbers diminish at once.

(From Zmutt you can cross the Zmuttbach for the trails to Stafelalp, Schwarzsee, the Hornlihütte, and the various little hamlets below the Matterhorn: Zum See, Winkelmatten, Blatten, and Furi. You can also return to Zermatt on the high route, via Hubel and Herbrigg. And you can continue on to Kalbermatten and the Schönbielhütte.)

2. ZMUTT HAMLET, THE HIGH ROUTE

Rating: moderate
Distance loop trip: 5 km
High point: 2020 m
Total climb: 425 m
Time: 2 hours 40 minutes
Map: pages 62–63

This route is a rather more demanding walk to Zmutt, with more extensive views. It's a good training walk for conditioning leg muscles and for altitude acclimatization.

From the village church, walk south along the street toward the Matterhorn for a couple of minutes. After the street bends slightly, watch for a sign on your right indicating Herbrigg, 30 minutes, Hubel, 1 hour 15 minutes, and Zmutt, 2 hours. Turn right and walk up past a few houses. The footpath climbs at a moderate grade above the village and then becomes steeper as you walk through small fields used for pastures and haymaking. Herbrigg (1755 meters) and Hubel (1946 meters) are clusters of wooden granaries (mazots) erected on short stone stilts, with flat round stones set under the barn floors to keep out rodents.

Above Hubel the path turns to the right (west), rises 75 meters, and then levels out somewhat onto a fine grassy shelf at 2020 meters with good views of the Matterhorn, the Rimpfischhorn, the Mischabel range, and the mountains above the Gorner glacier. Ramble along this shelf for 20 minutes or so, then turn left (south) at the fork for the descent to Zmutt.

3. SCHÖNBIELHÜTTE

Rating: strenuous
Distance round trip: 22 km
High point: 2694 m
Total climb: 1090 m
Time: 4 hours 30 minutes up, 3 hours down
Map: pages 62–63

A full day's walk with a substantial change of altitude. Magnificent scenery: one of the grandest walks in Switzerland. No retreats or mechanical aids are available, so wait for a good day. You can break up this walk by staying overnight at the hut.

Begin by taking the low route to Zmutt (page 65), where a sign indicates the way to Schönbiel. Leave the hamlet, following the footpath westward through a strip of meadow below the massive wall of Höhbalmen, which rises above on your right. Below, on your left, is the Stafelalp dam, fed by the Zmuttbach and the Zmutt glacier, and part of the Grande Dixence system. (This is one of the most complex hydroelectric projects in the world. A series of installations collects water from all over the Valaisian Alps—from the Saas valley to Martigny. Via tunnels drilled through the mountains, the water is pumped up to the Lac des Dix, where power is then generated as the water falls 1600 meters to the Rhône valley.) Except for an occasional concrete tunnel entrance on the Höhbalmen slopes above you and of course the dam itself, there is little visual evidence of the immense hydroelectric works. After passing the dam, you see the milky, gray-green Zmuttbach and then the broad moraine of the

The Swiss Alpine Club's Schönbielhütte

glacier. Towering above on your left is the immense, forbidding north wall of the Matterhorn.

The trail mounts gradually. An hour past Zmutt, you come to the tiny Kalbermatten restaurant (2105 meters), a simple little room in a wood cabin. Beyond this, in the moraine to your left, is more evidence of the Grande Dixence works: a basin and some concrete sluices. Ascend steadily below some rock walls. Pass the first of several junctions for trails that turn left (south) to Stafelalp. The trail then enters a cleft to the right, climbs beside a long waterfall, and emerges above the fall at the point where the Höhbalmen trail descends to the Zmutt valley. Cross a wooden footbridge. A sign points toward the route to the hut. Continue to the right of the stream (or take the gravel motorcycle track to the left of the stream). Shortly after this, the deep Arben valley cuts its way between the Höhbalmen massif and the mountains on the Schönbiel side. (The Arben bivouac hut, used for climbing the Ober Gabelhorn, perches above the first tier of the glaciers that hang over the Arbental.)

Follow the signpost to Schönbiel. The route leads onto the moraine, with the stream below to your right, and then climbs up onto the knife-edge crest of the moraine, where the path becomes very narrow and finally joins the slope on your right. Leave the moraine and climb switchbacks up to the hut. This last steep section takes 20 to 30 minutes.

The Schönbielhütte (2694 meters) is a stone building with a little terrace in front, which sits on a grassy shelf. The view is panoramic and breathtaking. If you face south you'll see, from east to west, the northwest ridge (the Zmuttgrat) and the west face of the Matterhorn, the Tête de Lion, the beautiful Dent d'Hérens with its arched, glittering white crest, the Tête de Valpelline, Col de Valpelline, Tête Blanche, Col d'Hérens, and the Wandfluehorn. To the north, above the hut, rise the Dent Blanche and the Pointe de Zinal. Around you, a sea of glaciers: the Schönbiel, Stockji, and Tiefmatten—hanging glaciers in serrated steps that tumble over the passes and descend to the smoother Zmutt glacier. All of this is astonishingly close. From this hut, climbers ascend any of these peaks or make glacier crossings over the Col de Valpelline and the Col de la Tête Blanche to the Val d'Hérens.

The Schönbielhütte, like most Alpine Club huts, is placed near the bivouac site of early Victorian climbers. Oscar Eckenstein, the inventor of the modern crampon, used to camp on the Schönbiel glacier, using crevasses as cold-storage lockers for his food. Today, the hutkeeper may occasionally give someone permission to camp near the hut, but the fragile alpine area is free of the tents and campfire sites found in the North American backcountry.

As you must count on at least 3 hours to walk back to Zermatt, time your departure so that you will have plenty of daylight for your return.

TRIFT REGION

The walks from Trift are all magnificent. When you emerge above the deep, narrow Trift gorge, you'll be in a high bowl surrounded by mountains and glaciers. A chain of high mountains sweeps around you from west to north and then east: the Ober Gabelhorn, Wellenkuppe, Triifthorn, Zinalrothorn, the two Äschhorn peaks, and the Platthorn—one of the greatest sights near Zermatt. Trift is the starting point for walks that take you deep into this high alpine region.

4. TRIFT

Rating: moderate
Distance round trip: 4.5 Km
High point: 2337 m
Total climb: 740 m
Time: 2 hours 15 minutes up, 1 hour 45 minutes down
Map: pages 62–63

Walking south on the main street before you reach the village church, look for a side street to your right (to the east) labeled Chrum. This street enters the main street across from Hotel Poste, between Café Beck and a shoe store. A small sign posted rather high above the wall of Café Beck indicates Edelweiss and the other Trift walks.

Near the Hotel Romantika, the route to Täsch diverges to your right. Continue up the lane toward Trift. The lane rises steeply, and in a few minutes you'll pass the last of the houses. The paved lane gives way to a dirt footpath. This takes you up by little switchbacks through a small parcel of fields to the Triftbach. Keep to the main path, which crosses the river on a sturdy wooden bridge. This river is used for the Grande Dixence project, and between here and the Trift Hotel, numerous signs in several languages warn that wading anywhere in the Triftbach is extremely dangerous, for water levels can fluctuate suddenly.

Across the bridge, the path ascends steeply in switchbacks through trees, turning at the cliffs between the fields below and the little platform at Alterhaupt (1961 meters), where Café Edelweiss is perched. This is a fairly popular walk, and provides hikers and tourists with good views of Zermatt and the Zermatt valley.

To continue from Edelweiss to Trift, walk past the restaurant, where the trail levels out for a short passage, shaded by trees, and then resumes its steep ascent of the gorge. It crosses the turbulent Triftbach on a bridge

Trift mountain inn

inues an almost relentless ascent on the right side of the stream,
deep crack of the gorge. The morning sun shines right into the
nd, as there is no shade above Edelweiss and the path is steep, this
ascent can be hot work. Therefore, try to make this walk in the cooler
morning hours.

After 45 minutes or so, you see the Wellenkuppe peak above you and
a few power lines on wooden crossbars (there is little else visible of the
massive hydroelectric works around you). In another 15 minutes reach the
broad, level plateau above with the Trift Hotel immediately on your right.

The view from the plateau is superb. You face a cirque of mountains
and glaciers: the Ober Gabelhorn (its southeast ridge curving like a long
arm, punctuated by the Mittel and Unter Gabelhorns), Wellenkuppe,
Trifthorn, and Zinalrothorn rise above the Gabelhorn and Trift glaciers
like a semicircle of presiding giants. The plateau is hemmed in on three
sides: the cirque to the west, the great shoulder of Höhbalmen (the arm of
land supporting the Mittel and Unter Gabelhorns) to the south, and another shoulder (roughly parallel to Höhbalmen) to the north. The plateau
itself is large, open, and grassy, and the streams that feed the turbulent
Triftbach below are shallow and tame here. An ideal picnic spot.

The Trift Hotel is a Victorian structure that for many years stood
abandoned and derelict. Now renovated, it's a simple mountain inn (Berg-
gasthaus) offering snacks, drinks, and basic meals. Matratzenlager and private rooms are available. The hotel lies on the route to both the
Rothornhütte and the Mettelhorn, which both require a long, steep ascent from Zermatt. Climbers descending from the mountains often stop
here for refreshments before heading down the gorge to Zermatt; hikers
can now break up the climb to the Mettelhorn by spending the night here.

5. HÖHBALMEN

Rating: strenuous
Distance loop trip: 18 km
High point: 2748 m
Total climb: 1250 m
Time: 7 to 8 hours
Map: pages 62–63

This and the walk to the Schönbielhütte are the two finest excursions
in the Zermatt region and are among the most spectacular walks anywhere
in the Alps. As with the walk to Schönbiel, no mechanical aids and no
retreats are available, so choose a fine day.

Ascend to the Trift Hotel (above), where you'll see a sign that points left (south) to Höhbalmen. Cross the stream on a bridge, walk across the meadow, and ascend the slope in front of you, where the trail, traversing up and left, is plainly visible. The trail, occasionally narrow, mounts steadily toward the southeast. After 1 hour (3 hours from Zermatt), reach the shoulder of Höhbalmen (2609 meters), where the path swings over the shoulder and around to your right. The Matterhorn heaves into view as you turn the shoulder. You emerge onto a sloping terrace (an excellent lunch spot) with phenomenal views.

Though the mountains are not as close to you here as they are at Schönbiel, you see a far greater number of them and of glaciers as well. Look east across the Zermatt valley to the Mischabel range (Dom, Täschhorn, Alphubel, Allalinhorn, Rimpfischhorn, Strahlhorn), then southeast across the Findel glacier to the Riffelberg, Stockhorn, and Monte Rosa, across the Gorner glacier to the chain of mountains (Lyskamm, Castor and Pollux, Breithorn) that culminates with the Matterhorn, then southwest down the Zmutt valley to the Dent d'Hérens and the mountains near Schönbiel, then above you to the Ober Gabelhorn, Zinalrothorn, and the peaks around them, and finally, northward to the distant but quite visible Bernese Oberland. A full circle, with 4000-meter peaks in every direction of the compass. The broad sweep of the Findel and the Gorner glaciers, resembling vast rivers of ice, are especially impressive from this viewpoint.

Your climbing is essentially done, as the trail mounts only slightly from here. Follow the slight track, broken in places but generally unmistakable, that leads around the shoulder, first southwest and then west. You'll then traverse the great body of the Gabelhorn massif, with the north face of the Matterhorn to your left. The track continues on narrow grass meadows parallel to the route to Zmutt but 600 meters above it; you'll need 1 to 2 hours to complete the traverse. As you move westward the views are mainly of the Schönbiel region.

Finally the trail begins to descend as you reach the Arben valley, and you walk down through meadows on the east side of the Arben. Descend the switchbacks beside the waterfall and join the trail to the Schönbielhütte. Turn left at this junction to return to Zermatt via Kalbermatten and Zmutt. Turn right if you want to go to the Schönbielhütte to spend the night. From this junction it will take you at least 1 hour 30 minutes to reach the hut, 2 to 3 hours to return to Zermatt.

6. ROTHORNHÜTTE

Rating: strenuous
Distance round trip: 10 km

High point: 3198 m
Total climb: 1610 m
Time: 5 hours up, 3 hours 30 minutes down
Map: pages 62–63

The Rothornhütte is located on a small promontory between the Trift and the Rothorn glaciers, which are very close to the hut. Moreover, this is as close as the hiker can get to some of the major peaks above Zermatt: the Ober Gabelhorn and Zinalrothorn, and the slightly lower Wellenkuppe, Triftborn, and Pointe du Mountet. In addition, the view across the Zermatt valley to the Mischabel range is breathtaking. Though this is a tiring walk, the spectacular views from the hut repay the effort.

Ascend to the Trift Hotel (page 74), where a sign points to the right (northwest) for the Rothornhütte and the Mettelhorn. Note that the same trail leads at first toward both but splits later. Continue straight on past the Trift Hotel, across the meadows—angling slightly toward the right—and cross the stream just below a waterfall. Just before the waterfall, the trail forks. Bear left here. (A sign points to the right for Schweifinen, 45 minutes and Zermatt, 2 hours, with a warning in German: "Nur für gute Wanderer"—for experienced hikers only.)

Continue past the waterfall. A few sluices and one short power line are the only evidence here of the Grande Dixence project. Ascend a small rise and follow the well-worn trail to your right. At this point you are walking toward the Zinalrothorn. At 2460 meters, about 20 minutes past the Trift Hotel, the trail forks, and a sign points you left (northwest) for the Rothornhütte. The trail leads you up to a narrow crest on the moraine. The final ascent—directly up the moraine crest—is steep and tiring. The hut (3198 meters) sits on a small rock shelf in a semicircle created by the Rothorn and Trift glaciers, and offers fine views not only to the north but also across the valley to the Monte Rosa and other mountains.

This hut is popular with individual climbers and climbing groups or clubs. During weekends in the high season or in good weather, it may be crowded.

7. METTELHORN

Rating: very strenuous
Distance round trip: 12 km
High point: 3406 m
Total climb: 1820 m
Time: 6 hours up, 4 hours down
Map: pages 62–63

As the Mettelhorn is a small peak, this is actually a climb rather than a hike, but one that presents no technical difficulty or rock climbing. Because it's so long and requires endurance, this trip is often used as a training climb, but the mountain is primarily climbed by hikers. You must cross a small glacier covered with permanent snow (névé) just below the peak. Although we strongly advise hikers to keep off glaciers, this is one of the very few that is considered safe. Check in at the Guides' Office (on Zermatt's main street) before you take this trip to inquire about conditions and to be sure that no recent caution has been issued.

Avoid this route after heavy fresh snow and remember that what falls as rain in Zermatt is snow at high altitudes. Rent an ice-ax (available at numerous sport shops in Zermatt) for this route and learn how to use it before you take this trip.

As this trip is long and fairly tiring and leads you up to a considerable altitude, you should not only wait for a good day but be sure you feel fresh and in good condition. You can break up the climb by staying overnight at the Trift Hotel. If you start from Zermatt, however, you must leave quite early in the morning—not later than 6 a.m.

At the Trift Hotel, the trail to both the Rothornhütte and the Mettelhorn points you to the right, across the meadows of the Trift plateau. Cross the bridge below the waterfall and continue straight (do not bear right at the fork in the trail where a sign points to Schweifinen and Zermatt). Ascend a little rise. Twenty minutes past the Trift Hotel the trail forks (2460 meters); take the path to the right (east), which is marked with a sign to the Mettelhorn.

Climb a fairly steep rise, up grassy slopes with a stream to your right. Eventually you'll come to a long meadow, less steep than the slope you just climbed up. The view is already magnificent: a sweep of glaciers above you, the chain of mountains from the Ober Gabelhorn to the Zinalrothorn, and eventually, as you rise, the Matterhorn. As you climb still higher, the mountains stretching from the Matterhorn to the Monte Rosa also appear. The trail fades from time to time, but there are cairn markers, and the direction you must take is fairly obvious—up through the long, grassy narrow valley (kumme) toward a dark notch or saddle that you see to the north. Keep more to the right than the left of the kumme.

To the right of the notch to which you are heading are two contiguous rock peaks, both gray, with swelling, round shapes. The one closest to the notch has a little nubbin on top. Neither of these is the Mettelhorn; you cannot see the Mettelhorn from the kumme. Nevertheless, the trail keeps to the right, as if you are heading for the gray rock peak, which is the Platthorn. As you approach the notch, traverse left up a stony area, then traverse right, to the top of the notch. From the notch, you see the snowfield névé and, to your right (east), the cone of the Mettelhorn. Cross the snowfield (there should be a track, unless fresh snow has fallen and no parties have crossed before you) and ascend the shaly cone on a narrow track with switchbacks. Climbing this rock pile takes about 15 minutes. The summit (3406 meters) is tiny and rather pointed, like a child's picture of an Alp.

From the summit, spectacular views around the compass—a real climber's view: the Weisshorn close at hand, the Zinalrothorn, Ober Gabelhorn, the Matterhorn, the Monte Rosa group, the Mischabel range, and the Bernese Oberland at the end of the Zermatt valley.

MATTERHORN PLATEAU

Hiking on the Matterhorn Plateau is fairly limited, and the main attractions are the Schwarzsee and the Hornlihütte, which is the climbing hut for the Matterhorn. From the Hotel Schwarzsee there's a superb view of the Monte Rosa, and the Hornlihütte is an interesting place, filled with parties of climbers and a sense of history. However, the view of the Matterhorn, from the plateau and the hut, is foreshortened, so these are not the best places from which to view the mountain. Those who have only a few days to spend in Zermatt should probably forego this trip.

The first stage of the Matterhorn lifts begins in Zermatt just above (and east of) the river at the south end of town. Here you take a cable car (télépherique) up to Furi (1864 meters). At Furi you can take a lift up to Schwarzsee on the Matterhorn plateau. The lift station is at 2582 meters, just above the lake. Although there is a second lift to Trockener Steg (2939 meters), the lift to Schwarzsee serves the Hornlihütte and is taken by most Matterhorn climbers. (A new lift from Trockener Steg continues south up to the Kleine Matterhorn at 3883 meters. There are superb views from this lift, but no hiking.)

8. HORNLIHÜTTE

Rating: strenuous
Distance round trip: 16 km
High point: 3260 m
Total climb: 1695 m
Time: 5 hours 30 minutes up, 3 hours 30 minutes down
Optional transportation: lift
Map: pages 62–63

The Schwarzsee is a charming small lake on the Matterhorn plateau, a grassy terrace below the northeast ridge of the Matterhorn. From there, you can continue up to the Hornlihütte at the base of the ridge, which is as close as the hiker can get to the famous mountain. The walk up to the Schwarzsee is a moderate excursion, but beyond the little lake the route becomes much more strenuous and difficult. Nevertheless, from the hut one can look up the ridge and see the climbers on the rock. There are also good close views of the edge of the north wall as it veers away from the ridge.

From Zermatt, several trails meander up through the meadows from which the Matterhorn plateau rises. These well-marked paths lead through the hamlets of Blatten and Zum See to Furi. A broad trail (crossing a jeep road) ascends in switchbacks, to the right of the ridge and later to the left and presents views of the Gorner glacier below. The trail passes under the lift up to Schwarzsee. A pleasant alternative route that avoids the overhead cable car and ascends more gradually is the one via Stafelalp.

The Schwarzsee (2552 meters) is pretty and during fine weather you are likely to find many tourists here, most of whom come up on the lift. The tiny chapel on the edge of the lake was built in fulfilment of a vow: a group of men crossing the pass from Italy became lost in a blinding snowstorm and promised to build a chapel to the Virgin Mary if their lives were saved. The sky then cleared, and the men were able to descend safely to Zermatt. Fine views from the Schwarzsee of the Dent Blanche, the Ober Gabelhorn, and Wellenkuppe, and the peak of the Weisshorn. From the viewpoint just past Hotel Schwarzsee there's a grand view of the Monte Rosa, the Gorner glacier, and the mountains between the Matterhorn and the Monte Rosa, as well as the Mischabel chain.

To continue to the Hornlihütte, walk to the left of the lake, where a signpost points to the trail to the hut. The sign indicates that the walking time is 2 hours, but 2 hours 30 minutes is more reasonable.

The trail is well marked and clearly visible, and gets a lot of traffic. Ascend a long rocky ridge, with numerous zigzags and one final, steep section. The trail has been improved in recent years; metal stairs and platforms have been installed over a few eroded, exposed places, where the route was once a little tricky. In good weather the route is not difficult; in snow, however, there are sections that require caution.

At the Hornlihütte, you'll find two adjoining buildings: the SAC hut with overnight accommodations for climbers, and the Belvedere Hotel, which was built by the Zermatt Burghers. The hotel has simple overnight accommodations and restaurant facilities.

FINDELN—SUNNEGGA—TUFTERN REGION

If you look at an aerial map or depiction of the Zermatt area, you will see a large massif to the east of the town, rising between the valley of the

Täschbach and the Findel glacier. This massif has numerous walking trails, a small mountain that hikers can climb, several lakes, and a chain of lifts (Sunnegga-Blauherd-Unter Rothorn) that can be used for any route on the whole massif.

The first leg of these lifts is an underground funicular train, the Sunnegga Express. This was built to replace an older chairlift that could barely accommodate winter ski crowds. The station is located on the east side of the Visp river as it flows through Zermatt (the embankments are now paved), roughly halfway between the cemetery and the Gornergrat cog railway. At Sunnegga (2288 meters), you emerge above ground. Here you can continue by gondola to Blauherd (2522 meters) where you can transfer to a cable car up to the Unter Rothorn (3103 meters). The Sunnegga Express takes about 7 minutes, the Blauherd gondola about 10 minutes, and the Unter Rothorn télépherique, which runs every half hour, another 10 minutes.

You can also begin the walks in this region by ascending on foot from Zermatt to either Findeln, Sunnegga, or Tuftern.

9. FINDELN

Rating: easy
Distance round trip: 7 km
High point: 2069 m
Total climb: 460 m
Time: 1 hour 30 minutes up, 1 hour down
Map: page 81

Findeln (2069 meters) is a hamlet, mainly abandoned now, of old wooden barns and houses. There are a couple of simple restaurants serving lunches, drinks, and snacks to hikers. This is a traditional spot for those calendar-perfect photographs of the Matterhorn's north and east faces and the sharply defined Hornli ridge.

Walk south down Zermatt's main street and turn left between the Zermatterhof Hotel and the church, with the cemetery on your left. Cross the bridge, continue straight on past the Old Zermatt restaurant and a "Végé" market (on your right). At the next corner (Hotel Julen), turn right at the signpost indicating the way to Winkelmatten, Findeln, and other points south and east. Walk south to Winkelmatten, a hamlet lying just beyond Zermatt. At Winkelmatten there is a tiny white church and a little square, with signposts. For Findeln, turn left (east). Walk up a paved lane to a waterfall, turning left (northeast) just before the falls. Cross the tracks of the Gornergrat cog railway and continue up the other side. At

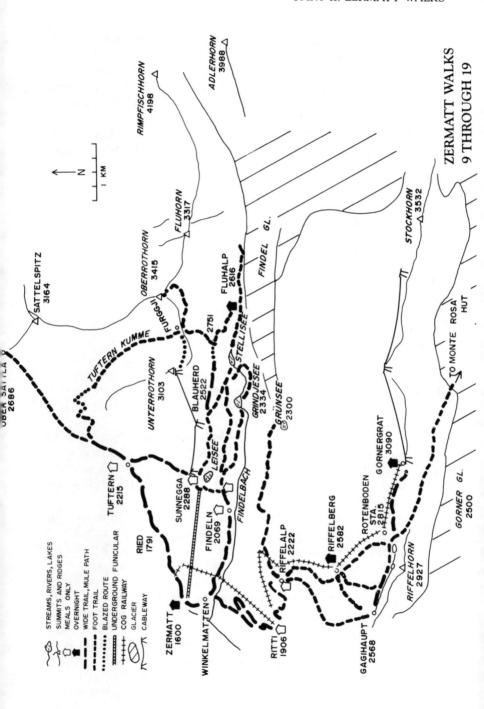

ZERMATT WALKS
9 THROUGH 19

RIMPFISCHHORN 4198

ADLERHORN 3988

FLUHORN 3317

OBERROTHORN 3415

STOCKHORN 3532

SATTELSPITZ 3164

OBER SATTLA 2686

FURGGJI

2751

FLUHALP 2616

FINDEL GL.

STELLISEE

TUFTERN KUMME

UNTERROTHORN 3103

BLAUHERD 2522

GRINDJESEE 2334

GRÜNSEE 2300

TO MONTE ROSA HUT

N
1 KM

LEISEE

FINDELBACH

GORNERGRAT 3090

TUFTERN 2215

SUNNEGGA 2288

ROTENBODEN STA. 2815

GORNER GL. 2500

RIED 1791

FINDELN 2069

RIFFELALP 2222

RIFFELBERG 2582

RITTI 1906

RIFFELHORN 2927

ZERMATT 1600

WINKELMATTEN

GAGIHAUPT 2568

STREAMS, RIVERS, LAKES
SUMMITS AND RIDGES
MEALS ONLY
OVERNIGHT
WIDE TRAIL, MULE PATH
FOOT TRAIL
BLAZED ROUTE
UNDERGROUND FUNICULAR
COG RAILWAY
GLACIER
CABLEWAY

81

1900 meters there's a fork in the trail and a sign indicating that you can either turn left or continue straight ahead for Findeln and Sunnegga. The path straight ahead is more direct.

The wide trail climbs on broad switchbacks up through woods, emerging into the open and bending to the left as it meets the shoulder of the massif. Here you turn east into the valley, high above the Findelbach, into which the Findel glacier drains.

There is another cluster of old barns and houses a little beyond Findeln at a location called Eggen (2177 meters). From Findeln or Eggen you can walk up to Sunnegga in 30 minutes.

10. SUNNEGGA, VIA TUFTERN

Rating: moderate
Distance round trip: 8 km
High point: 2288 m
Total climb: 700 m
Time: 2 to 3 hours up, 1 hour 30 minutes to 2 hours down
Optional transportation: lift
Map: page 81

This walk, mostly through forest, takes you up to the tiny cluster of barns and houses at Tuftern, which is just above the treeline on the eastern slope of the Zermatt valley. You'll have a good view from here westward across the valley to the mountains above Trift.

Start this trail by setting out as you did for Findeln (page 80), but when you get to the corner where the Hotel Julen is located, follow the sign that points straight ahead to Tiefenmatten, Ried, Tuftern, and Sunnegga. This street bends around to the left, taking you north. You are now on Riedweg street.

For another approach, head south on the main street from the train station. Shortly after passing the Gornergrat cog rail station, turn left for the town sport field (tennis courts). Pass the courts on your left and the Migros store on your right. Cross the river and continue straight ahead. Pass the Hotel Beau-Site on your left. Cross the Gornergrat cog railway tracks, and arrive at Riedweg street, where you turn left (northeast). There's a signpost here for Ried, 45 minutes, Tuftern, 2 hours 15 minutes, and Sunnegga, 3 hours.

The street climbs above Zermatt, heading northeast, until you reach the edge of town and a pine woods. Here you have a choice, which is clearly marked. The more gradual, slightly longer route takes you up on broad switchbacks through woods and then fields to Ried and then to

Tuftern. The steeper, more direct trail ascends through the woods. From Tuftern (2215 meters), a tiny cluster of wooden barns and houses and a simple restaurant, you can turn right and walk another 30 minutes southward, almost on the level, to Sunnegga at 2288 meters.

11. GRINDJESEE, VIA FINDELN

Rating: easy
Distance round trip: 4 km
High point: 2334 m
Total climb: 289 m
Time: 1 hour up, 45 minutes down
Optional transportation: lift
Map: page 81

Grindjesee with the Matterhorn in the background

There are five small lakes above the Findel glacier: the Stellisee, Leisee, Grindjesee, Mosjesee, and Grünsee. Of these, the Stellisee is the most popular, but we also like the Grindjesee very much. Hidden in a deep fold between the slope of the massif and the glacial moraine, it is a beautiful, refreshing spot, not much frequented, and perfect for a warm afternoon. Though the surrounding area is well above treeline, there are trees on one bank of the lake; you can hear birds and see fish in the lake here. A sparkling stream runs from the waterfall above the lake through meadows to the Grindjesee. You can dip your toes in the lake, lie on the grass, read a book, or simply gaze at the Matterhorn.

To reach the Grindjesee take the route to Findeln (page 80). At Findeln, continue straight ahead, following signs for Stellisee and Fluhalp, until you reach Restaurant Paradies.

Just past Paradies is another fork, which indicates that Leisee and Sunnegga are to the left and Stellisee and Fluhalp are to the right. Take the right fork and proceed straight on the footpath. Note that the milky gray-green lake visible below to your right is the Mosjesee, not the Grindjesee. The path climbs slowly through meadows and 20 minutes past Paradies, forks again. This is the junction for Stellisee (to the left) and Grindjesee (bear right). The trail continues on the right side of the slope, with the Findel glacier moraine and the Findelbach below. About 30 minutes past Paradies you will see a waterfall and then the Grindjesee (2334 meters).

12. FLUHALP FROM SUNNEGGA

Rating: easy
Distance round trip: 8 km
High point: 2616 m
Total climb: 565 m
Time: 1 hour 30 minutes up, 40 minutes down
Optional transportation: lift
Map: page 81

This is a very popular walk—because of the Sunnegga lift, it is also an easy one, and you will see families with small children, and older people. The path leads first to a pretty little lake, the Stellisee, from which there are superb views of the Matterhorn, the mountains above Trift, the Schönbiel mountains, and the Gornergrat ridge. Just a few minutes beyond the lake is a mountain inn, Hotel Fluhalp, which serves as the climbing hut for the Rimpfischhorn, Strahlhorn, Adlerhorn, and the glacier crossings to Saas-Fee.

To reach Stellisee, walk up to Sunnegga or take the Sunnegga Express (page 80). From Sunnegga a signposted path, broad and well marked, ascends at a moderate grade to the east, below the cliffs that separate Sunnegga from Blauherd. The path then proceeds along a grass shelf to Stellisee (2537 meters). (You can also reach Stellisee from the Blauherd lift station, from which a jeep road descends, signposted for Stellisee and Fluhalp, and then joins the path from Sunnegga to Stellisee.)

The Stellisee is a favorite picnic spot. The little lake is set among high meadows, well above treeline, with long, extensive views. To reach Fluhalp, continue walking to the east. After 15 minutes you'll come upon a rather tall old wooden building, Hotel Fluhalp (2616 meters), with a pleasant stone terrace in front. Because it is easily accessible, Fluhalp is a popular spot for hikers and strollers for lunches, drinks, and snacks. Beyond Fluhalp you can see an older, abandoned mid-nineteenth century mountain inn. You can walk through a fine meadow eastward past the old hotel toward the Rimpfischhorn or up to the moraine for views of the Findel glacier.

If you walk up to Fluhalp from Zermatt you have a 1020-meter ascent; from the Blauherd lift station, an 80-meter ascent.

13. OBERROTHORN

Rating: very strenuous
Distance round trip: 12 km
High point: 3415 m
Total climb: 1200 m
Time: 4 hours 30 minutes up, 3 hours down
Recommended transportation: lift
Map: page 81

Along with the Mettelhorn, the Oberrothorn is the most common endurance-training climb in Zermatt (the Riffelhorn is used for technical rock-climbing training). At 3415 meters, the Oberrothorn is a scant 9 meters higher than the Mettelhorn. The Mettelhorn, however, must be climbed solely through your own exertions, whereas most hikers approach the Oberrothorn from the lift at Sunnegga or Blauherd.

A signpost at Sunnegga indicates the way to Blauherd. The path is direct and rather steep and stays close to the lift line. Reach Blauherd station in about 45 minutes.

From Blauherd, follow the sign to "Rothorn," which points to the east. (Do not take the path to the left, which rises in steep switchbacks up the west face of the Unterrothorn, under the lift line.) Continue eastward on the jeep road that gradually bends around the south shoulder of the Unterrothorn. You are traversing below the rocky wall of the Rotewang, which is the south face of the Unterrothorn. The jeep road narrows, climbing gradually to 2751 meters, where you'll see a metal sign on a large boulder that points to Berghütte Fluhalp.

Walk past the boulder and turn left (north), keeping to the right of the bulldozed ski slope. Ascend a jeep track that rises gradually to the northeast. After 10 minutes the track turns left (north) toward the notch or saddle, which is clearly visible. The Furggsattel (or, on some maps, the Furggji) links the Unterrothorn to your left (west) with the Oberrothorn to your right (east). Keep right of the downhill ski trail, marked with red posts, as you climb through a green bowl to the saddle above you. Reach this saddle at 2981 meters (1 hour 30 minutes from Fluhalp, not much less from Blauherd).

From the Furggsattel, the Oberrothorn summit looks like an arc of reddish rock. Take the narrow footpath to your right (east). (Do not attempt to climb up the steep west face—the side that faces the Unterrothorn.) The path traverses the south face at first (facing the Monte Rosa), ascends in switchbacks, and then ascends more steeply up the east ridge. There are fixed ropes at a few steep passages. The way up the shaly slope is steep and narrow, but presents no technical difficulties unless there is fresh snow. There is often a little snow at the summit, but if there is snow on the face and ridge below, the ascent to the summit would require special care and would be inadvisable for children. From the summit (3415 meters) you'll have splendid views of the Mischabel chain, the Matterhorn, and the Gabelhorn-Zinalrothorn group across the Zermatt valley.

Return to Zermatt on the same route or via Findeln or the Tufternkumme. If you walk up from Zermatt instead of using the Sunnegga Express add 8 kilometers to the trip and 620 meters to the total climb. Walking all the way from Zermatt to the Oberrothorn will add 2 hours up and 1 hour 30 minutes down to the length of the trip.

14. TUFTERNKUMME

Rating: moderate
Distance loop trip: 12 km
High point: 2981 m
Total climb: 480 m
Time: 5 hours 15 minutes
Recommended transportation: lifts
Map: page 81

The Tufternkumme (Tufterchumme on some maps) is a long, empty valley, scooped out between the Ober and Unterrothorns. The kumme is quite wild—few hikers know of its rugged beauty.

Starting from Blauherd head toward the Oberrothorn (page 85), climbing the Furggsattel at 2981 meters. Ascend to the center of the saddle. The trail will now head north—not through the center of the valley, but a short way up on the right slope (along the lower slope of the Oberrothorn).

It's an attractive route, with long green slopes and the scoured rock of the Oberrothorn wall curving down to the floor of the kumme. As the two shoulders on either side of the kumme gradually level out, you emerge onto a broad grassy plateau. If there's lots of snow in the kumme, as is the case early in the season or in snowy years, the going can be very slow and strenuous. Be sure to take gaiters to close the tops of your boots. A ski pole or ice ax will also be useful early in the year.

Turn left (to the southwest) onto a broad path for the trail to Tuftern. From there walk down to Zermatt or proceed southward to the Sunnegga Express station, 30 minutes from Tuftern.

15. OBER SATTLA

Rating: moderate
Distance round trip: 11.5 km
High point: 2686 m
Total climb: 410 m
Time: 2 hours 30 minutes up, 1 hour 30 minutes down
Recommended transportation: lift
Map: page 81

This excursion leads you northward up the Mattertal and provides views you can't see from Zermatt. The Ober Sattla is a high, grassy perch from which you are well positioned to see the Weisshorn (4505 meters). The Weisshorn is a difficult climb, and some consider it one of the most beautiful mountains in the Alps. From the Ober Sattla there is also a fine view of several peaks in the Mischabel chain, which separates the Zermatt and Saas valleys.

From the Sunnegga Express station, walk to Tuftern. At Tuftern, continue straight ahead (north). (If you walk up from Zermatt to Tuftern, turn left at Tuftern.) A broad path leads you through the pastures above Tuftern and in the direction of the Tufternkumme, which rises to your right.

As the shelf on which you're proceeding narrows, the broad track becomes a footpath. Enter a pretty, enfolded valley, slung below one of the ridges of the Oberrothorn. The trail, ascending gradually upward to the end of this valley, grows still more narrow and traverses a steep, stony slope on which you must cross several boulder slides; walk with care. This rather long traverse will take you 30 minutes (there are fixed cables near the end to help you). The trail turns upward for a short, steep section and leads out onto the grassy shoulder of the Ober Sattla (2686 meters). There are generally several parties of hikers here, spread about on the shoulder at lunchtime.

Besides a superb view of the Weisshorn, you'll see the best view available from the Zermatt region of the Dom, the highest mountain entirely within Swiss borders, and of adjoining peaks in the Mischabel range. The tall pointed mountain you see to the north across the Rhône valley toward the Bernese Oberland is the Bietschorn. You can also see the Täschhütte across the valley of the Täschbach—the hut is used for climbs of the Rimpfischhorn, Allalinhorn, Alphubel, and Täschhorn to the east. You can return the way you came or walk down to Zermatt via Tuftern (page 82).

RIFFELBERG-GORNERGRAT REGION

This region consists of the massif between the Findel glacier to the north and the Gorner glacier to the south; it descends to the Zermatt valley (near the foot of the Matterhorn) to the west and rises to the Stockhorn and Monte Rosa peaks to the east. The region offers several walking routes, and the Gornergrat cog railway can provide hikers with transportation. The cog railway runs between Zermatt and Gornergrat, with a stop just above Winkelmatten at Findelbach and intermediate stations at Riffelalp, Riffelberg, and Rotenboden.

16. RIFFELALP

Rating: easy
Distance round trip: 8 km
High point: 2222 m
Total climb: 625 m
Time: 1 hour 45 minutes up, 1 hour 30 minutes down
Optional transportation: cog railway
Map: page 81

Riffelalp is the first stage of the way up to the Gornergrat. At Riffelalp you emerge from the forested lower slopes of the Riffelberg onto a grassy terrace.

Walk to Winkelmatten (page 80), the hamlet just south of Zermatt. At Winkelmatten, walk past the church and cross the stream which has two bridges: the upper one is metal, the lower is an old wooden footbridge. There's a trail up to Riffelalp from the upper, metal bridge, but a more attractive approach starts from the old wooden footbridge. Cross the wooden bridge, where a sign directs you to Riffelalp and Gornergrat. Go straight ahead on the footpath up a meadow. At one point the meadow trail intersects a loop of a paved road. Cross the road, continuing on the dirt trail.

After 10 minutes you'll see a sign that points in two different directions for the same destinations: Riffelalp, Riffelberg, and Gornergrat.

The trail to the left takes you up broad switchbacks on a paved road, which turns into a trail; the one to the right is steeper and narrower, and takes you past the little forest restaurant at Ritti. Both trails ascend through woods and then emerge at the pastures of Riffelalp (2222 meters). Note that Station Riffelalp (2211 meters) is about 10 minutes northeast of Riffelalp. At Riffelalp there are two old chapels, one Catholic and the other Protestant, and the remains of a hotel.

If you wish to continue past Riffelalp, you have two choices: you can walk up to Riffelberg or to Gagihaupt (which is also called Gakihaupt or Gagenhaupt on various signposts and maps). From either Riffelberg or Gagihaupt you can proceed up to the Gornergrat, which is a high, rocky ridge extending eastward from the Riffelberg, between several massive glaciers.

17. RIFFELBERG

Rating: easy
Distance round trip: 2.6 km
High point: 2582 m
Total climb: 360 m
Time: 1 hour 15 minutes up, 40 minutes down
Optional transportation: cog railway
Map: page 81

The high, sloping plateau called Riffelberg rises above the steep cliffs at Riffelalp. The Riffelberg is a large, open, grassy area with excellent views, especially to the west and southwest. To the southeast rises the high ridge of the Gornergrat.

Walk to Riffelalp or take the cog railway from Zermatt (page 88). The trail from Riffelalp to Riffelberg (2582 meters) begins between the two chapels and rises directly east through the green bowl before you; then it turns to the south, and heads up a steep slope on a well-marked trail with switchbacks. You'll arrive at Riffelberg in 1 hour 15 minutes, emerging above the cliff onto a broad plateau. At Riffelberg there is a mountain hotel, built in the nineteenth century by the Burghers of Zermatt.

From Riffelberg, you can continue across the plateau: there's a fork just past the Riffelberg station. The trail to your right takes you south, where you can join the route up to the Gornergrat at a point about midway between Gagihaupt to the west and the Rotenboden station (2815 meters) to the east. The trail to your left crosses the plateau a little higher and to the east, and then leads you down to the Rotenboden station or allows you to continue straight up to Gornergrat (3090 meters). From Riffelberg you can walk to Gornergrat in another hour and 30 minutes.

18. ROTENBODEN, VIA GAGIHAUPT

Rating: moderate
Distance round trip: 7.5 km
High point: 2815 m
Total climb: 600 m
Time: 2 hours 15 minutes up, 1 hour down
Optional transportation: cog railway
Map: page 81

This very scenic walk winds around the southwestern shoulder of the Riffelberg and provides you with excellent views of the mountains up the Zmutt valley and of the Matterhorn and Breithorn. The route takes you past the Riffelhorn and then to Rotenboden, from which you can continue up to the Gornergrat.

Walk or take the cog railroad to Riffelalp (page 88).

At Riffelalp pass the old Protestant and Catholic chapels, heading south on a trail marked for Gagihaupt (Gagenhaupt), Rotenboden, and Gornergletscher. Cross a stream, pass a few trees, and continue left at a fork. (Avoid the trail to the right, which descends to the Gornergletscher.) You will then traverse the west face of the Riffelberg massif, climbing gradually. The trail is fairly narrow but quite good and always clear. Head southward, toward the Matterhorn; as you round the shoulder, the trail will turn toward the southeast. At Gagihaupt, a rocky outcrop, chamois (small antelope) may occasionally be seen in the morning. The trail then proceeds eastward above the Gorner glacier and toward the Monte Rosa. Here you'll enter a narrow valley situated between the Riffelhorn to your right and the higher ground of the Riffelberg plateau to your left (north).

The trail continues toward the Riffelhorn, which rises before you: a dark rock tower with a flat top. The rock is reddish or in places greenish-black. This little mountain serves as the rock-training climb for Zermatt. There are numerous routes to the summit, both easy and very difficult. None of these should be attempted by the hiker, unless he or she is in the company of a Zermatt guide.

The trail climbs to the Riffelsee (2757 meters), a little lake that lies below the north face of the Riffelhorn. Pass to the north side (left) of the little lake, with the Riffelhorn on your right between you and the glacier below. The view toward the Matterhorn with the Riffelsee in the foreground is one of the standard postcard views of the Zermatt area.

For the Rotenboden station (2815 meters), continue eastward briefly; a signpost then directs you left (north). The station has a small shelter but no other facilities.

19. GORNERGRAT FROM ROTENBODEN

Rating: easy
Distance round trip: 3.5 km
High point: 3090 m
Total climb: 300 m
Time: 1 hour up, 30 minutes down *Short*
Map: page 81

The Gornergrat is arguably the best high mountain viewpoint in the Alps that can be reached by lift or train. Masses of tourists mill around the terrace outside the Gornergrat hotel, all enjoying a spectacular view that almost defies description. From the Monte Rosa in the east to the Matterhorn in the west, half a dozen glaciers sweep past half a dozen peaks (each over 4000 meters) and pour into the massive Gorner glacier, which looks like a Mississippi of ice.

Walk or take the cog railway to Rotenboden (above). From the Rotenboden station a signpost directs you eastward to the Gornergrat. (Do not confuse Gornergrat with Gornergletscher, which is the glacier below you.) The signpost also indicates the route to the Monte Rosa hut, which involves a glacier crossing that you should not attempt unless you have glacier experience and equipment. Arrive at the Gornergrat (3090 meters) in 1 hour. There's a cog railway station and a hotel with cafeteria service, rooms and Matratzenlager. There is also an observatory, but it is not open to the public.

The Monte Rosa—so enormous that it has two summits, the Dufourspitze and the Nordend—fills the sky to your left. And then your eye ranges over the Lyskamm, Castor, Pollux, Breithorn, the Kleine Matterhorn and the Matterhorn. Turn the other way and you see the Mischabel chain.

If you walk to Gornergrat from Zermatt, expect the climb to take you at least 4 hours 30 minutes—the total climb is 1535 meters. To walk back to Zermatt, you have to return to Rotenboden, where you can choose to walk down or take the Gornergrat railway.

6

SAAS-FEE WALKS

The Zermatt and Saas valleys are separated by the Mischabel chain, which includes the Dom—the highest mountain entirely within Swiss borders. Saas-Fee, to the east of Zermatt, is perched on a shelf near the south ern end of the Saastal (the Saas valley), at the relatively high altitude of 1800 meters. Beyond the southern end of the village, pastures extend for about a quarter of a mile—then, abruptly, a gigantic wall of glaciers and mountains heaves up, curving around the village: a glacier cirque. The great Saas glacier and, above it, the peaks of the Mischabel chain, seem to rise vertically above the town. In the aggregate, the mountains around Zermatt surpass the ones above Saas—there are more of them and as they rise from a lower base, they look more impressive—but you cannot see most of them until you climb above Zermatt. Saas sits directly below a wall of ice, snow, and rock, with a magnificent view of mountains and glaciers from every street in the village.

The Mischabel range, curving around Saas-Fee, presents a dozen peaks over 4000 meters high, and Saas is a great center for climbing, hiking, and skiing. But while Zermatt is an international resort, Saas-Fee, in the next valley, is scarcely known outside of Switzerland and Germany. It's a much quieter and smaller place, and less stylish than Zermatt. No crowds, no day-trippers; here, in fact, you will scarcely meet any visitors but Swiss and Germans.

The valley contains a string of villages with the prefix Saas: Saas-Fee, Saas-Balen, Saas-Grund, and Saas-Almagell. There are various claims as to the meaning of "Saas": beech tree, willow, or steep, wooded slope.

The Swiss Alpine Club's Britanniahütte

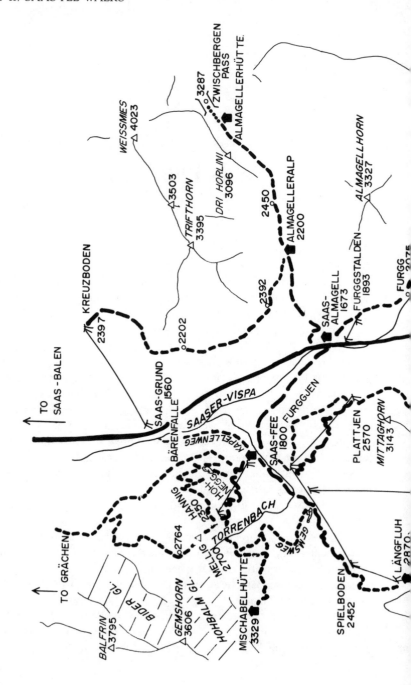

~~Seko~~ I. U.

Schloss ((Castle)
mittersill

N.A. Off — 414-886-9084
Fax 414-886-9074

Phone 43-6562-45230
Fax- 43-6562-452350

A-5730
mittersill, Austria

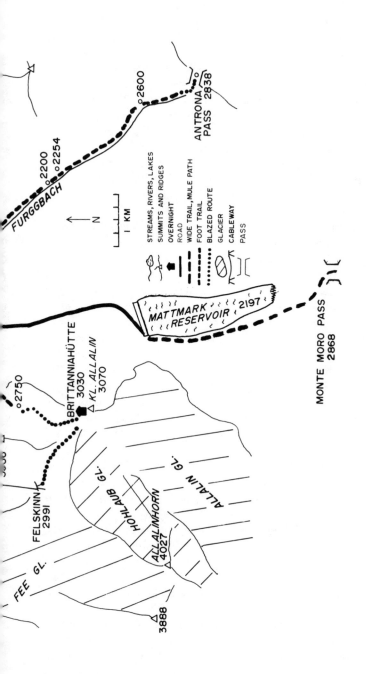

FURGGBACH

o 2200
o 2254

o 2600

ANTRONA PASS 2838

STREAMS, RIVERS, LAKES
SUMMITS AND RIDGES
OVERNIGHT
ROAD
WIDE TRAIL, MULE PATH
FOOT TRAIL
BLAZED ROUTE
GLACIER
CABLEWAY
PASS

← N   1 KM

MATTMARK RESERVOIR 2197

MONTE MORO PASS 2868

o 2750

BRITTANNIAHÜTTE 3030

KL. ALLALIN 3070

FELSKINN 2991

FEE GL.

HOHLAUB GL.

ALLALIN GL.

ALLALINHORN 4027

3888

SAAS-FEE WALKS

95

"Fee" may derive from a word meaning lambs or flocks of sheep. Up on a shelf above the main valley, and more difficult to reach, Saas-Fee was once among the least significant of these villages; there are no records of a village there before the thirteenth century, when a few families from the Saas valley evidently moved up to live year-round near the high pastures. But Saas-Fee, which has the most spectacular location, is the only one of the Saastal villages to have become an important ski resort and summer climbing center, and Saas, used alone, now refers to Saas-Fee.

The entire Saas valley was remote and undeveloped until recently, though the Antrona Pass route was used from Roman to medieval times. The road up the valley from Stalden was begun in the 1930s and construction was interrupted during World War II. Until the last section was completed in 1951, you could reach Saas-Fee only by mule. Since prosperity came so recently, traces of the old way of life are still in evidence. Some of the elderly women in Saas-Fee (and even more of them in Saas-Grund and Saas-Balen) go about their daily chores in old-fashioned dress: embroidered jackets, aprons, printed scarfs.

Saas-Fee is an agreeable mixture: an attractive, small resort that has retained the looks and the effect of a village. In the summer, Saas is filled with families and children. Although there is summer skiing here, most people come in summer for the hiking; it is delightful to see people of every age in the streets in hiking boots and packs. An evening entertainment is going out for dessert or wine after dinner, and once a week, everyone turns out when the village band plays in the square. At the main intersection in Saas there's a small supermarket, a fruit and grocery store, and a bookstore. There are good hotels but none in the luxury class. (Zermatt has two five-star hotels; Saas has none.) Ask about unusual restaurants.

Saas had a period of relative overdevelopment in the late 1970s. New chalets were built rather too close together in the village center, each one vying for a view of the Saas glacier from its balconies. Development, however, is now under tighter control, expansion has been limited, and restrictions are placed on building height and design in order to preserve the visual quality of the village. There are still streets bordered by pastures, and houses scattered in the fields, only 10 minutes from the village center. And like Zermatt, Saas-Fee has banned automobile traffic. Visitors must park at the entrance to the village, in a parking lot or one of several new garages.

Saas has fewer walks than Zermatt, in total, and no single walk that can match the grandeur of the best Zermatt walks. Yet there's plenty to do here: we list a dozen walks for Saas. The mountains that seem to heave straight up from Saas make for some rather steep paths, but there are also a number of easy and relatively level walks around the village. There are several very fine long walks as well. The high route from Saas-Fee to Grächen can be done in one day and is one of the attractions of the region. There are superb long walks from Saas-Almagell (an hour's walk or 20 minutes by bus from Saas-Fee) to the Zwischbergen and Antrona passes.

To reach Saas-Fee, take the train to Brig and change there to the PTT bus for Saas. You should phone ahead to the PTT office at Brig (tel. 028 23 66 57) for bus reservations, which are necessary for weekends. When you're ready to leave Saas, make reservations at the station there.

To reach Saas-Fee from Zermatt, take the train to Stalden, then change to the PTT bus at the station.

The recommended topographic map for all Saas-Fee walks is Wanderkarte Saastal, 1:25000: Hallwag AG Bern.

1. SAAS-GRUND, VIA THE KAPELLENWEG

Rating: easy
Distance round trip: 6.5 km
High point: 1800 m
Total climb: 250 m
Time: 1 hour down, 1 hour 30 minutes return
Optional transportation: bus
Map: pages 94–95

This is one of several short walks that can be taken from Saas-Fee by families with small children or people who just want an easy walk while acclimatizing to the altitude. This route to Saas-Grund is called the Kapellenweg (or Path of the Chapels) because it leads past 15 little chapels.

Walk behind the PTT, where a path descends toward the Feevispa river, heading northeast. The path continues above the river, with views into its rocky gorge. Along the route are a string of little chapels—the first built in 1687 and the rest in 1709—each of which contains a group of carved and painted wooden figures, the work of an anonymous artist. Collectively the chapels represent the 15 "Mysteries of the Rosary." (A short detour also leads to another chapel, "Zur Hohen-Stiege," which was built in 1685.)

2. LÄNGFLUH, VIA SPIELBODEN

Rating: moderate
Distance round trip: 9 km
High point: 2870 m

Villagers haying

Total climb: 1070 m
Time: 3 hours 30 minutes up, 2 hours 15 minutes down
Optional transportation: lift
Map: pages 94–95

A narrow strip of land reaches up the lower part of the Fee glacier like a crooked finger. On this little strip, flanked on either side by crevassed ice, is a lift line and a trail. The lift has two stops, first at Spielboden and then at Längfluh. The trail is well marked and easy, but it's a long, steep climb to the top. Spectacular views of the glacier around you and of the Mischabel chain curving above, as well as of the mountains across the valley.

The trail leaves from the south end of Saas-Fee. Cross the pastures and take one of the several easy, well-marked trails that lead up to Gletscheralp, an hour's walk. From there, it's another hour to Spielboden (2452 meters). The route presents no difficulties except that the way is steep. (The optional lift goes directly to Spielboden.)

Spielboden, the lower lift stop, is also the home of a rather tame colony of marmots, who scurry out of their burrows and sit upright to accept food. A favorite spot for children. (Signs request that one feed them only nuts, carrots, and apples—no fresh bread and no sweets.)

The well-marked trail that continues on to Längfluh (2870 meters) climbs steeply up the promontory of rocky land extending between banks of ice. Several precautions are in order. If you ride up all the way by lift, you are likely to feel the altitude when you step out. Walk slowly on top. Also, no matter how fascinating and inviting the glacier looks, do not step out onto it. The Fee glacier is crevassed and dangerous. If you want a glacier excursion here, you must have a guide.

At the end of the promontory is the upper terminus of the Längfluh lift and a mountain hotel that serves climbers (you can't take any walks from here, only technical climbs across the glaciers). Längfluh is a popular day excursion because it gives hikers and tourists extremely close views of the Fee glacier and a panoramic view of the Mischabel range, curving above the glacier.

3. PLATTJEN

Rating: moderate
Distance round trip: 6 km
High point: 2570 m
Total climb: 770 m
Time: 2 hours 30 minutes up, 1 hour 30 minutes down
Optional transportation: lift
Map: pages 94–95

This route leads you to a high shoulder under the Mittaghorn, the mountain overlooking Saas-Fee from the southeast. From here you'll have panoramic views of the Mischabel range and the Saas valley. This walk is the starting point for the route to the Britanniahütte.

Walk past the village church on the main street heading south, toward the mountains. Follow the street across the bridge to the outskirts of the town, where you see the Plattjen-Längfluh lift station. You can walk up to Plattjen (or take a gondola).

A signpost just before the lift station points you toward Plattjen, to the southeast. There are two routes: a direct, steep ascent on short switchbacks, and a trail via Furggjen that ascends more gently on broad switchbacks. Both start from the lift station on a level path that heads southwest for Plattjen. At the first signposted junction you have a choice of turning to the left (southeast) and following the steep short switchbacks directly to Plattjen or of continuing on the more gradually ascending path that will turn almost 180 degrees a little farther ahead and intersect the steeper trail at 1893 meters. At the signpost at 1893 meters, turn left (east) for Furggjen. The Furggjen route ascends on an old, broad mule path that leads through woods and boulders up to timberline. At 2000 meters the Furggjen trail forks; follow the path to your left (south), which continues up on switchbacks to Berghaus Plattjen, a mountain restaurant at 2411 meters, and then to the Plattjen lift station at 2570 meters.

4. BRITANNIAHÜTTE, VIA PLATTJEN

Rating: strenuous
Distance round trip: 9 km
High point: 3030 m
Total climb: 1270 meters
Time: 4 hours 30 minutes up, 1 hour 30 minutes down
Optional transportation: lift
Map: pages 94–95

Although this route and the next one (page 103) have the same termination point and may be combined into one loop trip, they are such different excursions that we are describing them as two walks. This route can take the whole day, especially if you don't use the lift. For the route via Felskinn we strongly advise using the lift and then taking a very short walk on the glacier. (It's the kind of attractive short excursion that fits perfectly if you're tired from some previous exertions, or if the weather is bad in the morning and then clears after lunch.)

The Britanniahütte, which flies the Union Jack as well as the Swiss flag, was built in 1912 by the Association of British members of the SAC and presented to the club's Geneva section. The Britanniahütte is located on a glacier at the southeast edge of the Mischabel chain; just east of the hut, this massif descends abruptly to the Saastal floor. Local authorities have determined that the Chessjengletscher is safe, and many hikers cross the glacier every day. No rope is needed. Dark glasses and sunblock, however, are essential.

At Plattjen (2570 meters), the trail begins behind the restaurant and heads south. It leads you in a long traverse below the Mittaghorn and the Egginer and high above the valley floor. The first part of this walk is occasionally quite exposed, but the trail is about 1 meter wide and is always distinct. To your left (east) you look down, almost 900 meters, into the deep, narrow valley of the Saastal, and you'll be able to see the village of Saas-Almagell below you. Across the valley, above Saas-Almagell, is a fine view of the Almagellertal, which ends in the Zwischbergen Pass. Farther southeast is the Furggtal, which ends in the Antrona Pass (although you cannot see that pass from here). Before you, farther south, are the Mattmark dam, the Monte Moro Pass, and Italy.

Continue this traverse below the rock wall for just over an hour. At 2750 meters the hut comes into view to the south. The trail descends about 40 meters and then turns right (west), skirting the base of the Egginer, which appears on your right as a great square-topped reddish rock tower. The trail turns the corner of the Egginer and then climbs steeply up a broad snow field. The hut (3030 meters) sits on a small saddle between

The Rimpfischhorn and glaciers, from the Klein Allalinhorn

the solitary little cone of the Kleine Allalinhorn to the left (east) and the longer ridge of the Hinter Allalinhorn to the right (west).

From the hut, there are superb views of the Allalinhorn and Rimpfischhorn to the southwest and across the Mischabel range. The rock cone of the Kleine Allalinhorn (3070 meters), just behind the hut, is an easy scramble that takes about 15 minutes. From the top you can see the tip of the Monte Rosa.

To return to Saas-Fee, reverse the route back to Plattjen. The scenery is just as remarkable in the return direction. You can use the Plattjen lift to Saas-Fee to shorten the trip. You can also make this a loop trip by taking the Felskinn lift down to Saas-Fee.

5.   BRITANNIAHÜTTE VIA FELSKINN

Rating: moderate
Distance round trip: 3.5 km
High point: 3030 m
Total climb: 40 m
Time: 50 minutes up, 40 minutes down
Recommended transportation: lift
Map: pages 94–95

The walk from the Felskinn lift station across the glacier to the Britanniahütte is a fairly easy one, nearly level and very short. The glacier route is usually safe and requires no other equipment than dark glasses and sunblock. (If conditions were to change, warning signs would be posted at the Felskinn lift station.) Because this is a short walk, it is perfect for a half-day—for example, when the weather clears after a rainy morning. Or it can be combined with another short trip.

The route between Saas and Felskinn is mainly on scree and moraine, so we recommend that you take the lift up to Felskinn (2991 meters). On a nice day you'll find a small crowd around the outdoor terrace next to the lift station at Felskinn, because of the summer skiing on the glacier. This is also the point where people change from the Felskinn lift to the new underground "Metro" that goes to the top of the Mittel Allalinhorn. (Go up for the view, but there are no walks from the top.)

Outside the lift station, turn left (southeast): a signpost indicates the route. Follow a broad track, which is frequently groomed by a snowcat. Stay on the track: don't wander off onto the glacier! As you trudge along, you may be able to see crevasses in the slope above you with blue ice glinting in the narrow, deep cracks.

The snow track passes between the Hinter Allalin to the right and the

Egginer—a reddish rock tower (3366 meters) with a square, flat top—to the left. It then climbs the little saddle, the Egginerjoch, between them, where there's a tiny ski lift. Stay on the broad snowtrack, which narrows to a path and turns slightly to the right (southeast). The hut is now in view above you.

6. HANNIG AND MELLIG

Rating: moderate
Distance round trip: 10 km
High point: 2700 m
Total climb: 900 m
Time: 3 hours up, 1 hour 30 minutes down
Optional transportation: lift
Map: pages 94–95

Hannig and Mellig are points on the lower slope of the Gemshorn, which is at the northern edge of the Mischabel chain, between the Ulrichshorn and the Balfrin. This walk is quite different in character from other walks in Saas; it takes you up into interesting terrain as you approach Mellig, where there is a series of rocky mounds.

There are two approaches to the trail to Hannig and Mellig. One starts just north of the Hannig lift station in Saas-Fee. From the church, walk north up the main street, away from the glacier cirque. The shops thin out and soon disappear. About 100 meters past this point, turn left (west). The lift station, clearly marked, is a short distance up the slope, and the trail is just beyond the station. The other approach starts just past the church, to your right (west) as you face the cirque.

The route, via the hamlet of Hohnegg (1950 meters), proceeds up broad switchbacks at a gentle grade. At first it ascends north through the woods, then traverses the slope in switchbacks, with a final short, steeper section to Hannig (2350 meters). Signposts at every trail junction indicate the routes.

At Hannig, walk behind the lift station, where you'll see a sign that points you to the right (northeast) for Mellig (also spelled Mällig). The trail is well marked, with switchbacks ascending directly up from the lift station. Reach Mellig (2700 meters) in 30 minutes. You'll have fine views of the Mischabel range and the Hohbalm glacier below the Lenzspitze and of the Weissmies group across the Saas valley. On the slopes at Mellig is an old stone wall, fancifully designated the "Chinesische Mauer"—the Chinese Wall, which makes a nice attraction for children.

7. BIDERGLETSCHER

Rating: strenuous
Distance loop trip: 8 km
High point: 2764 m
Total climb: 1065 m
Time: 7 hours
Optional transportation: lift
Map: pages 94–95

This is a long walk through lonely, wild country that offers superb views of the Mischabel range: the glacier cirque to the south and the Hohbalm glacier curving between the Lenzspitze, Nadelhorn, and Ulrichshorn above you (to the west). As you walk, extensive views unfold of the Weissmies group to the east. Return through a beautiful pine forest.

Take the lift or walk up to Hannig and then proceed up to Mellig (page 104). There, a signpost points you to the right (northwest) to Biderwald and Gebidem. An hour from the Hannig lift station, reach a mound of boulders. The route passes to the left of this mound, dips a little, and then ascends again to a second mound or crest. After 1 hour 15 minutes, emerge onto a small, level area with a stone wall to your right. Superb views of the entire Mischabel range, the Hohbalm glacier below the Lenzspitze, and the Weissmies group.

Continue straight ahead on the trail along another rise of boulders. Reach Gebidem (2764 meters), marked by a signpost and a cairn on top of the highest rock. The sign points to the right (northeast) to Biderwald. The trail continues to the north, along the crest of a ridge parallel to the long rock wall on your left. High above you to the southwest, ice climbers can sometimes be seen on the final ascent to the summit of the Lenzspitze. Views of the Bernese Oberland to the north.

After an initial steep section, the trail levels out, then turns right on a flat traverse. It then descends on narrow, exposed switchbacks—the trail is very steep and narrow—for about 100 meters. Two hours 30 minutes past the lift, at 2150 meters, come to an unmarked junction with the Saas-Fee–Grächen trail at a stone with a red and white diamond blaze and arrows pointing both left and right. Left of that is another blazed stone. Grächen is to the left (north); Saas-Fee is to the right (southeast).

Return to Saas, passing the signposted Senggboden junction (2150 meters). At the junction to Bärenfalle, follow the signs to the right (west) for Saas-Fee via Hohnegg and Melchboden. As you come out onto a broad jeep road, 3 hours 15 minutes past the Hannig lift station, turn left. The road comes out at the pond and playground at Melchboden. From here, follow the signposted road on the eastern edge of the pond to Saas, 20 minutes distant.

8. GEMSWEG

Rating: moderate
Distance loop trip: 9 km
High point: 2350 m
Total climb: 550 m
Time: 4 hours
Optional transportation: lift
Map: pages 94–95

The Gemsweg, the "chamois path," sweeps in a semicircle from Hannig to Plattjen, dipping in the middle to the little lake called Gletschersee at the foot of the Saas glacier, just south of the town. The most interesting part, however, is the section between this point and Hannig, and you can pick up the trail or terminate it at this lowest point.

Walk or take the lift from Saas-Fee to Hannig (page 104). At Hannig, a sign points you left (south) for Gemsweg and Plattjen. The trail begins to descend; after 15 minutes you'll reach a fork, where a sign points you left (southeast) to Gemsweg and Plattjen. (The other trail, ascending to the south, connects with the steep trail up to the Mischabelhütte.) The Gemsweg trail descends on switchbacks and then crosses a bridge, where a sign warns hikers to watch for falling rock. You are in the cleft between the ridge of the Gemshorn and that of the Lenzspitze, with magnificent views of the Hohbalmgletscher, a hanging glacier, towering above you. After crossing the bridge, turn left (northwest) at the next signposted junction and descend—the trail is marked by yellow and black blazes.

After 30 minutes come to a junction with the trail to the Mischabelhütte. A sign points left for the Gemsweg. The Mischabelhütte trail ascends very steeply to the right (west), and the Gemsweg descends to the left (east). The trail descends very steeply, on tiny switchbacks. You'll reach a signposted junction 45 minutes from Hannig. You can turn left (east) here and walk to Saas-Fee, but this is a poor trail—it's very steep and narrow. If you want to return to Saas, it's better to continue on the Gemsweg trail toward Plattjen, which lies straight in front of you (south). The Gemsweg trail descends just below the Gletschersee (1904 meters), then intersects the trail between Saas and the Gletschergrotte restaurant. You can return to Saas-Fee by turning left here and walking back on the easy, well-marked path.

You can continue along the Gemsweg route to Plattjen, climbing up on switchbacks, sometimes steep, to Berghaus Plattjen (2411 meters). In reverse, you can take the lift up to Plattjen, walk the semicircle, and return by the Hannig lift.

9. GRÄCHEN, THE HIGH ROUTE (HÖHENWEG BALFRIN)

Rating: very strenuous
Distance one way: 14.5 km
High point: 2364 m
Ascent/descent: 600 m/1000 m
Time: 6 hours 30 minutes to 7 hours
Recommended transportation: bus, lift
Map: pages 94–95

The Höhenweg Balfrin, one of the most famous high routes in Switzerland, connects Saas with the village of Grächen in the next valley to the west. It was built on traces of old shepherds' trails, but required blasting and some tunneling to open traverses across some of the rocky walls. After tremendous effort, the route was opened in 1954. A plaque attached to the rock near Rote Biel dedicates this "Weg in die Stille" (path in the silence of the mountains) to all who love wandering.

The route winds high above the Saastal at an average elevation of 2000 meters, along the eastern slope of the long north ridge of the Mischabel chain. To the west, the route is dominated by the Balfrin, with grand views of it and the Bidergletscher.

The Höhenweg Balfrin is a strenuous walk, requiring a whole day. The trail continually dips up and down, so the accumulated ascent is considerable, and boulders en route make it a rather athletic as well as long hike. The signposts indicate 5 hours 30 minutes for the walk, but count on 6 or 7 hours. We recommend that you take the bus to Grächen and walk back to Saas-Fee. There is neither village, farm, nor mountain restaurant on the Höhenweg, and no way off it once you're well underway. This route should on no account be undertaken in snow or bad weather, or by persons not feeling fresh and in good condition. The trail is fairly exposed in places and is occasionally rather narrow, with long drops to the valley floor, so this route is not advisable for those suffering from vertigo. Nevertheless, this is a very popular walk, and on a fine day one encounters many parties on the route, including families.

A special PTT bus leaves Saas for Grächen at 8 a.m. Call or stop at the PTT office in advance to reserve places on the bus. The trip takes 1 hour and the cost for the bus, which includes the fee for the Hannigbahn lift, is moderate.

In Grächen there are two lifts. For the Höhenweg route to Saas, nearly all hikers take the Hannigbahn. The other lift to Seetalhorn (3037 meters) takes you up higher, but adds a steep descent in snow or scree and cuts out about a third of the walk.

From Grächen (1618 meters) take the lift to Hannigalp (2114 meters), where there is a restaurant with Matratzenlager. From here you can see the Matterhorn, small but very distinct, to your left (south). A sign points out the direction for the Höhenweg.

The trail first crosses the pastures of Hannigalp, then leads through woods. It turns along the flank of the mountain and proceeds south-southeast, high above the Saas valley. After 1 hour you'll arrive at a rocky promontory called Stock (2491 meters) on maps. The trail swings in and out following the contours of the slope, which are like the innumerable folds of a curtain. Pass some fixed cables; then after 1 hour 20 minutes, at 2350 meters, you'll walk past a wooden bench. Looking north toward the Bernese Oberland you can see the unmistakable pyramid of the Bietschorn and other Oberland peaks. The Weissmies, Lagginhorn, and Fletschhorn are to your left, and the Antrona Pass is visible beyond them.

The trail continually climbs, descends, and climbs again. It is sometimes very exposed, but not continually so. After 1 hour 40 minutes follow a well-marked diversion, blazed in red, over boulders through a washed-out section of trail. At 2360 meters the trail descending from Seetal and the Seetalhorn lift joins on your right (southwest).

After 3 hours emerge onto a wide shoulder, the Rote Biel, which has fine views of the Balfrin glacier towering above. The Schweibbach stream is visible in a bowl below. This shoulder is a good spot for a lunch break. From Rote Biel descend to 2100 meters and cross the Schweibbach on rocks or boards. The Balfrin moraine is just above you, to the right. After 3 hours 30 minutes come upon a boulder slide; watching for the paint blazes, cross this on the level as much as possible and pick up the footpath on the other side.

Continue through the numerous folds of the slope, crossing the bridge over the Biderbach at 2167 meters. Saas-Grund is now visible on the valley floor below, and there's a good view of the Mittaghorn thrusting between the Saaser Vispa and its little tributary, the Feevispa, flowing down from the Saas glacier. Saas-Fee is visible on its shelf 250 meters above the Saastal. You can see the valley as it hooks to the southeast and the Antrona and Monte Moro passes in the distance.

The trail begins a long, gradual descent, entering a beautiful area of Arolla pines, thick grass, and Alpenrosen, which bloom from about mid-July to the first week of August. At 2000 meters the trail forks, left toward Bärenfalle and right toward Hohnegg and Melchboden. Either route will take you to Saas-Fee.

Several of the finest excursions in the area are made from Saas-Almagell, the last and southernmost village of the valley. It is easy to reach this village from Saas-Fee either on foot or by bus. Take the PTT bus to Saas-Grund and change there to the bus for Saas-Almagell. The ride to Saas-Grund takes 10 minutes, and to Saas-Almagell, 8 minutes. Buses are frequent, and the connections are excellent. The walk is an easy one, descending from Saas-Fee (1800 meters) to Saas-Almagell (1673 meters). The path leaves Saas-Fee to the east, just past the village. A broad, easy trail descends gently through the forest, and in 45 minutes you'll reach Saas-Almagell, a quiet, pretty little village on the banks of the Saaser Vispa.

10. ANTRONA PASS

Rating: strenuous
Distance round trip: 17 km
High point: 2838 m
Total climb: 1200 m
Time: 4 hours up, 2 hours 45 minutes down
Recommended transportation: bus; **optional transportation,** lift
Map: pages 94–95

This is a beautiful walk into a long, wild, deserted valley, the Furggtal, that climbs to the Italian border. In the Middle Ages this was an important trading route, and in several places on or near the present trail sections of paving from medieval times are still visible. You can also see the remains of a salt depot near the pass. With the exception of a small spillway for the Mattmark dam, there is no other sign of human use or habitation once you walk past the farm at the opening of the valley.

Take the PTT bus or walk from Saas-Fee to Saas-Almagell (above). From the Saas-Almagell village square, follow the signs for Furggstalden (1893 meters): the path starts near the church and climbs up through the woods, emerging into the open pastures of Furggstalden after 45 minutes. Families with small children or hikers who wish to conserve their energy for the pass may prefer to take the lift to Furggstalden, which saves you 200 meters of climbing. The little chairlift is located just off the square. Be sure to check the sign at the little ticket office for the last descent time.

At Furggstalden the trail for the Antrona Pass starts to the right (southeast) of Restaurant Furggstalden. The trail rises through pastures, climbing very gradually. Walk through the gate of a fence, then cross a very broad meadow and pass under a ski lift. To the right is a very small wooden granary (mazot) in front of a gigantic boulder. To the west, facing the opening of the Furggtal, is the huge black wall of the Egginer and the Mittaghorn, with a long waterfall shining on its face.

Continue up the gentle gradient through thin woods on the blazed trail. The path broadens, turns right, then curves leftward around the shoulder of the Almagellhorn. Pass under a second ski lift and continue around the shoulder, still to the left (southeast). At 2075 meters is the little farm of Furgg, with the Furggtal before you.

The trail proceeds up the left (north) side of the valley. Do not cross the valley or its stream, the Furggbach, where another farm is visible, as the trail to the pass keeps to the northern bank. Emerge from the trees and head southeast up the Furggtal, with the stream always to your right. The valley is very lovely, with the Furggbach running between grassy banks and walls of rock curving down on both sides. At first the gradient is very gentle.

The trail rises over a wall of scree. Ascend again on grass and then walk up a second wall of scree. Here you'll find a concrete spillway on the stream. Look for traces of medieval paving on the trail to your right, below the spillway. The Stellihorn points upward at the end of the valley, to the south, and the Antrona Pass is above you, to the southeast.

The valley rises toward the pass, and the ground becomes stony. Ascend long slopes of broken rock and glacial rubble. Again, watch for traces of the old paving: the stones are laid vertically into the ground, like bricks laid on their side. Though the trail is washed out in a few places, the way is marked both by paint blazes and by cairns. You'll cross a few broad slabs of rock just before you arrive at the utterly deserted Antrona Pass.

11. ALMAGELLERALP, THE HIGH ROUTE

Rating: moderate
Distance loop trip: 10 km
High point: 2397 m
Total climb: 830 m
Time: 3 hours 30 minutes
Recommended transportation: bus, lift
Map: pages 94–95

East of Saas-Fee, on the other side of the Saastal, rises a group of mountains, the Fletschhorn, Lagginhorn, and Weissmies. This route, the Höhenweg Almagelleralp, takes you up the base of the highest (4023 meters) of these, the Weissmies, and around its southwestern shoulder. The trail curves around the lower slopes of the mountain into the valley to the south, the Almagellertal. From there you return to Saas-Fee via Saas-Almagell.

Take the bus to Saas-Grund for the Kreuzboden-Hohsaas lift and ride up to the first station at Kreuzboden (2397 meters). Good views of the Weissmies group and of the Mischabel Alps across the valley. (If you ride up to the top station, Hohsaas, you can reach the Weissmieshütte at 2726 meters.)

Just outside the lift station, a sign points to the left (south) for the Höhenweg Almagelleralp. (Don't pay much attention to the times posted on the signs at the beginning of this route—they are inconsistent.) For the first few minutes, the route is not attractive: the broad, dusty path descends dry slopes covered with gravel. After crossing the loops of the lift construction road, the path joins a dirt jeep road. As you descend and turn the first shoulder of the Weissmies massif, bearing left, there are superb views of the whole Saas-Fee cirque, and to the northwest you see the Bernese Oberland.

After 30 minutes' descent, reach a signposted junction at Grundberg (2202 meters). From here a dirt road descends to the right (north) to Trift-alp and Saas-Grund. Continue straight ahead (south) for the Almagelleralp route. From here, you have a full view of the dam and long lake in the Mattmark valley. After another 10 minutes the route diverges from the jeep road to the right (west), onto a broad mule path that continues south. After a couple of minutes, come to another signposted fork in the trail. Another trail to Saas-Grund descends to the right (west), but the Höhenweg Almagelleralp continues to descend gradually to the south. At several places there are other signposted junctions from which paths descend westward to Saas-Grund; however, continue south for Almagelleralp.

After crossing some grassy slopes, the route traverses long slabs of dark rock below the west ridge and face of the Trifthorn. The trail is narrow but still good. Rounding the Trifthorn, the trail begins to climb. The route is still clear but narrow, uphill, and hard work. At 2280 meters, cross a boulder field.

About 2 hours past Kreuzboden the trail reaches 2392 meters and turns to the east to enter the Almagellertal. The trail starts out high above the valley, but descends gradually down the grassy slopes below the Trifthorn. The Almagellertal is a lovely valley with a stream bordered by meadows, a contrast to the harsher, rocky slope you traversed around the Trifthorn. Descend to the Almagelleralp mountain inn (2200 meters), situated on a green bank just above the stream. This is a cheerful little place where in fine weather hikers and climbers sit outside for snacks or meals, or picnic out on the meadows. The hotel is supplied by mule rather than helicopter, and you can often see the creature either resting on the grass or trudging up the path, crates of soft drinks tied to its back. (Portrait of the owner and his mule in the dining room.) From the inn you'll have fine views of the long Portjengrat ridge above a terraced glacier to the east and the little pointed Sonnighorn to the southeast. Looking west to the mouth of the valley, there's a fine view of the Mischabel chain.

From Almagelleralp the return to Saas-Almagell is an hour's walk. Head west down the valley on an excellent path, cross the stream on the bridge, and descend in switchbacks through pine woods. Part way down, at 1780 meters, there's a fork. The little path to the left (south) cuts across to Furggstalden. Continue down the main trail to Saas-Almagell, where you can catch a PTT bus in the square for the return to Saas-Grund and Saas-Fee. Or you can choose to walk back to Saas-Fee.

12. ALMAGELLERHÜTTE AND ZWISCHBERGEN PASS

Rating: very strenuous
Distance round trip: 16 km
High point: 3287 m
Total climb: 1700 m
Time: 5 hours up, 3 hours 30 minutes down
Recommended transportation: bus
Map: pages 94–95

This route offers a long, steep ascent from Saas-Almagell through some wild, remote country to a pass near the Italian border. To get to the pass requires great exertion but the views are extensive and utterly spectacular. Until the construction of the Almagellerhütte in 1982 (which the SAC has decided is its last new hut), there was almost no one up here, except for an occasional party making a bivouac to climb the Dri Horlini, the Portjengrat, or a tricky southern ascent of the Weissmies. This is a full day's hike (leave early!), but you can now break it up by staying at the hut, an hour below the pass, or at the Almagelleralp mountain inn.

Take the bus from Saas-Fee to Saas-Almagell. The square in the village (which is also the bus stop) contains a signpost for walks in various directions. For the Almagellertal, walk east across the village. In a moment or two you'll be out of the village and on a moderately steep path that ascends in switchbacks beside a waterfall. Climb through woods that thin out as you reach the Almagellertal, where the trail levels out considerably. Cross the bridge and proceed on the left (north) side of the Almagellerbach, heading east. Occasionally, you'll see "Z Pass" blazed on rocks.

The walk up the valley is very pleasant. After about 20 minutes, reach

Almagelleralp mountain inn (2200 m), a simple, cheery establishment that serves meals both indoors and out (Matratzenlager available).

From the mountain inn there are two ways to proceed up the valley—either will do. A small trail starts behind the hotel, climbs northeast and then east, traversing the slope north of the hotel. It then ascends in steep switchbacks to the little Rottalbach, which you cross on a bridge. A more gradual though longer route is the one that continues in front of the hotel, heading east above the Almagellerbach. This trail climbs west in a broad switchback up a moderately steep step, arriving at a shallow terrace above. You are now to the right (east) of the Rottalbach stream. Both trails merge at this point.

Head east and then northeast, entering the lovely Wysstal, a valley that is rather steep but grassy and green. To your right (east), above a glacier, is the long rocky wall of the Portjengrat. To your left, the Dri Horlini comes into view, a rocky ridge with three peaks. Continue to the northeast, past the Dri Horlini, climbing steadily up the rather steep trail until you reach the Almagellerhütte (2900 meters). To your right is the Portjenhorn.

The walk from the hut to the top of the pass takes another hour. Climb northeast to the top of the Wysstal, which becomes narrow and stony, filled with boulders. This is a route rather than a trail, so watch for the blazes. If you lose the way, just head for the lowest point in the pass, which is visible before you. The Zwischbergen Pass is a low, curving, rocky wall linking the southeast ridge of the Weissmies and the Portjenhorn: Zwischbergen means "between the mountains." Arrive at the pass (3287 meters) 3 hours 30 minutes from the mountain inn, 5 hours from Saas-Almagell. You will feel perched on top of the world with magnificent views not only of the Mischabel chain but also of the Monte Rosa.

7

VAL D'HÉRENS WALKS

The Val d'Hérens, like the Zermatt and Saas valleys, begins high in the Valaisian Alps near the Italian border and descends northward to the Rhône valley. The scenery in the mountains that surround the Val d'Hérens is impressive—the Valaisian Alps here are almost a match for the mountains at Zermatt, and the walks give marvelous close-up views of the mountains and glaciers that are characteristic of this valley. Moreover, there are few tourists here, so if you want to climb and ramble in high alpine country, while meeting very few other hikers on the trails, consider staying here. The Val d'Hérens is rather off the beaten track and is well loved for precisely that reason by some Swiss and Europeans who prize the combination of the grand Valaisian Alps and quiet, unassuming, and unspoiled villages.

At Les Haudères, for example, on August First, villagers and visitors celebrate the Swiss national day by marching down the road behind the village band from the church to the square in the evening. After speeches by the mayor and a high school teacher, everyone in the square is served a glass or two of wine. Following a tumultuous fireworks display (each family brings its own, and sets them off in the square), everyone troops off to the school athletic field for an old-fashioned Swiss bonfire.

Compared to the villages in the Val d'Hérens, Saas-Fee is large and very smart. Evolène, Les Haudères, and Arolla are not resorts, but simple mountain villages. Les Haudères, because of its topography, has not a single ski lift, and Evolène has only one. Consequently, these villages were untouched by the downhill ski boom and remain much as they were

An alp above La Forclaz on the way to the Col de Bréona

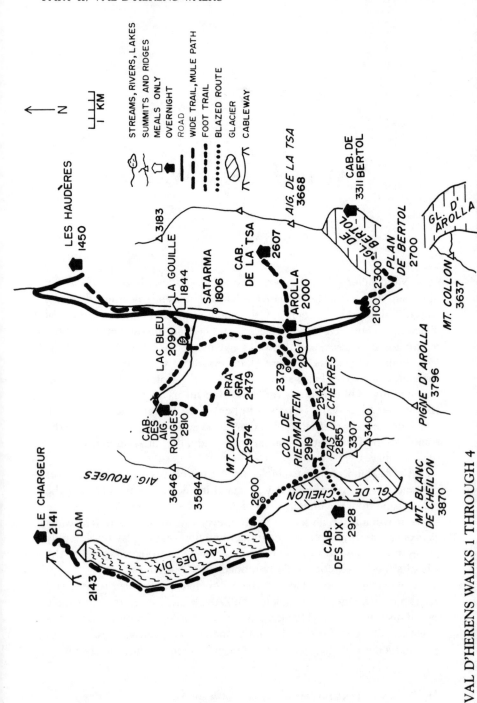

← N

1 KM

STREAMS, RIVERS, LAKES
SUMMITS AND RIDGES
MEALS ONLY
OVERNIGHT
ROAD
WIDE TRAIL, MULE PATH
FOOT TRAIL
BLAZED ROUTE
GLACIER
CABLEWAY

LES HAUDÈRES 1450

LE CHARGEUR 2141

DAM

2143

LAC DES DIX

2600

AIG. ROUGES
3646
3584

MT. DOLIN 2974

CAB. DES AIG. ROUGES 2810

LAC BLEU 2090

LA GOUILLE 1844

SATARMA 1806

3183

CAB. DE LA TSA 2607

AIG. DE LA TSA 3668

AROLLA 2000

PRA GRA 2479

COL DE RIEDMATTEN 2919

2379 2067

2542

PAS DE CHÈVRES 2855

3307

3400

GL. DE CHEILON

MT. BLANC DE CHEILON 3870

CAB. DES DIX 2928

PIGNE D'AROLLA 3796

MT. COLLON 3637

PLAN DE BERTOL 2700

2100 2300

CAB. DE BERTOL 3311

GL. D' AROLLA

VAL D'HÉRENS WALKS 1 THROUGH 4

116

50 years ago. When you walk through a village like Les Haudères (1450 meters), you can see what Zermatt was like long ago.

It's delightful to wander through the streets and lanes of these little villages. Most of the houses are the traditional old Valaisian wood chalets with tiny kitchen gardens full of lettuces and scallions, and some of the houses are several hundred years old. Women of 45 or 50 and older in Evolène and Les Haudères still wear traditional dress for everyday work. They mow grass, tossing and raking it for hay, in black skirts, white blouses, black bodices, and the traditional red kerchiefs. Older women in the villages go about in quite long black skirts and embroidered jackets, and some still wear the little black hats, tilted up at both ends, that look like coal scuttles.

Evolène (1346 meters) is a little larger than Les Haudères, and Arolla is barely a hamlet. Evolène has a bit of a main street; Les Haudères has only a rather sleepy little square. Evolène now has a couple of modern, concrete houses; Les Haudères has none. If you rent an apartment in either of these villages, you're most likely to get one in an old-fashioned chalet—comfortable, of course, clean and well provided.

Arolla (2000 meters) doesn't even rank as a village: it's more of a mountain outpost—a "station de montagne," a base for winter skiing and summer climbing. Arolla has two ski lifts, neither of which operates in the summer. It's at a higher elevation than the other villages and sits up at the valley's end, where it has a marvelous view of Mont Collon. Arolla has no streets—only the road and a few paths. There's a little square, with the post office, office du tourisme, a couple of simple hotels, a tiny grocery, and two sporting goods stores. Nevertheless, you can rent an apartment here. A couple of older houses have apartments, and a group of modern vacation apartments called "Les Marmottes" was recently constructed about 50 meters above the square. If you don't have a car, the owner of the little grocery shop will deliver loads of groceries to apartments up the hill.

Each of these villages has hotels and restaurants, none of them fancy. Evenings in the Val d'Hérens are very quiet. If you want to go out for something other than a stroll, you can always do as the Swiss do: go to a restaurant after dinner for wine or dessert. During the summer there's a little concert series in the valley, spread about among local churches; read the posters for the dates and locations.

There is also a string of very small villages just above Les Haudères: La Sage, Villaz, and La Forclaz, where you can stay either in a vacation apartment or a hotel. They are connected with the rest of the valley by bus.

The language in this valley is French, and the people speak both standard French and a fairly impenetrable local dialect. Fewer people speak English in the Val d'Hérens than in Zermatt or Saas-Fee, but you can write to the various offices de tourisme in English.

European visitors drive to the valley in their own cars, stay in one village, and drive to the others for the hikes there. But you can stay in any of the three villages and use the PTT buses to get about. The buses are frequent and the rides are short. If you stay at Les Haudères, for example, you can easily catch a morning bus and be in Arolla in 25 minutes. The ride between Evolène and Les Haudères takes about 9 minutes. And at Les Haudères, there are good connections to the little villages above: Villaz, La Sage, La Forclaz, and Ferpècle. So all of the walks are easily accessible from any of the various villages.

To get to the Val d'Hérens, take the train to Sion and change there for the PTT bus to Evolène and Les Haudères; you may have to change at Les Haudères for the bus to Arolla. If you don't have a Swiss Holiday Card, you can buy a special bus pass (abonnement) at the PTT bus station in Sion that will provide you with unlimited travel for a week or two.

Arolla has a spectacular location, near the foot of the Arolla glacier and below the 3637-meter Mont Collon—a peak lower than the highest Valaisian Alps, but nonetheless a formidable sight with its nearly vertical rock walls and snowy head. Just to the west is the equally impressive Pigne d'Arolla, named for the Arolla pine, which grows abundantly here. Those who love glaciers especially prize Arolla, for a number of glaciers are easily accessible from the village. On a topographic map, the area just south of the hamlet looks like a delta, with glaciers instead of rivers.

The recommended topographic maps for all Val d'Hérens walks are Arolla 1:50000, Carte pédestre, Editions MPA Verlag; or Carte touristique de la region Evolène 1:40000, Editée par les Sociétés de Développement d'Evolène-Les Haudères-Arolla-La Sage.

1. PLAN BERTOL

Rating: moderate
Distance round trip: 10 km
High point: 2730 m
Total climb: 730 m
Time: 3 hours up, 1 hour 30 minutes down
Map: page 116

This is a nice walk of medium length that leads up to a good viewing point for the Haut (Upper) Glacier d'Arolla and Mont Collon, the massive pile of rock and snow that rather abruptly closes the valley. The route takes you out to the moraine of the Bas (lower) Glacier d'Arolla, and then rises above this glacier along rocky slopes to the east, ending at the Plan Bertol, a high, rather level area between two long ridges. The trail is part of the route for the Cabane de Bertol, an SAC hut. Between the Plan Bertol and the hut, however, is the crevassed Glacier de Bertol, which you should not cross without proper equipment and training.

From the little square in Arolla, walk down the road to Arolla Sport, a shop that sells ski and mountain equipment. Keep right, continuing on the paved road toward Mont Collon and the glacier. This road, at first blacktop and then gravel, was built for the Grande Dixence system, one of the most complex hydroelectric projects in the world. (This series of installations collects water from all over the Valaisian Alps—from the Saas valley to Martigny. Water is pumped up to the Lac des Dix through tunnels drilled under the mountains. Power is then generated as the water falls 1600 meters to the Rhône valley.) As you continue toward the glacier, you'll pass a big wooden bridge on your left and a construction lift on your right. Just past this lift you'll see a pumping plant and a schematic display of the hydroelectric project.

Come to a second bridge, with a metal railing, on your left. Cross this bridge and bear left. A red sign points to Cabane de Bertol; here the trail begins to climb. At the first fork, bear left—even though there is no signpost. Both trails from this fork are blazed, but the trail to the right is a shortcut and has washed-out sections.

The trail ascends on big switchbacks, occasionally over boulder slides. At 2440 meters there's a junction, marked by red signs—continue to the left for the Cabane de Bertol and pass concrete buttresses set into the cliff—more evidence of the Grande Dixence works. Shortly after this, the trail turns left and climbs a steep ridge. In a couple of sections the trail is quite eroded and very exposed, so go slowly over this difficult part. Continue up to the top of the ridge, where the trail levels out near a tiny stone cabin (2730 meters). You'll be in a high, grassy area with a good view of the Glacier du Mont Collon—huge, crevassed, and full of toothy seracs—tumbling between Mont Collon and Pigne d'Arolla. You can continue walking northeast for about another half hour on the trail toward the Cabane de Bertol, turning around when you reach the glacier.

2. PAS DE CHÈVRES

Rating: moderate
Distance round trip: 10 km
High point: 2855 m
Total climb: 880 m
Time: 3 hours up, 1 hour 30 minutes down
Map: page 116

This is a fine walk crossing the high meadows to the north of the Pigne d'Arolla, with superb views of this mountain, the Glacier de Tsijiore

Nouve, Mont Collon, and the chain of mountains that runs northward on the other side of Arolla. The Pas de Chèvres (goat's path) is a little notch in the rock wall overlooking the Glacier de Cheilon. The Cabane des Dix is on a little rocky point overlooking the west bank of the glacier. (Do not cross this glacier without proper equipment and training.)

From the square, walk up the paved road toward Les Marmottes, but turn left at the yellow diamond blaze onto the footpath for the Grand Hotel and Kurhaus. From the hotel continue on this path with yellow blazes. You'll see a sign to Pas de Chèvres, Col de Riedmatten, and Vignettes.

Follow the blazed trail and ascend the grassy slope northwest on switchbacks. On top of the slope (at 2379 meters) the trail bears left (southwest), where it joins a wider trail. Come out on a gravel road, where you turn left (southwest); you'll pass another sign to Col de Riedmatten and Pas de Chèvres.

As you climb, heading west to the Pas de Chèvres, Mont Collon is on your left. The trail rises steeply through a meadow. After 1 hour 10 minutes you'll pass three or four abandoned stone farm buildings. The trail will intersect a dirt road leading right (north) to Pra Gra. Continue up the footpath, crossing over the dirt road and climb through meadows. The rock point before you is Les Monts Rouges; the rock peak to your right is Mont Dolin.

At 2542 meters cross the stream, which has been running on your left, on an old plank bridge. Turn right onto an old construction road for about 30 meters, then turn left onto a narrow trail at a very large boulder. The trail forks at 2780 meters: the path to the left (west) leads to the Pas de Chèvres; the right fork (north) leads to the Col de Riedmatten. Continue west toward Les Monts Rouges. The Pigne d'Arolla and the big Glacier de Tsijiore Nouve are to your left.

Traverse up the steep saddle to the top. From here you can look down to the Glacier de Cheilon below and across the glacier to the Cabane des Dix on a small moraine. To the south is the Mont Blanc de Cheilon, a huge black wedge topped by snow, and to the north, the Lac des Dix. Fixed ladders below the pass allow climbers to descend to the glacier. Do not descend here unless you are experienced and equipped for the glacier.

3. LE CHARGEUR

Rating: Very strenuous
Distance one way: 17 km
High point: 2919 m
Ascent/descent: 970 m/810 m

Time: 8 hours
Recommended transportation: bus; **optional transportation:** lift
Map: page 116

This is a very long and adventurous walk requiring a full day. The views are varied and magnificent. From the Col de Riedmatten you can cross over to the Val des Dix without going onto the glacier, then descend to the southern end of the Lac des Dix, the huge artificial lake for which the Grande Dixence power system is named. The walk takes you along the lake to the Grande Dixence dam (the highest in the world) and descends to Le Chargeur, where you can catch a bus for the return to Arolla.

The Col de Riedmatten is 64 meters higher than the Pas de Chèvres and 150 meters to the north of it. The routes are the same for the first part of the trip. Begin as for Pas de Chèvres (page 119), except turn right at the junction just before the final ascent to the pass. Climb on steep switchbacks up the long stony wall to the Col de Riedmatten (2919 meters). Magnificent view of the mountains that almost encircle Arolla. From the pass, the view to your left is a little blocked, and not as good as the one from the Pas de Chèvres.

Descend from the Col west to the moraine below. This route down the wall is very steep at first—a narrow trail with tiny switchbacks on shale and dirt. Take care with footing. Do not attempt the descent in snow or ice unless you have climbing experience and appropriate equipment. You soon descend to the moraine where the going is easier. Turn right (northwest). The trail now proceeds up the right (northeast) side of a very wide valley, well above the glacier ice.

The blazed route proceeds over boulders at first and then eventually off the moraine onto meadows. Grand view over your shoulder of Mont Blanc de Cheilon and the end of the moraine, with rock slabs and waterfalls. The valley, beneath a wall of red cliffs, is wild and desolate. One hour 30 minutes past the Col the trail turns left (west) and descends sharply. Climb down a fixed steel staircase to a metal suspension bridge over an inlet to the lake. The bridge is new, well engineered, and fixed by many steel cables, but this is not for the fainthearted!

Walk around the blunt south end of the lake, then turn right (north). Cross another bridge, which is upstream from the path, and proceed along the left bank for the entire length of this lake (6.5 kilometers). The route, though long, is almost level. At the end, you must walk through several dark tunnels, the last of which has electric lights (as you enter the tunnel, press a button, which will keep the lights on for 5 minutes). The walk from the suspension bridge to the end of the lake takes from 1 hour 30 minutes to 2 hours. A cable car runs from the huge dam wall down to Le Chargeur (the cost is small and the cars run until 18:30 hours). Le

An *alp above* Arolla *at* Pra Gra

Chargeur has a large hotel and a bus stop, where you get the bus to Vex. The Holiday Card is not valid on this route, but the fare is moderate. In Vex you'll need to change to a PTT bus for the Val d'Hérens.

4. CABANE DES AIGUILLES ROUGES

Rating: strenuous
Distance loop trip: 13 km
High point: 2810 m

Total climb: 900 m
Time: 6 hours
Map: page 116

The Aiguilles Rouges (red needles) is a long rocky ridge separating the Val d'Hérens from the Val des Dix. This is a very fine walk to an SAC hut in a glorious location with extensive views. From Arolla, you can make a circular trip.

From the Arolla square, walk uphill on the paved road toward Les Marmottes, the group of chalets. Turn right (northeast) at the yellow sign for the Cabane and climb a short, rather steep section up to Pra Gra (2479

123

meters), a beautiful area of summer farms and alpine pastures, with superb views of Mont Collon and the Pigne d'Arolla. Turn right (north)—a yellow sign indicates the route to the Cabane. The trail also has red blazes. It crosses over a shoulder, then turns left, proceeding northwest into a very wild place: stony, full of boulders and streams. The trail crosses a stream, then bends to the right (north). One small section has some exposure and a few difficult steps, but there's a fixed chain to aid you. The trip to the Cabane (2810 meters) will take 3 hours, and you'll have spectacular views, with the long, rocky wall of the Aiguilles Rouges, the glaciers behind it, and Mont Collon to the south. Across the valley to the east is the Aiguille de la Tsa and its lateral peaks and, farther, the Tête de Valpelline and Dent Blanche.

From the Cabane you can continue the loop by descending to Lac Bleu, then to Arolla. Pick up the trail behind (west of) the hut. The descent provides new and very fine views. Lac Bleu (2090 meters) is a small, clear, intensely blue mountain lake—glacier-fed and too cold for a dip. From Lac Bleu you can walk down to either Satarma or La Gouille and pick up the bus to Arolla or Les Haudères. Or, you can traverse the slopes between Lac Bleu and Arolla.

For the traverse, walk to the valley end of Lac Bleu, where there's a little log bridge at the outlet of the lake—this is at the opposite end from the waterfall. Turn right after you cross the bridge and find an unmarked narrow trail that leads south. Soon after leaving the lake, cross a stream. This trail, with blue blazes, jogs up and down and traverses the wooded slope about 200 meters above the valley. Near the entrance to Arolla there's a fork: take the upper path (the lower path leads to the village dump). It will take you about 1 hour 15 minutes to walk to Arolla.

Les Haudères is situated at a fork in the upper Val d'Hérens, where the streams flowing north from Arolla and Ferpècle join. Between the two streams is a massif topped by a number of peaks, including the Grande Dent de Veisivi and the Aiguille de la Tsa. To the east of Les Haudères there are several trails leading up to cols or notches in the long, high ridge that separates the Val d'Hérens from the Val de Moiry. To the southeast, beyond Ferpècle, is the trail to Bricola and Les Manzettes, which offers superb views of glaciers and the Dent Blanche. Evolène, a few kilometers north of Les Haudères, is well positioned for the climb up the Pic d'Artsinol, a favorite excursion in this region.

5. LA GOUILLE

Rating: easy
Distance round trip: 7.5 km

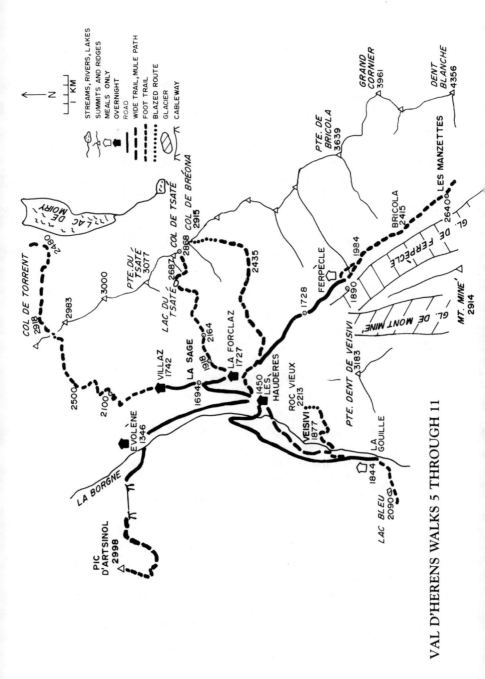

VAL D'HERENS WALKS 5 THROUGH 11

High point: 1884 m
Total climb: 400 m
Time: 2 hours
Map: page 125

With its passages through pine forest and views of the stream, this is a pleasant walk for a late summer's afternoon or if the weather clears after a mostly rainy day. The route follows a gentle gradient through woods and fields, slightly above the west bank of the Borgne d'Arolla.

Leave Les Haudères from the south on the road to Arolla and cross the bridge on the highway. Do not turn left onto a gravel road, marked by a red blaze. Instead, cross the second bridge to the right; immediately after that a sign points you left to Arolla, Lac Bleu, Veisivi, and Roc Vieux. Proceed down a wide cart or jeep track, which passes through meadows and woods. Walk for 1 hour 15 minutes until you pass under a high tension pylon; a wide gravel road then diverges to your left (southeast). This is the road to Veisivi and Roc Vieux. Instead, continue straight ahead, climbing slightly, and emerge on the highway near St. Barthélemy. La Gouille is to the south.

6. ROC VIEUX

Rating: moderate
Distance round trip: 11 km
High point: 2213 m
Total climb: 825 m
Time: 3 hours up, 1 hour 30 minutes down
Map: page 125

Roc Vieux is the endpoint of the massif separating the Arolla and Ferpècle valleys. From the Roc Vieux viewpoint there's a precipitous drop down to Les Haudères and a correspondingly good view, not only of the village but also of various peaks and passes on either side.

Begin as for La Gouille (above). (Note that if you take this walk from Arolla, you can take the bus to St. Barthélemy and from there walk downhill until you pick up the trail at 1740 meters. The topographic maps indicate two trails from Les Haudères to Veisivi: one along the east, the other along the west bank of the Borgne d'Arolla. Do not take the east bank route, in either direction. It is extremely steep, narrow, and muddy, and would be dangerous when wet.)

Proceed down the west bank of the Borgne d'Arolla. Pass under the pylon and then turn left (southeast) onto the gravel road that leads down to the stream. Cross the stream and head north up the east bank. The trail soon crosses two smaller streams and turns east, then northeast. Ascend through the woods until you emerge into the meadow at Veisivi (1877 meters), an alp with several farm buildings. Here the trail ascends east and then north. Arrive at Roc Vieux (2213 meters) in another 50 minutes, emerging onto a ridge below the large cross that can be seen from across the valley. Good views of the summits all around: Dent Blanche, Mont Collon, Pigne d'Arolla, and others.

You can walk back down to Veisivi in 30 minutes. "St. Bart" is painted in red on a rock, indicating the good trail down; do not take the path to your right (north) at Veisivi, as that's the dangerous east bank route. Descend the way you came up, crossing the Borgne d'Arolla and then heading to the right for Les Haudères or left for St. Barthélemy, La Gouille, or Arolla.

7. BRICOLA AND LES MANZETTES

Rating: moderate
Distance round trip: 13 km
High point: 2800 m
Total climb: 1050 m
Time: 3 hours up, 1 hour 30 minutes down
Recommended transportation: bus
Map: page 125

One of the best of all glacier views. This route takes you up to a high ridge of land from which there are astonishingly close, spectacular views of two hanging glaciers and of the Dent Blanche.

Take the bus from Les Haudères to Ferpècle (1766 meters), a minuscule hamlet southeast of Les Haudères. Continue up the road from the bus stop. In 10 minutes you'll pass a steel bridge on your right; don't cross it. At the next junction, take the bend to the left, following the direction of the red arrow you'll see painted on a rock. In another 10 minutes you'll pass a small café, Chez Joseph & Henriette, on your right.

From here you can continue in one of two ways. Two minutes past the café, you'll see a blue arrow painted on a rock, pointing up to the left of the paved road. This path climbs eastward, at first through a few woods, then into the open. Blazes read "Les Rosses," "Bricola," or are just blue arrows painted on rocks. Cross a stream. Forty-five minutes past the bus stop, this trail joins the second one.

A second option is to continue past the blue arrow on the rock near the café. A few minutes farther up the paved road you'll see two yellow metal signs in front of a large boulder. These signs point left to Cabane Rossier and Bivouac Dent Blanche. Ascend gradually southeastward. Soon, the first trail merges with this one.

The route has blue or white or white-red-white blazes. The Glacier de Ferpècle lies in front of you and the Glacier du Mont Miné is to your right (west). As you climb, you can see the solitary, three-story building that marks Bricola on the shoulder above you. At a junction before you cross the stream, take the upper path (blazed "Bricola") to the left. As you reach the waterfall, don't cross at the lower point, where the rock is wet and slabby; the safer crossing is the upper one. On the other side of the stream the trail, marked by red arrows, descends, bears left around the shoulder, and leads up to Bricola (2415 meters), where there were once shepherds' huts. Just beyond this point, past a low stone building left over from the hydroelectric works, there's a level area—an excellent lunch place. Magnificent views of the two glaciers, with the black Mont Miné between them, and the Dent Blanche towering above.

To continue to Les Manzettes, a high ridge between the Ferpècle and Manzette glaciers, walk back to the three-storey stone house and take the jeep road left from the Grande Dixence construction. As you face the Dent Blanche, the track rises to your left (east).

The route proceeds through empty, tundralike meadows. You'll pass the fork for the Bivouac Dent Blanche on your left, but walk straight ahead, toward the Cabane Rossiers. Climb several hundred meters up a moderate grade and reach the high crest of the moraine that climbs toward Dent Blanche. Caution: the crest is steep, and the trail, ascending in switchbacks, is narrow and tricky—watch your footing. And do not climb up the crest if there's snow. From here you'll have fine views of glaciers and the Dent Blanche. Note: the moraine below this crest rests on ice—you can see the crevasses between the boulders. Stay off it.

The eastern wall of the Val d'Hérens is topped by a long ridge, running from northwest to southeast. On the grassy slopes below this long ridge are the villages of Evolène, Villaz, La Sage, La Forclaz, Les Haudères, and Ferpècle. There are several notches (cols) in this long ridge, passes with trails descending into the Val de Moiry to the east. These include the Col de Torrent, Col de la Tsa, and Col de Bréona. Note that you can gain a little altitude for these walks by taking the bus up to one of the higher villages.

8. COL DE BRÉONA

Rating: strenuous
Distance round trip: 12 km
High point: 2915 m
Total climb: 1250 m
Time: 4 hours up, 2 hours 30 minutes down
Recommended transportation: bus
Map: page 125

This route requires a great deal of ascent, but leads up to a magnificent vantage point above a wild, lonely, and splendid high pasture.

Take the bus from Les Haudères to La Forclaz (1727 meters). Walk through the tiny village toward the Dent Blanche (southeast) and pick up the trail to the Col de Bréona between Café la Promenade and Le Grenier. You'll walk past groups of farmhouses and then alps. The trail is blazed red and white in some places, red, white, and blue in others. At the last cluster of farm buildings, the Alpage de Bréona (2435 meters), the blazed trail ends.

Head straight up the slope (northeast) on the left edge of the ridge. Below, on your right, is a very steep valley, almost a gully. After about 10 minutes, near the top of the slope you're ascending, turn left onto a wide jeep road. Turn right (to the east) on the jeep road and continue up for a few hundred meters.

Come to a fork from which you can see a metal-roofed shed below to your right. At this fork, turn left (north) onto a narrow, rough dirt tractor road that climbs higher up the slope. Just below the last farm, which has a corral, a couple of sheds, and a house, the tractor road forks (2520 meters). Turn left (north) onto a second narrow, rough road. This leads you up to the final green shelf—almost a basin between steep walls. It's a large, empty, and beautiful place, giving you a sense of great space and wildness. From this high green meadow, full of wildflowers, you see glaciers strewn about on either side. You will find very few other hikers up here.

To your left is a greenish ridge with a smooth summit line and lots of pebbles strewn down its slope. To your right (east) is a wall of black rock with a very jagged, pointed summit line and rough scree below the rock wall. The path to the Col is on your extreme left (near the slope with the smooth summit line, not the black rock wall with the jagged top). Stay to the left (west), pass a small cairn, and go almost due north (20 degrees on a compass). The route is very steep for the last 300 meters. Continue climbing and aim for the spot between the black rocks and the rounder, greener shoulder on your left. Ascend steadily till you see the Col, which is the lowest notch between the rounded shoulder and the rock wall. From the Col (2915 meters), grand views of the Zinalrothorn, Trifthorn, Wellenkuppe, and Ober Gabelhorn (all considered Zermatt peaks), Lac de Moiry in the next valley to the east, the mountains above the Ferpècle and Mont Miné glaciers, and the Arolla mountains: Pigne d'Arolla and Aiguilles Rouges.

(Note: the topographic map indicates a traverse from the Col northeast to the Col du Tsaté. The trail, however, is vague, requires some ascent on rock, and follows an extremely exposed ridge—all of which are excellent reasons for not going. Also, do not try to climb the Couronne de

Bréona, the black rock wall on the right (southwest) of the Col; it's narrow, exposed, and dangerous.)

9. COL DU TSATÉ

Rating: strenuous
Distance round trip: 9 km
High point: 2868 m
Total climb: 1200 m
Time: 3 hours 30 minutes up, 2 hours down
Recommended transportation: bus
Map: page 125

The views from this col are not as grand as those from the Col de Bréona, but the walk is less fatiguing. (On the signs painted on rocks, Tsaté is also spelled Tzaté.) Above the steep slopes is a little farm, amid lovely high meadows, and the little Lac du Tsaté is charming. The route up to the Col enters a wild, stony terrain with its own savage beauty.

Take the bus to La Forclaz, getting off at the Col de Forclaz stop just before the bus reaches the village center. You have a choice of two ways to ascend. A jeep road climbs the slope in broad switchbacks. You can follow this entirely or in part. The grade is gentler, but the distance much longer. There's also a path that ascends very steeply and directly. The best way is to combine the two routes.

At the bus stop, with your back to the village center, turn right (east) for Tsaté-Motau. Ascend a few meters to a junction, where a sign points left (north) to Motau. Walk up a small cart road past a few chalets, then ascend through pine woods. After 15 minutes you'll see a sign in blue, pointing right (southeast) for Tsaté. Follow this onto a dirt tractor road, and climb on switchbacks through pleasant woods. After another 15 minutes the trail emerges into a meadow and continues uphill. The view to your right will be of the glacier.

After passing a few alps, about 40 minutes from the start, you'll come to a fork (1874 meters). The path to the right (south) leads to Bréona. Continue straight ahead and, immediately after this fork, turn left and cross the stream. At Motau (1800 meters), there's another fork. A blue sign on a rock indicates Zaté to the right (south). The blazes here are sometimes blue, sometimes white-red-white.

After 1 hour 20 minutes, pass a cluster of abandoned barns and houses. There's a fork here, and a sign points left to Prélet and La Sage. Continue climbing through this cluster of buildings to the dirt road above, which swings to the left (north), then northeast. Head up through the meadows toward the cross you can see on the notch above you, between the waterfall and the little peak on your left. Follow the path to the right (east) just after two concrete manholes. It ascends steeply through the meadows, with the stream flowing to your right. Look hard for switchbacks, to make this less steep. Pass a solitary abandoned house with a metal roof. Continue up the slope and then take the gravel jeep road to the right, which is much easier to walk on at this point than the farm path. Ascend to another gravel jeep road, which you'll reach 2 hours from the start (it's actually the same jeep road ascending in long switchbacks from La Forclaz). Turn to the right and follow the jeep road, which swings to the left and then ascends to the alp above.

After 2 hours 15 minutes come to an alp with cows and a dairy barn—a pretty place with big meadows. Ascend to the right of the alp, above the dairy. The path will head east, then north to the little Lac du Tsaté (2687 meters). There are nice views of the valley and the mountains above Arolla and Ferpècle.

The 1-hour walk that continues to the Col du Tsaté (2868 meters) proceeds from the southern end of the lake straight up the slope on a little path on your right (east). Reach a junction 15 minutes above the lake. The path to your right (south) continues on up to the Col du Tsaté, first on a path, then on a track that sometimes disappears for a few feet. Ascend on grass and over rocks, heading generally eastward. At 2750 meters climb over a ridge of scree that runs from northeast to southwest. Then the track bears left. The Col is directly in front of you, to the east: a high, dark wall. The track climbs on the left (north) side of the Col, ascending gradually at first, then steeply up the last 100 meters of the narrow valley (kumme) on switchbacks. Do not go onto the scree to your right (south). The view from the top is down the steep slopes of the Val de Moiry.

In descending, after you pass the dairy barn, you can take the gravel jeep road to your left. It takes you down in wide, easy switchbacks. Pass the solitary abandoned farm building with the metal roof and then the abandoned hamlet. Here, you can choose to descend the center of the slope on the trail, which is quicker and straighter but steeper. Or you can walk on the jeep road, which takes you to the Motau-Tsaté junction you passed just after the Col de Forclaz bus stop; reach La Forclaz in 2 hours.

10. COL DE TORRENT

Rating: strenuous
Distance round trip: 9 km
High point: 2918 m

On the way to the Col de Torrent

At a "mazot" (granary) in Evolène

Total climb: 1200 m
Time: 3 hours 30 minutes up, 2 hours 30 minutes down
Recommended transportation: bus
Map: page 125

This is a fine climb up long meadows, with views of the Dent Blanche and the Ferpècle glaciers beyond the green slopes. From the narrow Col there are long views across the Val de Moiry.

You can walk this as a day trip to the Col and return to the Val d'Hérens or cross over the pass and descend to the Lac de Moiry and then Grimentz (18 km, 6 hours 30 minutes) (page 214).

Take the bus from Les Haudères to Villaz. The bus stops in front of the Café Col de Torrent. From the café, walk back about 50 meters in the direction from which the bus came—that is, between the Villaz and Bozza bus stops. The trail starts to your left, heading northeast.

At first, the path is marked for Volorons. After passing a farmhouse, it turns sharply left (north). Follow the red and white blazes up the slope. The blazes are infrequent, but you can't miss the trail. Climb up beautiful green meadows, past chalets and barns. (Among the farm buildings of the Cotter alp are stones with prehistoric engravings. To see them, keep walking northwest at the first switchback, instead of turning right.) Ascend steadily on broad switchbacks, with fine views of the Dent Blanche, Dent d'Hérens, and the glaciers. Near the Col the path turns to the east and climbs more steeply to the summit ridge line. The route to the Col (2918 meters) takes 3 hours 30 minutes. It has no torrent, but does offer sweeping views.

11. PIC D'ARTSINOL

Rating: moderate
Distance round trip: 8.5 km
High point: 2998 m
Total climb: 900 m
Time: 2 hours 30 minutes up, 1 hour 30 minutes down
Recommended transportation: lift
Map: page 125

This climb to the summit of a small mountain, with panoramic views, is a favorite excursion in this region.

Start at Evolène and walk to Lana, a tiny hamlet across the river from Evolène to the northwest. The path starts at the center of Evolène near the Café Central, and the walk will take you 30 minutes. At Lana (also spelled Lannaz) there's a chairlift that you can take for a boost up to 2121 meters. The lift has a limited schedule in summer, running from 8 to 8:15 and from 11 to 11:15 each morning. You can take it down from 14 to 14:15 and from 17 to 17:15. The walk up follows a winding dirt jeep road that is used by automobiles. We recommend the lift.

From the station at the top of the chairlift, turn right and walk up a broad jeep road with wide switchbacks. The road turns and heads southwest. After 30 minutes a sign points left (west) to the Pic d'Artsinol and Col de la Meina. You can see the Pic: the rounder, rocky bump to the right of two such forms towering over the meadows. Here you leave the gravel jeep road and ascend on a small footpath, marked by blue blazes, through the meadow. This is a long, gradual ascent.

After 1 hour 15 minutes, at 2570 meters, there's a fork. The broader, lower path to the left (southwest) goes to the Col de la Meina; the steeper path heading up (west) goes directly to the Pic d'Artsinol. At 2700 meters the trail briefly disappears in a broad meadow—head northwest across this meadow to the trail that you can see above you. (On your return this way, head for the Dent Blanche.) Blue blazes mark the route. Climb steeply to the west, and reach the ridge. Then turn right (north), and continue ascending the ridge to the summit. At 2801 meters a trail from the Col de la Meina joins this trail on your left (south). The trail to the summit ridge winds up through slabs of rock but isn't exposed. Long and sweeping views from the summit in every direction: among the landmarks, you can see the Grande Dixence, Le Chargeur, the Matterhorn, Dent Blanche, and the Bernese Oberland.

8

GRINDELWALD WALKS

The mountains of the Bernese Oberland extend in a long chain running from east to west through the center of Switzerland. These mountains are not quite as high as the Valaisian Alps, but are nevertheless massive and splendid, glittering with ice and snow. The broadest glacier in Switzerland is located here, the Aletsch Gletscher; the point where five glaciers pour into a central ice field has been waggishly named "Konkordia Platz," for the Place de la Concorde in the center of Paris. Here also are three of the most famous mountains in Switzerland, the Eiger, Mönch, and Jungfrau.

The weather in the Oberland is considerably less certain than that in the Valais or the Engadine, which are drier and sunnier. Though beautiful days occur, clouds and rain are more likely here than elsewhere. Because of the increased moisture, however, this area has meadows of magnificent, thick grass and a profusion of wildflowers. The contrast of a shining green meadow before a backdrop of snowy peaks and glaciers makes the Oberland the image of Switzerland that you see on calendars and chocolate boxes.

People sometimes use Interlaken as a base for visiting these mountains. From Interlaken, however, you see almost nothing, and the train ride up the valley to places like Grindelwald, Mürren, or Wengen takes an hour. Though all these village are well positioned both for views and good walks, Grindelwald has the largest number of walks and perhaps the best views, though Mürren is a close second for scenery.

Though the Oberland is a long area, some of the most dramatic scenery in the whole chain is in this region. The rock wall comprising the

Cows grazing during a storm above Grosse Scheidegg

GRINDELWALD WALKS

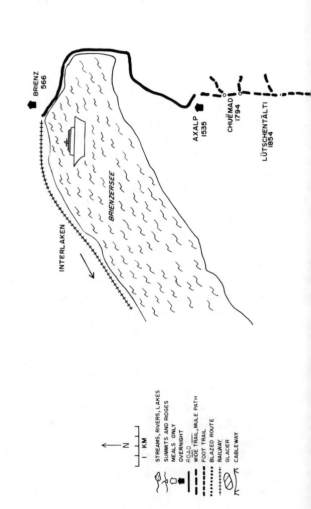

BRIENZ
566

AXALP
1535

CHUÉMAD
1794

LÜTSCHENTÄLTI
1854

BRIENZERSEE

INTERLAKEN

N

1 KM

STREAMS, RIVERS, LAKES
SUMMITS AND RIDGES
MEALS ONLY
OVERNIGHT
ROAD
WIDE TRAIL, MULE PATH
FOOT TRAIL
BLAZED ROUTE
RAILWAY
GLACIER
CABLEWAY

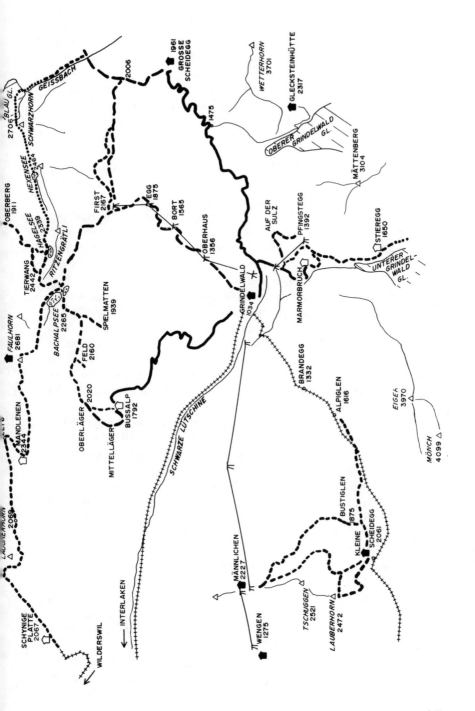

Wetterhorn-Mättenberg-Eiger is gigantic—not only high but immense, nearly 15 kilometers long (though cut through at two points by narrow glaciers). Turning the corner of the Eiger, you come upon an equally magnificent wall, but one of snow and ice instead of sheer rock. Grindelwald is sited at the foot of the Eiger, facing this stupendous rock wall. As one climbs the slope above the village the perspective deepens; the terrace on top of this slope is like a platform for one of the grandest views in the Swiss Alps: the Eiger, Mönch and Jungfrau, with the icy peaks of the Finsteraarhorn and Schreckhorn rising behind them—the great centerpiece of the Bernese Oberland.

Not only does Grindelwald have a stunning view, but also a setting that's something of a geographical curiosity. The village lies in a cleft between the Mättenberg-Eiger wall and an opposing slope that terminates in such lesser-known peaks as the Faulhorn and Schwarzhorn. To the east, this cleft is blocked by a high saddle, the Grosse Scheidegg; to the west, the Grindelwald valley is blocked by another saddle, the Kleine Scheidegg, where the mountain wall continues southwestward, as the Eiger is followed by the Mönch and the Jungfrau.

Grindelwald, like Zermatt, is internationally known, though a little less chic, and, as at Zermatt, many people come to look but not to hike. Grindelwald is a major mountaineering center, and, because of successful Japanese feats on the Eiger, Grindelwald is very popular with Japanese tourists. One of the great attractions here is the Jungfrau Express, which climbs up through tunnels inside the mountains and brings you out at an observation platform below the summit of the Jungfrau for a grand view of a sea of glaciers and mountains.

Unlike Zermatt and Saas-Fee, cars are allowed in Grindelwald. Most of the houses and all of the shops are concentrated in a shallow area, built close to the rather long main street. Above the main street, the slope rises fairly steeply to the north. Houses are built up this slope on several levels of terraces, but soon give way to small farms that continue up to nearly 1600 meters (the main street is at 1050 meters). The houses are snug and pretty, and the slope is carpeted with flowers. A road loops up the slope in broad switchbacks. If you rent an apartment in Grindelwald, bear this topography in mind, unless you choose to rent a car. When writing to the tourist office (Verkehrsbüro) you should inform them that you will not have a car and wish to rent an apartment close to the village.

Most people approach Grindelwald from Interlaken, where the trains stop at two stations: Interlaken Ost (east) and West. There are frequent trains between Interlaken Ost and Grindelwald; the trip takes about 40 minutes. You can also reach the town by bus from Meiringen.

The Oberland giants rise abruptly from the south bank of the Schwarze Lütschine river, on which Grindelwald is located, but the north bank rises more gradually. Many of the best walks from Grindelwald are found on this north side, on a shelf that you can easily reach by the lift to First. This very long lift extends 4355 meters and is a 30-minute ride. It has four sections: from Grindelwald you ascend to Oberhaus, then Bort, Egg, and First. Various excursion tickets are available locally that will reduce the price of lift tickets considerably. The Swiss Holiday Card gives you a 20% reduction on this lift, but if you intend to stay in Grindelwald for at least a week, a Regional Holiday Season Ticket might be a good buy (see "Transportation" in Chapter 1). This regional ticket gives you five days of free travel on this lift and almost unlimited travel in the region, and then a 50% reduction for an additional 10 days. It can be purchased only in Switzerland.

You can also walk all or part of the way up to First by several routes. The most direct (and steepest) path starts near the lift station, which is set back from Grindelwald's main street near the eastern end of town. There is also access to this path just above the main street, west of the railroad station. A path from the west end of the town ascends to Aellfluh and then traverses to Oberhaus, from which you climb more directly and steeply up to Bort and then past Egg to First. Or you can walk eastward through the town to Muhlebach (or even as far as Lauchbühl), and then turn northwest for Bort and First. Because of the height from Grindelwald to First, an ascent of 1120 meters, count on a walk of about 4 hours—and remember to add the extra 4 hours to the walks listed in this chapter.

The recommended topographic map for all Grindelwald walks is Wanderkarte Grindelwald, 1:25000, Schad + Frey AG Bern. Verlag: Gemeinde Grindelwald.

1. BACHALPSEE

Rating: easy
Distance round trip: 5.5 km
High point: 2265 m
Total climb: 100 m
Time: 1 hour up, 40 minutes down
Recommended transportation: lift
Map: pages 140–41

The Bachalpsee, also called the Bachsee, is a very pretty lake; the view across the water to the Eiger, Mönch, Jungfrau, and other Oberland peaks is one of the classic alpine panoramas. The lake is a lovely spot for a picnic lunch, a lazy afternoon or a first outing. Families with small children may prefer to turn around at the Bachalpsee—instead of continuing on to Bussalp—and return to First.

From behind the First lift station (2167 meters), walk northwest. There are numerous signposts and the trail is unmistakable. After jogging north for a short stretch, the trail once again heads northwest. After 1 hour come to a very tiny lake and a moment later to the Bachalpsee (2265 meters).

2. BUSSALP

Rating: moderate
Distance loop trip: 12.7 km
High point: 2265 m
Ascent/descent: 150 m/550 m
Time: 3 hours
Recommended transportation: lift, bus
Map: pages 140–41

The advantage of this walk is that it's not very long but leads through beautiful high country and has magnificent scenery.

Follow the route to the Bachalpsee (page 143), where a signpost points southwest to Bussalp. For the Bussalp trail, walk to the small lake just south of the Bachalpsee, and proceed along its western shore. The trail then bends to the right; it's blazed and always clear. A junction and signpost indicate a trail to Spielmatten and Grindelwald straight ahead (south) and the route to Feld and Bussalp to the right (west). (Don't take the trail to Grindelwald via Spielmatten, which is steep and has long, washed-out sections.) Turn right for Bussalp. Climb up on a dirt footpath, a little steep in places. There's a rock crack, like a tiny gorge, to your left. At a little notch (2350 meters) where a rock is blazed with a white diamond and a red stripe through its middle, turn left.

The trail descends through a steep, grassy area with big rocks strewn about. About 1 hour past Bachalpsee, a sign indicates Bussalp, straight ahead. Shortly after, at Feld (2160 meters), a second sign points to the right for Bussalp. The meadows here are breathtaking—sweeping slopes of green dotted with wildflowers. To your left there are great views of the Oberland giants across the valley. One hour 30 minutes from Bachalpsee a sign points left (south) for Mittelläger and straight ahead for Bussalp Oberläger. If you want to take the bus back to Grindelwald, turn left here on a small grass and then dirt path. Cross two very small brooks and reach Mittelläger in another 30 minutes. (The Bussalp mountain restaurant and bus stop are at Mittelläger.) The bus ride to Grindelwald takes 30 minutes. The last bus departs at 17:55, and the Holiday Card is not valid on this route.

To walk down to Grindelwald, follow the signposted trail to the southeast, through woods and fields, and reach the northwestern corner of Grindelwald in another 2 hours.

3. FAULHORN AND SCHYNIGE PLATTE

Rating: strenuous
Distance loop trip: 15 km
High point: 2681 m
Total climb: 800 m
Time: 6 hours 30 minutes
Recommended transportation: lift, railway
Map: pages 140–41

This is one of the finest walks in Switzerland—a high traverse above Grindelwald that gives you superb views of the Eiger, Mönch, and Jungfrau, the mountains behind them, and the continuation of the chain all the way to the Blümlisalp group. Some of the route signs claim you can walk this in 5 hours 30 minutes, but disregard them. This is a long excursion with some sections of exposed trail, and a passage through some wild and empty country. Do not take this route in bad or threatening weather, or if you are not in fit condition.

From the First lift station walk to Bachalpsee (page 143), following the signposts to Faulhorn. Proceed along the east side of the lake, climbing a stony, steep slope to the saddle above. The trail, through rubble, is not well marked (look for red and white blazes), but you should head for the saddle, which is clearly visible. At the saddle (2620 meters) there are magnificent views of the great Bernese Oberland wall and the expanse of peaks to the south. To your right (north) is the Faulhorn; the Faulhorn mountain inn is a 15-minute climb up the little peak.

Proceed westward below the Faulhorn. The trail is quite narrow and very exposed here—almost a knife-edged ridge—for 10 or 15 minutes. Spectacular views of the Eiger, Mönch, and Jungfrau to your left (south) and of the blue Brienzersee to your right (north), but watch your footing instead. The trail, clearly visible, becomes less exposed as a ridge of rock rises on your left side.

Proceed along this rather long, narrow, and elevated ridge. After 30 minutes the trail dips and descends to the right (north), below the rock ridge. After another 30 minutes, at Mandlenen (2344 meters), you come upon a tiny cabin, lashed down by a couple of cables—the Weber Hütte Gast Stübli, a surprising sight in this wild and empty mountain landscape. The front room is the size of a garden shed; the back room, half its size, al-

Herr Weber at the Weber Hütte Gast Stübli

most entirely filled by an old kitchen range. It's a cozy, jolly place; you may see more hikers concentrated in this hut than on the entire route. Herr Weber plays Swiss folk tunes on his accordian, evidently all afternoon, while Frau Weber serves drinks and simple snacks.

From here, 2 or 2 hours and 30 minutes to Schynige Platte. The route is always clear, with "SP" blazed on rocks. The trail passes behind the Weber Hütte and then turns right (north). It descends a little—be careful on a passage of slippery black rock—and then swings left (west) into the long, wild valley of the Sagistal. Continue down this valley, cross over at the end to the right, proceeding westward, and then turn south and west again into another deep valley. Fantastic rock shapes to your left. Finally begin to climb; the tiny Schynige Platte station is above on your right (2067 meters). Climb this last short slope to the station, where you can ride down to the Wilderswil rail station (1 hour) on a narrow-gauge cog railway that resembles the old cartoon creation, the Toonerville trolley. The last train leaves at about 18:00 hours, and the Holiday Card is not valid. In Wilderswil, you can take the train to Grindelwald (or Interlaken).

4. HAGELSEE, BLAU GLETSCHER, AND GROSSE SCHEIDEGG

Rating: strenuous
Distance loop trip: 14 km
High point: 2706 m
Ascent/descent: 700 m/ 900 m
Time: 5 hours 30 minutes
Recommended transportation: lift, bus
Map: pages 140– 41

This long, challenging route crosses through very wild, desolate, and rugged terrain. On the crest of the slope north of Grindelwald is a long rock wall running east to west; its highest point is the jagged Schwarzhorn. Various sections of this wall are called Ritzengrätli and Widderfeldgrätli on maps. This excursion takes you behind this rock wall and leads you in a long traverse, parallel to the wall, until you turn the end of the wall, where you head back to Grindelwald. Several cautions are in order. The route is difficult to follow in fog and should not be taken in poor or threatening weather. It is not recommended for small children, for people who are not in good physical condition, or for inexperienced hikers who might find steep terrain and snow difficult.

From the First lift station walk toward Bachalpsee (page 143). About 30 minutes after leaving First, pass a small stone building to the right of the path; then about 10 minutes after this, come to a small junction. Turn right (north) onto the trail with a signpost for Axalp, Brienz, Hagelsee, and Wildgärst. Pass a small pond to your left (west) and climb a moderately steep slope to a small saddle. Descend through some boulders in a few minutes to another junction (where you could turn left (west) for the Faulhorn). Keep to the right (east) for Axalp, Brienz, Hagelsee, and

Wildgärst. Here you reach the western end of the rock wall. As you pass behind the wall, at 2442 meters, the trail turns right (east) and begins the long traverse behind and parallel to the rock wall.

One hour 30 minutes past First, you'll reach a junction with a yellow signpost, at Hagelsee (2339 meters), a little blue lake often partially covered with ice. A trail heads left for Axalp; however, take a sharp right for Hexensee, Wart, and Wildgärst. The long rock wall, rough and striated, is always to your right. Several sections of the route involve descents or traverses on loose scree. You'll descend to a shallow depression, the Hühnertal, and pass another small lake, the Hexensee.

The trail continues upward, sometimes on long patches of snow, sometimes on rock and scree. Watch for the red and white blazes on the rocks and on boulders in the long patches of snow. Climb to the saddle called Wart (2706 meters) as the Schwarzhorn rises to your right; this grim tower of rock is the end point of the long wall.

At Wart, a trail leads left (north) to Wildgärst, but continue straight ahead (east) for Pfanni and Schwarzwaldalp. Turn the corner of the Schwarzhorn and walk down the left side of the Blau Gletscher, southeastward—a very steep descent. (The Grindelwald Verkehrsbüro considers this a safe glacier for unroped travel.) Descend first on snow, then on scree, and then on a rough surface of grass, dirt, and mud. The area is boggy; stay to the left of the stream.

The route intersects a dirt farm road—Schwarzwaldalp is to your left (east), Grosse Scheidegg to your right (southwest). Reach this junction 5 hours past the lift station at First. The farm road crosses the stream on a bridge, passes some farm buildings, then reaches a gate, a signpost (2006 meters), and a wide jeep road. This jeep road runs straight down to Grosse Scheidegg (1962 meters), which you can walk to in about 30 minutes.

At Grosse Scheidegg take a bus down to Grindelwald, a 35-minute trip. The last bus leaves at approximately 18 hours. The Holiday Card is not valid on this local bus. Alternately, you can return to the First lift station by turning right at the intersection (point 2006) and following the road or high path to First. This route will take you 1 hour 30 minutes. You can also follow the trail from Grosse Scheidegg down to Grindelwald. The trail bypasses many sections of the automobile road.

5. TIERWANG, AXALP, AND BRIENZ

Rating: strenuous
Distance loop trip: 10 km
High point: 2442 m
Ascent/descent: 300 m/900 m
Time: 4 hours

Recommended transportation: lift, bus, lake steamer and/or railway
Map: pages 140–41, and Wanderkarte Berner Oberland Ost 1:50000,
   Kümmerly + Frey

This walk provides an amazing variety of scenery as it takes you over the mountains from Grindelwald to the huge Brienzersee to the north. It also offers interesting transitions among the different landscapes: the alpine pastures above Grindelwald, the wild, rocky terrain of the ridge above, a descent to more pastures and alps, and then Brienz on its lovely lake. The trip back to Grindelwald can easily be made in the same day, using either the train or a combination of the lake steamer and the train. The hour-long ride on the steamer is a treat on a lovely day. (The Freilichtmuseum at Ballenberg, just west of Brienz, is an open-air museum that displays various types of Swiss farmhouses. A visit would require staying overnight in Brienz.)

Begin as for the Hagelsee, Blau Gletscher, and Grosse Scheidegg route (page 147). At the junction near the Hagelsee, turn left (northeast) for Axalp and Brienz. The trail cuts through this high valley to a small notch, then descends steeply to the Oberberg farm (1911 meters). On a couple of sections you'll have to scramble a little down some rock—though the route is not exposed, you must use your hands. Reach Oberberg in 1 hour past the Hagelsee junction.

Continue northward past the Oberberg farm and descend to a deep, grassy shelf enclosed by high rocky walls. You'll pass signposted junctions at the farms at Lütschentälti (1854 meters) and Chüemad (1794 meters). Keep to the left (north) at each of these junctions. At Axalp (1535 meters) there's a small community with a Kurhaus, 1 hour 20 minutes past Oberberg. At Axalp the trail will join a paved road, where you can catch the bus to Brienz.

The bus leaves at about 12, 15:30, and 17 hours, and the trip takes about 40 minutes. At Brienz take the train to Interlaken, changing at Interlaken Ost. If you catch the 15:30 bus from Axalp, you'll be back in Grindelwald by 18:21. The steamer between Brienz and Interlaken Ost will add about 45 minutes to the return trip. The steamer schedule as well as the bus and train schedules are listed in the Kursbuch, which you can consult at any railway station. You can also telephone (033 36 02 58) for the current steamer schedule and the train connections. If you wish to call about the current bus schedule from Axalp, phone 036 51 15 45.

We don't suggest the option of walking from Axalp to Brienz for this walk because the route prarallels paved roads, is 16 kilometers long, and would make the return trip to Grindelwald very rushed. It is not possible to walk back to Grindelwald from Brienz via the lake, Interlaken, and the Lauterbrunnental in one day.

6. PFINGSTEGG AND STIEREGG

Rating: moderate; easy with lift
Distance round trip: 10 km
High point: 1650 m
Total climb: 700 m
Time: 3 hours up, 1 hour 30 minutes down
Optional transportation: lift
Map: pages 140–41

The Unter Grindelwaldgletscher, extending between the Eiger and the Mättenberg, is one of two glaciers that break the great wall of rock facing Grindelwald. This walk, though fairly short (especially if you take the lift), takes you close to this very impressive glacier and to some of the mountains that tower above it. The route also provides the only view the hiker can get of the east face of the Eiger. The lift eliminates 400 meters of ascent.

For the Pfingstegg lift, walk east down Grindelwald's main street, passing the First lift station and the village church. A sign then points right for the Pfingsteggbahn, near the river. To walk up to Pfingstegg, continue past the lift station to the river, where a sign points left toward Pfingstegg, Gletscherschlucht (the gorge of the Lütschine river), and Marmorbruch. There are two paths up to Pfingstegg. The one to the left (north), via Auf der Sulz, is gradual, ascending to Pfingstegg in 1 hour 40 minutes. The other path climbs steeply through the woods and reaches Pfingstegg in 1 hour 20 minutes.

At Pfingstegg (1392 meters), turn right for Stieregg. The path is very clear; occasionally there's very deep exposure, but there's a good fence of wire and a climbing rope along the outside of the trail. As you climb, you have superb, fairly close views of the huge east face of the Eiger, a gigantic tower of rock, and a splendid view of the Unterer Grindelwaldgletscher below you. Before you are the hanging Fieschergletscher and, above that, the Fiescherhorn. The trail curves around a cliff and soon you arrive at Restaurant Stieregg at 1650 meters, with a very fine view of the glacier.

7. MÄNNLICHEN, LAUBERHORN, AND ALPIGLEN

Rating: easy
Distance loop trip: 11 km
High point: 2472 m
Ascent/descent: 300 m/860 m
Time: 6 hours
Recommended transportation: lift, railway
Map: pages 140–141

This is an easy walk that will take you from the Männlichen lift over an alpine moor to the summit of the Lauberhorn, from which there's an excellent view of the north wall of the Eiger, as well as a panorama of the region. To return to Grindelwald, you'll walk through meadows and past alps to the cog railroad station at Alpiglen.

Start by walking to the Männlichen lift station, which is near the Grund Station of the Kleine Scheidegg cog railroad. Signposts throughout Grindelwald will direct you to the lift, which is in the west end of the town just above the river. The lift ascends almost 1200 meters in two stages and takes 30 minutes. At the top station (2227 meters) there is a splendid view of Wengen far below the rocky cliff.

Follow the signposts for Kleine Scheidegg and the Lauberhorn—the well-defined, easy trail leads south. After walking 15 minutes, reach a signposted junction. The trail to the left (southeast) goes to Alpiglen; continue walking on the right fork (south) toward Kleine Scheidegg and the Lauberhorn. After another 30 minutes, reach another signposted junction. Take the right fork, which ascends to the Lauberhorn. Forty minutes later you'll join a trail that climbs from Kleine Scheidegg on the south summit ridge of the Lauberhorn. Turn right at this junction and head for the summit, which is apparent directly to the north. From the Lauberhorn (2472 meters) you can see the north face of the Eiger (to the south). The view in other directions is panoramic; on a clear day you can see the Thunsee in the distance.

To continue the loop, retrace the route back to the junction for Alpiglen, which you passed near the Männlichen lift. (You can also descend from the Lauberhorn to the Kleine Scheidegg cog railroad station, though the area around Kleine Scheidegg is usually swarming with crowds of tourists who have come up by train and are pointing their cameras at the north wall of the Eiger. To reach Kleine Scheidegg, don't take a sharp left turn at the first trail junction of the descent. Instead, continue ahead to the south, following the trail to Kleine Scheidegg. If you walk directly from Kleine Scheidegg to Alpiglen, you'll be walking parallel to the railroad tracks.)

If you walk back to Männlichen, turn sharp right (southeast) at the Alpiglen trail. At Bustiglen (1875 meters) you'll pass farm buildings and a signposted junction. Continue south following the Alpiglen signposts. The trail will swing left (east) and pass another alp. You'll arrive at the Alpiglen cog railroad station (1616 meters) about 10 minutes after the trail crosses the railroad tracks. You can walk down to Grindelwald in 2 hours but half of the route is on paved roads and streets, so we advise taking the train back from Alpiglen.

9

LOWER ENGADINE WALKS

The Engadine is one of the most interesting regions in Switzerland, much of it little known outside the country. The canton of Graubunden (Grisons or Grischun), which contains the Engadine, is the largest in Switzerland, lying in the southeast part of the country. The river En originates in the high mountains of the Upper Engadine and descends to the Lower Engadine. The Lower Engadine, though it lacks the grander mountains and broader glaciers of the Upper, is a more unusual region and one of great charm. You feel as if you're in a different world here: The "Engiadina Bassa" has preserved a small, proud, regional culture—with its own distinct language, unique architecture, and style of design.

The native languages of the Engadine are a group of related tongues known as Romansch or Ladin. Some variations exist between the Romansch spoken around Scuol (Romansch Vallader) and that of the Upper Engadine (Romansch Puter). Romansch descends from Rhaetic, a language derived from Latin, with some mixture of German. The dairy store, a "molkerei" in German Switzerland, is here a "lataria"; a bakery is a "furnaria." People greet each other by saying "Allegra"—joy to you—surely one of the most beautiful expressions of greeting. Romansch is a living language with a literature, and you will hear it spoken and read signs written in it in the Lower Engadine, where the indigenous culture remains (the clusters of international resorts in the Upper Engadine have practically driven out the local tongue there). You can attend church services in Romansch in Scuol and several villages. You can also get Romansch specialties in some restaurants—often various sorts of pan-

The village of Scuol

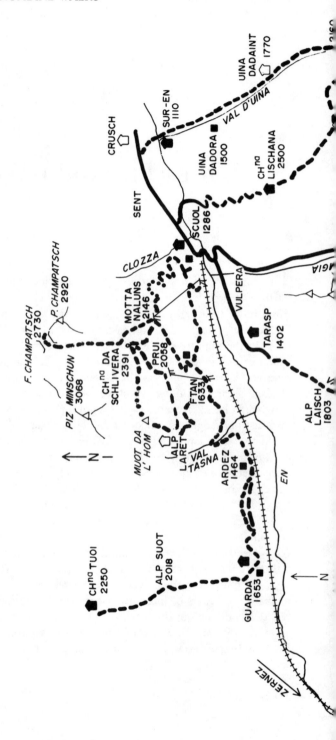

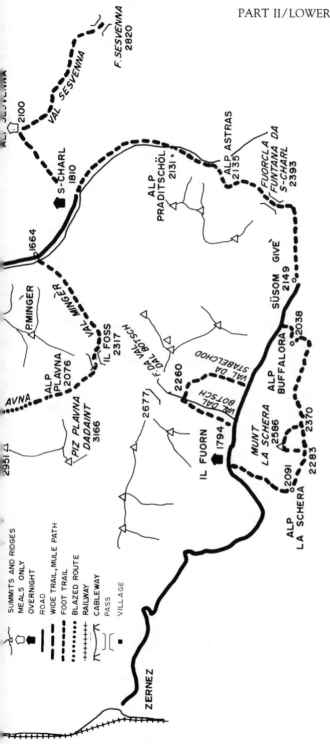

LOWER ENGADINE WALKS

SUMMITS AND RIDGES
MEALS ONLY
OVERNIGHT
ROAD
WIDE TRAIL, MULE PATH
FOOT TRAIL
BLAZED ROUTE
RAILWAY
CABLEWAY
PASS
VILLAGE

155

cakes, with potatoes or fruit. Speakers of Romansch also speak German, and it is easy for travelers to get around speaking English as well.

The Engadine villages, however, are the outstanding feature of the region. White-washed old houses on cobbled streets, surrounded by green mountains and fields, are lovely in themselves, but these houses are unique because of their design and decoration. Their facades are a collective display of a remarkable folk art, *sgraffito*. The house wall is first covered with a layer of gray or brown plaster, which is then covered with a coat of whitewash. The sgraffiti are then formed by incising through the exterior coat to let the gray or light brown designs show through. These designs are often abstract, consisting of geometric forms that appear in bands around windows and doors or in the midst of walls, but some sgraffiti are representational. In addition, designs or pictures are sometimes painted on house facades in vivid colors. The painted forms may be those of fish, mermaids, or mythical beasts, suns and stars, or scenes from the Bible. Texts or sayings are painted or carved on house fronts as well.

Besides their beautiful painting, the houses have an unusual construction. Rooms cluster around a huge entrance hall, through which hay wagons pass to the barn and stables in the back of the house. The broad house facades are divided, with one part of the wall projecting forward. These walls are very thick, with deeply cut windows, some with charming grilles; and many are delightful little corner or oriel windows. People in these villages show that they are up and about for the day by opening their front doors, and as you walk through the streets you can peer in and see the great front halls, often furnished with carved and painted chests.

Two of the most beautiful villages with the finest sgraffiti are Guarda and Ardez. You can rent a vacation apartment in either of them, and both have hotels, although accommodations are very limited. (Guarda has two attractive hotels, but you have to reserve a room months in advance.) You can also rent an apartment or stay in simple accommodations in the pretty farm hamlet of Bos-cha, just outside of Guarda. But although these villages are accessible by rail, it would be troublesome to get from them to other walks down or across the valley without a car. Therefore, we suggest that you make Scuol your base. Scuol, the capital of the Lower Engadine, is a pleasant and interesting large village with good rail and bus connections. It is therefore an excellent center from which to visit many of the extraordinary nearby villages: Ftan, Ardez, Guarda, Sent, Ramosch, and others, and also to hike in the mountains of the Lower Engadine. Scuol has a long history, much involved with fighting off the Austrians and establishing a Reformed church. During the Thirty Years' War, when an Austrian army marched on Scuol, the women fought along with the men to defend their town. Since then, the women of Scuol are allowed the privilege of sitting on the right hand side of the church, a place once reserved by custom for men. There are some very fine old houses decorated with sgraffiti in the old part of Scuol, Scuol Suot—between the main street and the river En. There is also the Museum d'Engiadina Bassa, which shows different typical interior rooms of Engadine houses, as well as a complete mill. And in nearby Tarasp there's a handsome old castle that you can visit. Scuol, Tarasp, and Vulpera together constitute a leading and still fashionable Swiss spa center, with various kinds of waters and such curious treatments as balneological therapy, fango packs, and kinesitherapy baths.

The Lower Engadine is part of the Italian Dolomites and the peaks, as on the Italian side, are jagged and rocky rather than snow-capped. Beautiful meadows and forests also characterize the region. In certain places the round, green mountains may remind visitors of the Scottish highlands (though the country here is not boggy).

In the high country southwest of Scuol is the Swiss National Park, founded in 1914. As Switzerland has no wilderness, this, the sole national park, is very precious. The land is left untouched: there is no foresting, no clearing of dead trees. The park is also a nature preserve, where deer, lynx, and various other species of wild animals may be seen. There are no bears, however, as the last one was killed in 1904. There are several good hiking trails through the park; no camping is allowed, but you can stay at a lodge or a hut within the park boundaries.

The chief attraction to spending a week or more in the Lower Engadine is the exceptional charm of the villages, the soft loveliness of the scenery, and the interest of the Romansch culture. Moreover, this region is not crowded with tourists—indeed, much of it is off the beaten track, which is an attraction in our opinion. If you have only one or two weeks for your stay in Switzerland, however, you would miss the grandest alpine scenery if you spent all your time here.

Some of the best excursions begin from the delightful hamlet of S-charl, south of Scuol and considerably higher. But there is good bus service between Scuol and S-charl, with morning buses at 7:35 and 9:20, so you can have a whole day to ramble in the country above S-charl. The trip to S-charl takes about 40 minutes, and the bus is full of hikers. You can also take a circular walk through the Swiss National Park, for which the PTT has instituted a special bus pick-up. There is one lift available in Scuol, from which you can climb into some wild and high country. And you can also walk through a string of charming villages, including Ardez and Guarda, and return by train to Scuol.

You can reach Scuol by rail from St. Moritz or Pontresina, changing at Samedan. You can also travel by PTT bus from Davos over the Flüela pass to Susch, then continue down the En valley to Scuol.

The recommended topographic map for all of the Lower Engadine walks is Wanderkarte Unterengadin: Samnaun - National Park - Val Mustair, 1:50000. Kummerly + Frey.

1. FTAN, ARDEZ, AND GUARDA

Rating: easy
Distance one way: 15 km
High point: 1664 m
Ascent/descent: 400 m/80 m
Time: 4 hours
Recommended transportation: bus, railway
Map: pages 154–55

This walk takes you through some of the prettiest Lower Engadine villages on the gentle slopes and terraces along the northern bank of the En river. On the southern bank the land generally rises abruptly and steeply, without space for villages and farms. In these villages you find superb old Engadine houses with their characteristic sgraffiti in geometric patterns or enchanting depictions of fanciful creatures.

For this route, walk westward from Scuol through Ftan and Ardez to Guarda, where you take the train back to Scuol. The most direct starting point for the route to Ftan is at the west end of the village near the Motta Naluns lift station. To find the lift, head for the railroad station (you can take a brief bus ride from the PTT station up to the railroad station, which is about 50 meters higher than the village). At the railroad station you'll find a sign that points right (northeast) to the Motta Naluns lift.

At the lift station, follow the road that ascends to the left (west). After 150 meters, a sign indicates the path to Ftan, diverging to the right of the road. Follow the ascending path, which turns right (northeast) until it is almost directly under the cables of the two lifts to Motta Naluns. The path to Ftan then turns to the left (west), where it joins a second path from Scuol.

Proceed directly ahead on the path, which continues westward. Ftan is comprised of two connected villages: Ftan-Pitschen (1644 meters) and, to the west, the larger Ftan-Grond (1633 meters). You may wish to linger in Ftan—which is 1 hour 30 minutes from Scuol—to look at some of the fine old Engadine houses.

For the most direct route to Ardez, take the road that winds around the southern end of Ftan-Grond. At the western end of the village a signpost indicates the route, which follows the gravel road. (A path from the northern end of Ftan-Grond to Ardez is pretty, though less direct.) Views to the left (south) of the castle of Tarasp across the broad En valley.

In the village of Ardez

The road continues almost on the level, gradually swinging to the north-west after it crosses a little stream.

After 10 minutes a signpost for Val Tasna and Ardez indicates the forest path, which diverges to the right of the road and rises about 40 meters above it. Both the road and the upper forest path lead northwest to the opening of the Val Tasna. For Ardez, turn left when you reach the river bank, walk downstream, cross the bridge, and then turn left (south) on the road. After 100 meters you'll see a signpost for Ardez and a path branching off to the right (west). Follow this path, which ascends another 50 meters to open meadows above Ardez. There are several signposted junctions and alternate trails that all lead to Ardez (1464 meters), enter-ing the village from the east. The walking time from Scuol to Ardez is 2 hours 15 minutes.

Although Guarda is better known, Ardez, with its superb examples of Lower Engadine architecture and sgraffiti, preserves more of the true char-acter of a village. The mural depicting Adam and Eve in the Garden of Eden is well known within Switzerland, but many other charming sgraffiti are scattered through the village: dragons, mermaids, fanciful creatures. To ramble through the village, allow yourself at least an hour. There are several simple restaurants in Ardez. From the Ardez station you can take the train back to Scuol.

To continue the walk to Guarda, follow the main street of Ardez to the west—look for a signpost indicating Bos-cha and Guarda on the wall in front of the church in the center of Ardez. At a signposted junction, a road diverges to the left, descending to the hamlet of Giarsun. Take the street to the right, which leads to Bos-cha and Guarda. After an ascent of 100 meters the road levels out and you'll find another junction with a signpost. The main route, along the old dirt road, continues west and gradually ascends to Bos-cha. The fork to the right (north) is a higher route to Guarda and Bos-cha via Pradasura: the signpost reads "Höhenweg Unterengadin." The higher route adds about 20 minutes to the walk, in-volves a steeper initial ascent on a narrow footpath, and about 50 meters of total ascent/descent. It's worth taking in early or midsummer, however, because it leads through fields that are then a mass of alpine flowers. After an ascent of 50 meters, this route intersects a signposted path that runs from Bos-cha to above Ardez. Turn left (west) to Bos-cha (1664 meters), a quiet and very pleasing little hamlet in the fields. The route then follows the contours of the open fields to Guarda (1653 meters).

Guarda is a little gem, with magnificent examples of Lower Engadine architecture and sgraffiti. Give yourself at least 30 minutes—though an hour or more would be better—for exploring the village. Guarda sits on a terrace overlooking the river En, but its railroad station is 250 meters be-low on the valley floor. The trail down to the station is steep and unin-teresting, but you can take a bus down from the PTT: check the timetable at the Post Office. The Holiday Card is not valid on this trip, but the cost of the ticket is low. The train trip back to Scuol takes about 15 minutes. You can get a train until 16 or 17 hours, but check the current schedule.

2. CHAMANNA TUOI

Rating: moderate
Distance round trip: 12 km
High point: 2250 m
Total climb: 700 m
Time: 2 hours 45 minutes up, 1 hour 45 minutes down
Recommended transportation: bus, railway
Map: pages 154–55

This is a very pleasant walk through one of the narrow, lateral valleys that punctuate the En river. The initial section is an easy stroll through country of gentle, pastoral charm, with fields and woods. The trail then rises to a beautiful valley (the Val Tuoi), in which a clear, pale blue stream meanders through wide, grassy banks. At the upper end of the valley, below a chain of rocky peaks, is the SAC Chamanna (hut in Romansch) Tuoi.

From Scuol, take the train to Guarda. Trains leave Scuol every hour (check the current schedule), and the trip takes 15 minutes. The railroad station at Guarda is 250 meters below the village, and you can either take a bus to the village or walk up. The walk to Guarda takes about 45 minutes whether you follow the 4-kilometer automobile road with its long switch-backs or take the steep, well-posted footpath. The signpost is directly behind the station, and the path ascends steeply to the north.

From Guarda village, follow the signposted route to Ardez, which heads eastward along the main street of the village. Part way through the village, a signpost points left (north) to the Chamanna Tuoi. The path ascends about 40 meters and reaches a fork where you take the path to the left (west) to Alp Suot and the Chamanna Tuoi. This is a lovely walk, at first through fields and then larches, with a stream below. The larches thin out and disappear, and you ascend through a meadow with steep walls of grass and rock on either side, though the mountains are quite low. The path gradually ascends for 2.5 kilometers. Shortly before you reach the barns of Alp Suot (2018 meters), 1 hour past Guarda, the path ascends fairly steeply to the right (east) of the alp, then continues to ascend gradually for another 2 kilometers, with a final steeper 100-meter ascent to the hut (2250 meters). Above the hut rises a wall of scree, then a glacier and the Piz Buin, a jagged tooth of rock. If you intend to stay overnight you should phone ahead (084 9 19 63).

3. CHAMPATSCH

Rating: moderate
Distance round trip: 9 km
High point: 2730 m
Total climb: 700 m
Time: 2 hours 30 minutes up, 1 hour 30 minutes down
Recommended transportation: lift
Map: pages 154– 55

This excursion leads north of Scuol to a high, desolate, moorlike landscape set among walls of rock.

To start this route from Scuol, take the lift up to Motta Naluns (2146 meters). The lift station is near the railroad station (page 158). (If you walk to Motta Naluns, add another 850 meters and 3 hours to the trip. The most direct route leaves from the east end of Scuol. Signposts on the main street near the bridge over the Clozza stream indicate the route.)

From the lift station at Motta Naluns follow the signposted path that heads northwest. The trail proceeds across rocky pastures on which flocks of sheep somehow find something to eat. A line of low peaks rises to your left as the trail swings toward the north. The blazed trail (white-red-white) climbs through boulder fields and then up through scree to the Fuorcla Champatsch (2730 meters), a saddle between the Piz Nair and the Piz Champatsch. A little snow is possible below the saddle. The country is barren and wild, with jagged, black basalt peaks and slopes of rock and scree.

At the Fuorcla Champatsch you can see down into the forested Val Laver. A rough trail also leads up from the Fuorcla eastward along a ridge of the Piz Champatsch to its summit. This route can be difficult if there's snow and should not be attempted if you have any doubts.

Return to Motta Naluns the way you came or descend to Ftan on foot from Motta Naluns by following the signposted trail to Prui, which starts to the left (southwest) of the lift station. Walking down to Ftan will take about 1 hour 30 minutes; from Ftan you can walk or take a PTT bus to Scuol.

4. MUOT DA L'HOM AND CHAMANNA DA SCHLIVERA

Rating: strenuous
Distance one way: 12 km
High point: 2512 m
Ascent/descent: 1000 m/1000 m

Time: 5 hours
Recommended transportation: bus, lift
Map: pages 154–55

This is one of the most attractive walks north of the En, and one with a great deal of variety. The trail leads through meadows and a lovely forest, then climbs up to a high terrace from which there is a grand panoramic view across the En valley. You can return from Alp Laret or continue on a poorly marked trail into high alpine country. Pick up a good trail again below Piz Clunas and return via Motta Naluns or Ftan to Scuol.

From Scuol take the PTT bus to the bus stop at the eastern end of Ftan-Grond village. Turn right as you leave the bus and you'll see a sign that points left (west) for Alp Laret and for the Alpine Töchterinstitut, a school that you'll reach in 10 minutes. At the junction soon after the school, continue straight (southwest) for Sass Majur and Alp Laret (the path to the right also leads to Alp Laret, but is steeper). Proceed along a jeep road through beautiful meadows, then head up into a forest. At a second junction, turn right onto a footpath for Sass Majur. The path climbs more steeply here, through lovely woods, then levels out after 40 minutes. Far below, on your left, is the stream of the Val Tasna.

At Sass Majur (1889 meters), a sign points straight ahead for Alp Laret. Enter a long, steep meadow and climb up a grass track. A small blazed rock is visible up the slope and, farther above, a blazed post. Switchback up to the top of this steep meadow—there are occasional traces of a footpath. Reach a small gravel road above the meadow and follow it as it winds through high meadows. There are beautiful, long views of the mountains across the En valley and to the north. This section of the route is part of the "Panorama Engiadina Bassa," a walk that parallels the river En. Two hours past Ftan, reach Alp Laret, where you can buy various drinks and cheese. Superb views from the alp across the En valley.

To continue this route, pick up the trail behind Alp Laret. At 2206 meters, a sign points toward the left for Muot da l'Hom, Piz Clunas, and the Chamanna da Schlivera; right for Prui. If you take the path to the right, you can walk on a fairly level path to Prui, then descend by lift or footpath to Ftan. For the longer route, which leads into wilder country, continue climbing up the slope behind Alp Laret. There are some blazes here and there, but aim for the high bump up the slope. Go to the left (west) of this large bump; look for blazed posts and some blazed rocks. As you walk around to the north side of the bump, turn toward the right (east), so that the bump is now on your right. To your left there's a much higher mountain. Here you are in beautiful, wild, empty high meadows.

Walk between two very small streams; a tiny cabin is visible up to your left. Reach a signpost, which points you straight ahead for Muot da l'Hom. The square-topped mountain to your left is Piz Minschun, and the one with snow fences is Piz Clunas. Continue eastward and come to some big snow fences. (If you should walk this route in reverse, from Naluns westward, keep to the right: don't go left on a plank bridge, at an unmarked junction. Head straight for the big, pointy mountain far in front of you.)

Pass the snow fence area and a cabin, cross a small stream on a bridge, then continue on a gravel jeep road. A signpost points straight ahead for Schlivera and Motta Naluns. You'll pass a shed on your right, then reach Alp Clunas (2444 meters) where you can buy milk.

From the alp, a gravel road snakes around various bumps in the terrain and descends to a junction; turn left (east) for Naluns and Schlivera.

At the next signposted junction continue to Naluns, taking the path to the left. After you pass Chamanna Naluns, the road turns. Go to the right (down the slope) for the Motta Naluns lift, which takes you directly to Scuol.

5. S-CHARL TO SÜSOM GIVÈ (PASS DAL FUORN).

Rating: moderate
Distance one way: 13 km
High point: 2393 m
Ascent/descent: 600 m/350 m
Time: 4 hours 30 minutes
Recommended transportation: bus
Map: pages 154–55

From Scuol, take a bus to S-charl, walk to Süsom Givè, and return by bus and train. This is easy to do as this route is one of the PTT's suggested excursions, and the connections were designed to accommodate hikers. The bus ride from Scuol to S-charl takes about 30 minutes and there are two morning buses. It may be necessary to reserve a place, which can be done the day before. For the 1 hour 30-minute return trip, take a PTT bus from Süsom Givè, which connects with the train at Zernez. This excursion from Scuol is a popular one, and there should be no difficulty in making connections.

The tiny, picturesque hamlet of S-charl (1810 meters) consists of about a dozen houses, including several very attractive inns and a little square with a fountain. The church dates from the twelfth century. S-charl is located in a narrow green valley between wooded slopes, with views at each end of the jagged Lower Engadine peaks: a place so pretty, quiet, and remote that you might well be tempted to spend a night here. It's hard to believe that S-charl was once a mining community four or five times its present size and played a historic role in the struggle of the Engadine people against the Austrians. In the little square are signposts for walks in several directions.

For this route, follow the sign for Süsom Givè. The trail is a broad dirt road that follows the gently curving Clemgia river southeast. The mountains here are low, with pine forests that extend fairly high up the slopes. To the north, the mountains are bare, green, and rounded, while to the south and east, the peaks are rocky, jagged, and gray—true Dolomites. The valley is wide and open despite the trees, with the lovely Clemgia running between grassy banks: peaceful, gentle, lovely country.

At 1994 meters (about 40 minutes from S-charl) reach a signposted junction. The trail to the left (east) leads to Alp Plazer, Cruschetta, and Taufers (Tubre)—the Italian border. Continue on the path to the right, heading south for Alp Praditschöl (2131 meters). The path crosses the stream on a bridge and continues along the valley below Alp Praditschöl to Alp Astras (2135 meters). A sign here points southwest, behind the alp. The track is visible in the grass, and soon there are blazed rocks.

The trail ascends more steeply to the Plan Matun (2303 meters), and then to the Fuorcla Funtana da S-charl (2393 meters), where you have a beautiful view into the Val Mustair. From the Fuorcla continue straight ahead (southwest), and soon reach the top of the pass.

At a marked junction after the pass, take the path to the right (west). Descend steeply to the meadows of the Plaun da l'Aua (2190 meters). The path goes through the pine forest and reaches another signposted junction at 2152 meters, where you follow the path to the right (north). There is a short stretch here with some exposure. Descend through the woods and reach the inn at Süsom Givè, which is on the Pass dal Fuorn (2149 meters). Take the PTT bus to Zernez, where you change for the train to Scuol.

6. S-CHARL TO FUORCLA SESVENNA

Rating: moderate
Distance round trip: 15 km
High point: 2660 m
Total climb: 550 m
Time: 4 hours up, 2 hours 30 minutes down
Recommended transportation: bus
Map: pages 154—55

This trail leads into the Val Sesvenna, a wild, empty valley that rises gently at first, then more steeply, and ends at a rocky wall that requires a strenuous scramble. You can turn around at the base of the wall or continue to the Fuorcla Sesvenna, a notch in the mountainous ridge that forms the Italian border to the east.

From Scuol, take the bus to S-charl. A signpost in the square points northeast to Alp Sesvenna and Fuorcla Sesvenna. A stream is on your left, and the trail is easy and wide, ascending a very gentle grade up through the woods. Cross a bridge, and continue through trees, then up grassy slopes. Climb up into a meadow that is partially surrounded by low, rocky mountains.

After 1 hour you'll reach Alp Sesvenna (which sells refreshments) in this big meadow. Next to the alp there's a huge boulder, blazed for several routes: left for Fora de l'Aua and right for Fuorcla Sesvenna. Head east and ascend through a round bowl, angling up to the right. Cross a slope of rock and scree; a rushing stream is on your right. Then climb more steeply, ascending into a narrow, uninhabited valley. The trees thin out and disappear. The footpath is generally clear and has occasional blazes. Climb steadily, the stream now well below you, into a higher bowl, very green and wild. You'll reach this second bowl about 2 hours from S-charl.

To continue to the pass, climb up on the left side of the valley—the trail is a little steep and occasionally blazed. Head southeast, climbing steadily. As you ascend, you must aim for the end of the valley, then to the right of that—walk in the direction of a high, dark, pointy rock peak that is visible to the right above the wall. Finally, you are faced with a steep, rock-strewn wall. Climb up on a poor, scanty track. Take care here, for there is loose rock. (This is the part of the route that calls for a strenuous trail rating.) Climbing this wall takes about 25 minutes. At the top (2660 meters) the country opens out, and you'll emerge into high alpine terrain: a stony basin with a little milky green lake, a glacier above it, and rocky mountains around.

Continue if the route is clear of snow and you can see blazes on the rocks. As few hikers come here, you may not find an evident track. The route climbs gradually; a half hour from the little lake, reach the Fuorcla Sesvenna on the Swiss-Italian border. There are several lakes in the valley below, which is narrow and flanked by rocky ridges.

The return to S-charl will take you at least two hours.

7. VAL MINGÈR, VAL PLAVNA, AND TARASP

Rating: strenuous
Distance loop trip: 14 km

High point: 2317 m
Total climb: 1100 m
Time: 5 hours 30 minutes
Recommended transportation: bus
Map: pages 154–55

This route takes you into the Swiss National Park. The first part of the route ascends a long, green valley, the Val Mingèr, rising to a pass called Il Foss outside the national park. Return through a very different landscape—the stony Val Plavna and the forest above Tarasp.

Take the bus to S-charl, but get off at the stop for Val Mingèr, just before S-charl. There's a concrete dam on the Clemgia at this bus stop. Cross the river on the concrete bridge. The trail starts on the other side and is very clearly marked. Here you enter the Swiss National Park: a set of signs announces the rules: you may not leave the trail, pick flowers, litter, make fires, etc. The fine for violations is heavy.

The gently graded trail begins through pine woods and leads through a pretty meadow, then back into the woods. Cross the stream several times, always on bridges. Eventually the trail turns to the right, away from the stream, and ascends a moderate grade. There are jagged rocky peaks above to your right and a big rocky mass behind you. Rejoin the stream bed, now to your left, and enter a long meadow. Before you is a solitary, pointed gray mountain, the Piz Plavna Dadaint. In this long meadow is a Rastplatz (place de repos) defined by posts, with picnic tables. Note, however, that you are not far from the pass, which is outside the national park, and where you may eat lunch wherever you like.

The valley here is broad and beautiful. Continue to the west, heading for the Piz Plavna Dadaint. Soon you climb above the last trees and reach Il Foss, a saddle (or pass) with fine views of the narrow valley below and its ring of jagged gray peaks. The tall Piz Plavna Dadaint is across the valley and the long, green Val Mingèr is behind you.

Turn left (south) at Il Foss for the route into the Val Plavna and on to Tarasp—a sign indicates the way. In 10 minutes reach a second signposted junction; turn to the right here for Alp Plavna.

Descend into a pretty valley with a braided stream and, to your left, jagged gray peaks. Alp Plavna (2076 meters), which sells refreshments, is set in a meadow. At the alp, a sign points left to Tarasp. Continue, heading north, on a narrow jeep road, with the stream to your left. You must then walk through an area of gravel—at first on the right bank, but then crossing a bridge to the left bank. Descend to a wide, flat area, like a lake bed full of white stones, giving the valley a strange appearance. Cross the stream again, on a plank bridge. You must then cross this "lake" of stones. At first, keep to the right side of the valley; there is no path really, and there are no blazes. Follow what looks like the shallow channel of a former torrent, which seems to cross to the middle of the lake. Finally, after 10 or 15 minutes, enter a thin wood, on a stony trail. Come out into a meadow, then come to another, smaller area of boulders, where you cross a dry stream bed. Proceed to the right, into thin woods again, then emerge and descend on a gravel road through the pine woods. At a junction here, a sign points you to the right to Tarasp. Descend a grass track through a meadow, then through woods, where it becomes a gravel track. At a second junction, keep to the right for Tarasp (don't take the bridge, sharply to the right, for Godplan and Funtana). Continue straight ahead, where you'll find a bridge that you must cross. The river is now to your left.

At a third junction, stay on the main trail, a gravel road. From here you can see the castle of Tarasp before you, high on its hill. As you enter Tarasp bear right at the first (and only) junction. Pass the Hotel Tarasp on your left, and soon reach the bus stop (Posta). Buses leave for Scuol at regular intervals until 18:40.

8. VAL D'UINA

Rating: moderate
Distance round trip: 19 km
High point: 2150 m
Total climb: 1050 m
Time: 5 hours 15 minutes up, 2 hours 30 minutes down
Recommended transportation: bus
Map: pages 154–55

This route is not particularly steep nor are there any technical difficulties, but it leads up to a spectacular gorge. There the trail is blasted out of a gigantic, vertical rock wall, which plunges about 600 meters to a turbulent river. The trail is adequately wide and has fixed cables or partial railings; however, persons suffering from vertigo should be forewarned. This is not a strenuous or difficult hike, but the tremendous exposure may frighten some people. Above this gorge the trail emerges into high, broad, beautiful meadows.

From Scuol, take the bus through Sent to Crusch (indicate to the driver that you want to get off there). Crusch is a cluster of three or four houses and a post office, just east of Sent. Walk back in the direction from which the bus came, past the next house. Just past this house is a narrow path that descends steeply to the river. Cross the covered bridge to the campground and turn right for Uina, passing the little hamlet of Sur-En.

At Restorant Val d'Uina, a signpost indicates Uina Dadaint, 1 hour 30 minutes (too little by 30 or 45 minutes) and Chamanna Lischana.

Walk up a dirt jeep road of moderate grade, through woods. You'll cross bridges over the river several times. Ascend through this narrow, wooded valley, entering a deep, rocky gorge. The trail is very good here, built out over the rock wall in places. About 1 hour from the start, emerge above this gorge to a more open place. Continue straight ahead—several more bridges cross the river. After another hour the trail becomes steeper and you climb up into a large meadow. Here you'll find Alp Uina Dadaint, which sells milk, yogurt, cheese, and other refreshments.

Beyond the alp, the gravel trail starts to climb up to the gorge and becomes very steep. The gorge is spectacular—a narrow, deep crack between two massive rock walls, with a wild torrent far below. The trail, blasted out of the rock, passes through some short tunnels. The exposure is severe, and there are fixed cables alternately on the inner side of the trail or against the rock, as well as sections of railing on the outer side, over the gorge. Every part of this section has something for you to hold onto.

This dramatic section takes 20 to 25 minutes to ascend. Then the trail levels out, and you emerge into a beautiful meadow—grassy and wide, with mountains rising around it. The stream here flows very gently. The contrast between this broad, pleasant, open place—on a sunny day the stream and meadows sparkle—and the dark, narrow gorge is a striking one.

From this meadow you could turn right on the trail (2180 meters) to the Lischana hut, but that's a very long route. Wander about in this high meadow for as long as you wish or have time, then return by the same route to Sur-En. Climbing back up from the En to the bus stop at Crusch will take you at least 20 minutes. The road to Scuol is served by both Swiss PTT and Austrian buses, on which the Swiss Holiday Card is valid. The Austrian buses are yellow, with no red band. You could also walk back to Scuol from Sur-En, taking a gentle trail westward along the En river. This would take you 1 hour 45 minutes.

9. SWISS NATIONAL PARK: IL FUORN, ALP LA SCHERA, AND ALP BUFFALORA

Rating: moderate
Distance one way: 11.5 km
High point: 2586 m
Total climb: 800 m
Time: 4 hours 30 minutes
Recommended transportation: train, bus
Map: pages 154–55

Switzerland's only national park was established in 1914, and the decision was made to let the area revert to a natural state, so that the Swiss people could have one such wilderness in their country and study the effects of natural processes left untouched by human disturbance. Everything in the park is protected: you may not pick a single flower, or leave the marked path, or make loud noises that might frighten the animals. No dogs are allowed, no camping, no fires, no leaving of trash. You may not stop to picnic except at the designated rest spots.

An automobile road traverses the park from west to east, entering at Zernez and reaching its high point at the Pass dal Fuorn or Ofenpass (2149 meters). Süsom Givè, one of the hiking stops, is located at the pass. There are several numbered parking lots along this road, from which hiking trails start.

At the park Headquarters and Information Center in Zernez, you can see exhibits about geology, plants, and wildlife and obtain literature and maps.

From Scuol, take the train to Zernez (33 minutes) and change there for the bus to Il Fuorn (30 minutes). Il Fuorn means oven (Ofen in German) and was the site of a blast furnace that was used for the production of iron as early as 1489 and perhaps even earlier. There is one very attractive hotel, Hotel Parc Naziunal, a modern establishment—though some of the walls of the present hotel date back to the fifteenth century. Matratzenlager are available, though the hotel does not advertise them. On the path to Grimmels, a 10-minute walk past the hotel, you can see one of the old furnaces that gave Il Fuorn its name.

From Hotel Parc Naziunal (1794 meters), turn right (west) and walk down the road a few hundred meters until you see the sign for Alp la Schera (at Parking Lot 5). Turn left (south) onto the path, which climbs gently through pine woods along the northwest slope of Munt la Schera and offers occasional glimpses of the mountains across the valley. Around the shoulder, the trail gradually rises out of the trees and turns out onto a sloping meadow with lovely views on three sides. This is Alp la Schera (2091 meters), where there is a designated rest spot and a ranger's cabin with water and simple toilet facilities. The trail continues eastward to 2283 meters, where you have the option of a short side trip: climbing 300 meters to Munt la Schera.

The route to Munt la Schera is a steep, clearly marked, and signposted trail that takes 1 hour; from the summit there's a fine view of the Val Livigno to the south. From the summit you can continue on a trail to the east that descends to the main trail at 2370 meters.

From the main trail you'll see valleys to your right and before you, and jagged, rocky, but fairly low mountains. The main trail continues eastward, gradually descending for 3 kilometers to some farm buildings at

2194 meters. The trail turns left (north) after this point. A deep bowl lies in front of you and to the right, and you gradually descend to the park boundary. After passing the barn at Alp Buffalora (2038 meters), reach the highway at Chasa dal Stradin (1968 meters), where you can catch a bus back to Il Fuorn or Zernez. (If you walk back to Il Fuorn it will take another hour.)

10. SWISS NATIONAL PARK: IL FUORN, VAL DAL BOTSCH, AND ALP STABELCHOD

Rating: moderate
Distance loop trip: 9 km
High point: 2328 m
Total climb: 600 m
Time: 3 hours
Map: pages 154–55

This walk takes you into the northern reaches of the Swiss National Park, with a variety of terrain within a short space: the national park forest and high slopes above treeline. As with all walks in the national park, there is a good possibility of seeing wildlife; however, the Val dal Botsch gives you an excellent chance of seeing deer and chamois.

From the Hotel Parc Naziunal (page 170), cross the highway and turn left (east), where you can take a path (the Naturlehrpfad or Nature-learning path) through the woods, parallel to the road toward Val dal Botsch. Various engraved steel signs carry information about the park's plants and animals. Turn left at the junction for Parking Lot 7 and cross the river. The trail up to the Fuorcla da Val dal Botsch begins across the road at the parking lot.

The trail starts through pine woods that gradually thin out and emerges into the open to the left (west) of a rocky stream bed. It crosses the stream at a signposted junction (2260 meters). The trail to the Fuorcla da Val dal Botsch is the left (north) fork. Take the right fork, which continues eastward to Stabelchod. The trail proceeds across steep slopes, with jagged peaks above. Climb to the high point of 2328 meters and then descend to the Val da Stabelchod and Alp Stabelchod (1958 meters). The park rangers frequently set up telescopes near their cabin at Alp Stabelchod to allow hikers to view wildlife. From the alp take the path to the right back toward the road and Parking Lot 8, where you can return on the path to the bus stop at Il Fuorn.

PART III

Walking Tours

between

Hotels, Mountain Inns, and Huts

10

LONG ROUTES AND
WALKING TOURS

A delightful way to walk in Switzerland is from point to point, to
"travel" on foot, as people did hundreds of years ago. Indeed, when you
walk this way in Switzerland, you're often following trails that are hundreds, sometimes even thousands, of years old. These paths were not made
by Trail Commissions; they were created by alpine farmers to connect one
village with the next, by a short (albeit arduous) route. Otherwise, the
journeys up and down the valleys, around the mountains, would take a
week. In this part of the book, we describe a selection of extended walking
routes and tours that you can take in different parts of Switzerland.

The practice of linking together these ancient pass routes and other
trails to make long-distance walking tours is at least 150 years old. James
Fenimore Cooper, who spent three years in Switzerland, described a walking tour from Lauterbrunnen to Meiringen in the Bernese Oberland. And
while foreign climbers, often English, were conquering the great alpine
peaks during the middle and late nineteenth century, numerous others
were following the series of tours that the Rev. Harry Jones called *The
Regular Swiss Round* (as he entitled his 1866 book on the subject). These
tours were then noted in the Baedeker guides to Switzerland published in
the late nineteenth century.

Unlike North American long-distance trails, these tours are not necessarily linear. But neither are they circular (with a few exceptions). Swiss
tours are shorter than the long-distance North American trails, matching
the proportions of Switzerland. And no Swiss trail takes you through a wilderness for days on end; there are no such extended wildernesses. The

Snow bridge and stream below the Oberhornsee, in the Bernese-Oberland

At the top of Höhturli in the Bernese Oberland

trails pass through villages. And, as we noted in the Introduction, hikers on Swiss trails do not camp: they stay in mountain inns, huts, or village hotels.

These conditions are the result of both Swiss history and geography. The configuration of the Swiss alpine landscape is quite different from that of most mountainous regions in North America. While the Swiss mountains are comparable in height to the Canadian Rockies, the valleys between ranges are generally narrower and steeper. Walks over the pass routes descend to valleys, and valleys have villages. In order to survive in the alpine environment, people developed the system of dual pastures: winter farms and summer alps, positioned as high on the slopes as the flocks could graze—up to 2500 meters. Flocks are led to the alps for summer grazing, and cheese is made there during the summer. Trails lead from villages up to alps, then over passes, and down to alps and the next villages.

Walking these long routes gives you a chance to see the total alpine environment. In one day, you can make the astonishing transition between villages, alpine pastureland and summer farms, and breathtaking alpine passes, often overhung by glaciers and snow-capped peaks. On your route you will often see flocks grazing at high altitudes, old wooden storage barns, and people cutting hay. In the traditional villages, people wear mountain boots as their daily outdoor footwear. (Shoes are for church and social occasions.)

You can actually walk from one end of Switzerland to the other. On some of the routes that we describe here, we suggest that you use buses or trains rather than walk the few sections that run on or parallel to roads. Your overnight stops will sometimes be in mountain inns, occasionally in huts, and sometimes in village hotels.

The longest tour that we describe is in the Bernese Oberland; we have *1 ·* selected what we consider the most scenic portion of the traditional traverse of the Oberland. This is a linear route that can be walked west to east or in reverse. It offers numerous overnight stops at mountain inns, as well as several optional stops in villages. We then describe a linear route *2 ·* that links several passes across the Valais, through both French- and German-speaking sections. For the Upper Engadine, we suggest a semicir- *3* cular tour around one of the region's major glaciers, with overnight stops at huts and inns. In the Italian-speaking Ticino, we describe a traditional *4.* route, the Strada Alta, which links the small villages above the Val Leventina. Finally, we describe a set of walks in the Emmental, a region *5.* which, although not alpine, has its own special appeal.

Walking from point to point like this is exhilarating. You can walk over mountain passes through spectacular scenery, on routes used since medieval and Roman times. You're carrying everything you need, and that turns out to be wonderfully little. This gives you a magnificent sense of freedom and self-sufficiency. You constantly meet new people, on the trail and at huts, inns, and hotels. Remarkable encounters occur. On walking tours we've met an American diplomat, a pair of Swiss cooks home on vacation from their job in Texas, a Dutch linguist, and the packaging manager of a Swiss supermarket chain. By the banks of a river we were invited to share a picnic lunch by a Swiss truck driver and his family—and lunch was no sandwich and cookie affair but a full-scale cookout with a portable raclette oven, coffee, and brandy.

Although you can walk from point to point and stay in a different place every night, you can also stay in a village hotel or a mountain inn for a couple of nights and make a few side trips in the area, then continue the walking tour (or take a bus or train) to another base. There are several advantages to this approach. If you know that you're going back to the same hotel, hut or inn, you can leave some of your things behind and hike with a lighter pack. There may be several good walks in one locality that you'd miss if you moved straight on. And you get more of a feel for the way of life in a particular place. There is nothing sacred about the always-on-the-move approach.

The Swiss way is to be flexible.

177

11

TOURING THE BERNESE OBERLAND

The Bernese Oberland exemplifies the classic image of Switzerland: snowy peaks, green meadows, herds of cows wearing cowbells. The Valaisian Alps are higher, but the Bernese Oberland has some of the most spectacular views in the Alps and some of the most famous mountains—the Eiger, Mönch, and Jungfrau. The Oberland gets more rain than the Valais or the Engadine, but this also makes the meadows noticeably more green and lush, with a dazzling profusion of wildflowers.

The Oberland is a mountain chain running from east to west, just north of the Rhône valley. You can traverse the Oberland from the Jochpass above Engelberg to Gstaad. The grandest part of the route extends between the Jochpass and Kandersteg, but you can do more if your time permits. This route encompasses almost the full range of alpine terrain of the Oberland: the gentle pastures and lake of Engstlenalp, the awesome mountain wall over Grindelwald, the savage, rocky Sefinenfurke, the isolated alpine farms above Griesalp, the glaciers and summits of Hohtürli, and the turquoise Oeschinensee below the glaciers near Kandersteg. Hordes of tourists swarm at Kleine Scheidegg near Grindelwald, to look at the Jungfrau and the north wall of the Eiger, but we propose a route that avoids the crowds while showing you the mountains in their full splendor. We also suggest that you use buses or trains on certain sections of the route that coincide with automobile roads. The time you save can be used in places that can be seen only on foot. Although we describe a westward course, you can just as easily walk this route (or any segment) from west to east.

Cowherd between Oberhornsee and Schmadrihütte

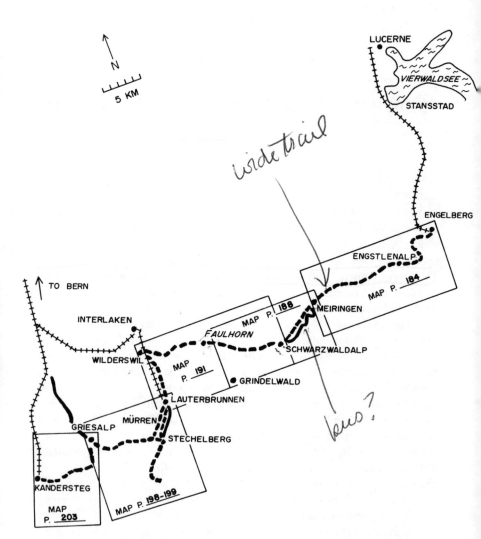

OVERVIEW OF BERNESE-OBERLAND TOUR

The route from east to west presents a series of walks that each requires progressively more physical effort. You begin at Engelberg, in the
canton of Obwalden, from which you can ascend to the Jochpass—which
has a comparatively low altitude—by lift. The Jochpass is the eastern
boundary of the canton of Bern. If you reach Engelberg by train in the afternoon, you can stay overnight at the mountain inn at Engstlenalp. Then
walk from Engstlenalp to Meiringen by a high or middle route. If you are
still adjusting to the altitude and don't quite have your hiking muscles in
tune, you can take the middle route. Stay overnight either at Meiringen,
an attractive little town at the foot of the Reichenbach Falls (where Pro-
fessor Moriarty wrestled Sherlock Holmes to his supposed demise), or you
can continue and stay overnight at the mountain inn at Rosenlaui. From
Meiringen we recommend that you take the PTT bus to either Rosenlaui
or Schwarzwaldalp, where you can walk on a high route to the First lift station above Grindelwald. From there you can descend to Grindelwald after
seeing the Bachalpsee. You can also stay overnight at the Faulhorn inn
and avoid a side trip to Grindelwald. From the Faulhorn, follow one of the
classic alpine walking routes to Schynige Platte, from which you descend
via cog railroad to Lauterbrunnen. These two sections of the route—from
Meiringen to Grindelwald and Grindelwald to Schynige Platte—are more
taxing than the earlier sections. If you have the time, we recommend a
side trip to Stechelberg with an overnight stay at one of the mountain inns
at Obersteinberg and a walk to the beautiful Oberhornsee. Otherwise, you
can proceed from Lauterbrunnen to Mürren via funicular. After an overnight stop at Mürren (there are mountain inns at Blumental, just outside
the village), you can continue on the route over the Sefinenfurke to
Griesalp (mountain inns). This section of the route is still more demanding. From Griesalp, the most strenuous section of the route continues to
Hohtürli and the Blümlisalphütte of the SAC. The route then descends
past the Oeschinensee to Kandersteg. (You can continue westward over
several more passes, which have lower altitudes, to Adelboden, Lenk, and
Gstaad.)

Since it often rains in the Bernese Oberland you should allow at least
10 days for the basic route. You also might want to take a rest day or two
on the basic route even if it doesn't rain, particularly if you walk this route
at the start of your vacation. If you have extra time you can take some of
the side trips or walk the sections on which we recommend that you take
buses and cog railroads.

1. ENGELBERG TO ENGSTLENALP

Rating: moderate
Distance one way: 9 km

High point: 2207 m
Ascent/descent: 1200 m/360 m
Time: 5 hours
Optional transportation: lifts
Map: page 184; also Landeskarte der Schweiz 1:25000, INNERT-
 KIRCHEN-1210

You can reach Engelberg easily from Lucerne, either directly by train
(in about 1 hour) or by lake steamer from Lucerne to Stanstad and then by
train to Engelberg (1 hour 30 minutes). The lake trip is delightful in fine
weather.

Cut off on three sides by mountains, Engelberg can be approached
only by rail or road from the north. The most famous peak here is the
Titlis. Not only is its location spectacular, but Engelberg is also a charming town with pretty gardens. At the edge of the town is the Kloster, a
Benedictine abbey founded in the twelfth century. The church and museum can be visited by guided tour at 10 or 16 hours on weekdays. The library can be visited only by special appointment and is open only to men.

You can walk from Engelberg to Meiringen in one day if you use the
lifts and get an early start. Or you can break up the walk with an overnight
stop en route. The advantage of doing it in two stages is that you can
spend a night at Engstlenalp, a lovely spot with a charming mountain inn.
From Engstlenalp, you have a choice of three routes to Meiringen—high,
middle and low. But first, you must ascend from Engelberg to the Jochpass
and then descend to Engstlenalp.

Unless you have a lot of time, we recommend that you use the lifts
and begin hiking at the pass: the lifts enable you to reach the Jochpass in 1
hour 30 minutes. The walk up from Engelberg to the Jochpass is not that
interesting because you're facing the mountain during the ascent, with the
views behind you or to the side, and the trail sometimes passes under or
near the lifts. Whether you plan to climb or to take the lifts, leave the
Engelberg train station and walk past the station telephones (on your right
as you leave the train platform). A sign indicates the way to both the trail
and the lift, which goes up in stages. Take the cable car (télépherique) to
Trübsee. At Trübsee, walk in front of the hotel, to your right, and then
around to the back of the terrace, where you'll see a signpost directing you
to the Jochpass. Walk past the lake (there are blazes on the cement walk)
to the Jochpass chairlift (Sesselbahn). The walk from Trübsee to the pass
takes 1 hour and the path rises in switchbacks under the chairlift. At the
pass there's a mountain restaurant with Matratzenlager.

From the Jochpass, the trail descends westward under a chairlift.
About 100 meters below the upper chairlift station, there's a junction. Al-

though the sign on the path to the right (north) indicates Engstlenalp and Melchsee-Frutt, that is a longer route. Instead, continue straight ahead to the west. Soon this trail diverges to the right of the chairlift; there are paint blazes on the route. Behind you to the left (southeast) you can see the round snow hump of the Titlis. After 40 minutes arrive at the Engstlensee and, in another 20, at Engstlenalp (1835 meters).

Engstlenalp isn't even a hamlet. It's an alp—a little group of summer farms. It also has a mountain inn, Hotel Engstlenalp (tel. 036 75 11 61), that John Tyndall, the Victorian scientist, described as "one of the most charming spots in the Alps" in 1866. To one side is the lake, with a blue-green color unusual in Switzerland. The lake is so clear that you can see the trout in it and so cold that one brief dip with your big toe will be enough. The region around the lake and to the south is a nature preserve. Camping, hunting, open fires, and flower picking are all strictly forbidden, but fishing is permitted. To the south, a wall of rock with slabs of snow and glaciers rises along the length of the lake; to the north, you'll see steep green slopes and the Graustock, a great outcrop of rock. To the east, superb waterfalls drain into the lake. And to the west, over the deep cleft of the narrow Gental, rises the huge, distant mass of the biggest mountains of the Bernese Oberland.

At about 16:30 hours every summer afternoon, the farmers' children drive the cows down to the barns for milking, a sight worth seeing—and hearing, as the cows each wear a bell of a different pitch. In the evening, the farmers often come to the inn for tea and schnapps.

If you decide to spend a second night at Engstlenalp, you could take a side trip to Melchsee-Frutt via Tannalp.

2. ENGSTLENALP TO MEIRINGEN

Rating: strenuous, moderate with lifts
Distance one way: 20 km, 9.5 km with lifts
High point: 2255 m
Ascent/descent: 520m/1645 m (no lifts)
Time: 6 to 7 hours
Optional transportation: lift
Map: page 184; also Landeskarte der Schweiz 1:25000, INNERT-KIRCHEN—1210

Leaving the inn at Engstlenalp, turn right from the door (northwest) and follow the sign indicating walks to Planplatten and Melchsee-Frutt. The well-marked footpath takes you through the cluster of summer farms and then below a cliff with long slabbed rock and a waterfall. Reach a

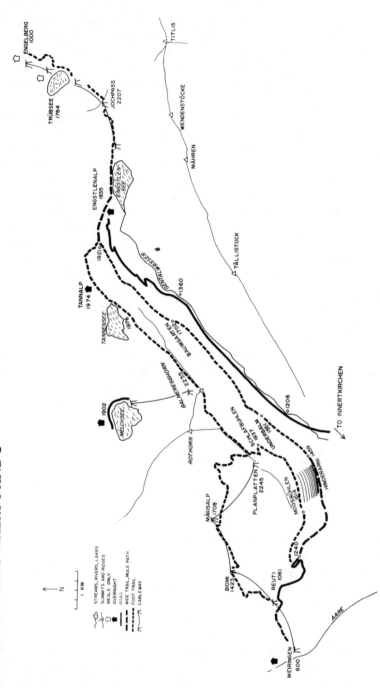

BERNESE-OBERLAND WALKS 1 AND 2

STREAMS, RIVERS, LAKES
SUMMITS AND RIDGES
MEALS ONLY
OVERNIGHT
ROAD
WIDE TRAIL, MULE PATH
FOOT TRAIL
CABLEWAY

1 KM

N

signposted junction (1921 meters) 15 minutes from the inn; take the path to the right, to Melchsee-Frutt, Planplatten, and Käserstatt. (The path to the left goes to Baumgartenalp and Hasliberg-Reuti.)

The path rises in switchbacks, steep at first and then moderate, up the rock wall that separates Engstlenalp from Tannenalp. After 50 minutes, arrive at Tannenalp (also called Tannalp), at 1976 meters. There is a little lake, the Tannensee, and a mountain inn, Berghaus Tannalp (tel. 041 67 12 41). At the lake, a signpost points left (southwest) toward Balmeregghorn and Planplatten. You'll see blazes on rocks and a distinct trail across and up the alpine meadows. Deep below on your left (south) is the Gental, and there are fine views eastward to the Jochpass and Titlis, south to the Grimsel and Furka passes, and west to the great wall of the Bernese Oberland. At 2280 meters there is a large cross and a bench. A path to the right (north) leads to Melchsee-Frutt. However, continue straight ahead (southwest) for Planplatten. Arrive at a chairlift terminal and the little peak of Balmeregghorn at 2255 meters after 1 hour 40 minutes. (The chairlift can be used for an emergency descent to Melchsee-Frutt, which has several hotels and a lift down to the Engelberg valley.)

The trail then descends about 100 meters. The route becomes very exposed and is not advisable in snow or bad weather. (To check on conditions early in the season or after a snowfall, call the tourist office in Meiringen, tel. 036 71 43 22, or the Meiringen-Hasliberg Bahnen, the lift company, tel. 036 71 36 22.) The trail is always distinct, though narrow in places.

Reach the Planplatten Sattel (or notch) at 2186 meters, where you'll find two benches and a signpost. You can then climb up a short distance to the Planplatten lift station, at 2245 meters, where you can take a series of lifts all the way down to Meiringen. Even using the lifts, the descent takes from 1 hour to 1 hour 30 minutes. The first stage of the descent is a chairlift to Mägisalp, then a gondola to Bidmi and Reuti, and finally a cable car to Meiringen.

The descent from Planplatten to Meiringen is 1645 meters. There are two choices if you decide to walk down—both start at Planplatten (2186 meters), where the signpost near the benches indicates the two trails.

If you take the route to the right (north), follow the easy path that leads to "Höhenweg: auf den Haggen 50 mins., Käserstatt 1.40." (These place names refer to a high route that ends at the Käserstatt lift station.) The path, which is easy to follow and clearly signposted, will lead to the Mägisalp station in 40 minutes, to the Bidmi station in 1 hour 15 minutes, to the Reuti station in 2 hours, and to Meiringen in 3 hours. You can follow the path and walk down past the farms below, through a pleasant green bowl, and pick up the lift part of the way down. If you take the lift at Reuti, you cut 460 meters off the route through the forest.

The alternative route down to Meiringen proceeds to the left (south) to Schlafbühlen (1937 meters), a small alp reached in 30 minutes. The trail continues to Moosbühlen (1614 meters) then joins a road on which it continues to the Reuti lift station in 2 hours 15 minutes. The view is of the Gental and the Oberland mountains, but of course from lower altitudes.

Alternate Route: Engstlenalp to Meiringen

Rating: moderate
Distance one way: 15 to 17 km
High point: 1921 m
Ascent/descent: 90 m/1330 m
Time: 5 hours
Optional transportation: lift
Map: page 184; also Landeskarte der Schweiz 1:25000, INNERT-
    KIRCHEN—1210

When snow conditions make the high route dangerous, this alternate middle route is an excellent way to walk from Engstlenalp to Meiringen. The scenery is not as grand, but there's little ascent and the trail is pleasant.

Begin as for the previous route. Just west of Engstlenalp at 1921 meters, where there's a signpost and junction, take the narrow path to the left for Baumgartenalp and Hasliberg-Reuti. The route is always distinct and traverses the long wall between Meiringen and Engstlenalp, descending gradually. Near the cluster of farm buildings at Baumgartenalp, the route joins a paved road for about 200 meters, but returns to a path at the point where the road makes a U-turn to the left. Follow the signposts to Underbalm. You'll pass a few abandoned farms and then a group of summer farms still in working use. We were offered fresh, warm milk here by some boys who were tending the farm for their family and who showed us their operations. One brother operated a hand churn; another dipped his hand into a huge cauldron simmering on a charcoal fire and showed us the new cheese forming. They poured the skimmed-off rennet through a chute to a trough outside, where several piglets greedily drank it.

You'll meet fewer people on this middle route than on the high route. It's wild and lonely, with good views of the mountains at each end and the stream on the floor of the Gental below.

The path joins a paved road about 20 minutes before Reuti, where you can take the lift down to Meiringen.

A second alternative, to be considered if a period of bad weather sets in while you're at Engstlenalp, is the low route, near the bottom of the

Gental. The walking route starts in front of the hotel at Engstlenalp, following the general direction of the paved road, mainly on a series of dirt roads and trails marked by signposts. This is the least interesting of the three routes, for it runs along the valley floor. At Innertkirchen the Gentalwasser flows into the Aare; turn right (northwest) toward Meiringen, which you reach in 5 hours. It is also possible to take a bus the whole distance. The bus leaves from in front of the Hotel Engstlenalp, and the ride takes 1 hour. The Holiday Card is not valid for this trip.

3. MEIRINGEN TO SCHWARZWALDALP

Rating: moderate
Distance one way: 10.5 km
High point: 1454 m
Ascent/descent: 860 m/0 m
Time: 3 hours 30 minutes
Optional transportation: bus
Map: page 188; also Wanderkarte Berner Oberland Ost 1:50000, Kummerly + Frey; Grindelwald Wanderkarte 1:25000; or Landeskarte der Schweiz 1:25000, Grindelwald–1229

You can walk this entire route or combine bus travel and walking. Riding the PTT bus between Meiringen and either Rosenlaui or Schwarzwaldalp is a practical option, for the trail from Meiringen to Rosenlaui is mostly in woods and very near the road. The road is so narrow and has such tight turns that the Post Office uses special buses for this route, with the driving wheel on the right hand side. The bus station in Meiringen is next to the railroad station. The bus runs several times each day and it takes about 30 minutes to reach Rosenlaui, another 10 for Schwarzwaldalp.

If you decide to walk, you'll find signs at the railroad station in Meiringen that point to Rosenlaui. Head south and cross the bridge over the Aare. The route soon begins to climb fairly steeply. Sections of the route follow the road, but sometimes the trail diverges, then loops across the road. The 8.5 kilometers to Rosenlaui will take you 3 hours. The trail continues in the same fashion and after another 2 kilometers reaches Schwarzwaldalp.

Rosenlaui, at 1328 meters, is located below a famous hanging glacier, the Rosenlaui Gletscher, with jagged, pale blue seracs. It's also the site of a notable waterfall. At Rosenlaui there's a Victorian hotel, the Hotel Rosenlaui (tel. 036 71 29 12, Matratzenlager and showers) and a climbing school. You can walk from Rosenlaui along the paved road to

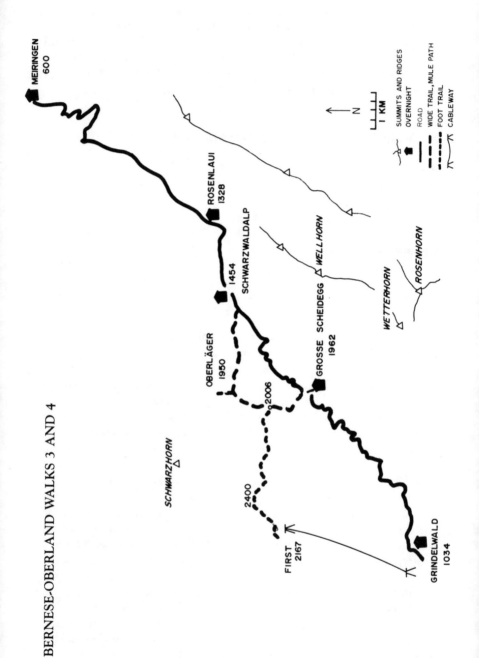

BERNESE-OBERLAND WALKS 3 AND 4

MEIRINGEN
600

ROSENLAUI
1328

SCHWARZWALDALP
1454

OBERLÄGER
1950

GROSSE
SCHEIDEGG
1962

WELL HORN

WETTERHORN

ROSENHORN

SCHWARZHORN

2006

2400

FIRST
2167

GRINDELWALD
1034

N

1 KM

SUMMITS AND RIDGES
OVERNIGHT
ROAD
WIDE TRAIL, MULE PATH
FOOT TRAIL
CABLEWAY

Schwarzwaldalp (1454 meters) in 35 minutes or take the bus which takes 5 minutes. The huge gray face of the Wetterhorn, streaked with innumerable waterfalls, dominates the entire route.

At Schwarzwaldalp there's a mountain inn with Matratzenlager, Hotel Schwarzwaldalp (tel. 036 71 35 15). From Schwarzwaldalp you can continue by bus to Grindelwald or walk by a direct route (southwest) up to Grosse Scheidegg (1962 meters), the high notch that separates the Grindelwald valley from the Reichenbach (or Rychenbach) valley, which contains Schwarzwaldalp and Rosenlaui. The trail between Schwarzwaldalp and Grosse Scheidegg is on the route of the ancient bridle path between Meiringen and Grindelwald. This pleasant route generally follows the road through the center of the valley, going through patches of woods, and sometimes cutting across the loops of the paved road. This portion of the route is 4 kilometers long, ascends 500 meters, and takes about 1 hour 45 minutes to walk.

At Grosse Scheidegg, which has a restaurant with Matratzenlager—the Hotel Grosse Scheidegg—you can take the bus down to Grindelwald.

4. SCHWARZWALDALP TO FIRST

Rating: moderate
Distance one way: 8 km
High point: 2400 m
Ascent/descent: 1000 m/250 m
Time: 3 hours 15 minutes
Optional transportation: lift
Map: page 188; also Wanderkarte Berner Oberland Ost 1:50000, Kummerly + Frey; Grindelwald Wanderkarte 1:25000; or Landeskarte der Schweiz 1:25000, Grindelwald—1229

Leave Schwarzwaldalp heading southwest and walk 15 minutes along the road toward Grosse Scheidegg. Turn off the road at a sign pointing right (northwest) toward Oberläger. This is a pleasant ascent on a good footpath, through pines and then up grassy slopes, to Scheidegg-Oberläger (1950 meters), which is 1 hour 30 minutes from Schwarzwaldalp. A signpost just before the cluster of farm buildings at Oberläger points you left (southwest) toward both Grosse Scheidegg and First. Continue along the dirt farm road. After 30 minutes reach a gate, a wide jeep road and a signpost (2006 meters) for the high route (Höhenweg) to the First lift station and on to the Faulhorn. Turn sharply to the right, on a blazed trail that starts close to the fence. Don't take the wide jeep road, which also leads to First, but is not as interesting a route.

The path ascends gradually to 2400 meters, traversing grassy slopes that give you increasingly fine views of the Schreckhorn, Finsteraarhorn, and Eiger across the valley. The route rises and falls, and you'll arrive at First (2167 meters) after an additional hour and 30 minutes. From this plateau the views of the Eiger (3970 meters) and the surrounding peaks are superb.

At First you find the topmost station of the Grindelwald lift and can make the side trip to Grindelwald by taking the lift down, a long descent of 1100 meters, or you can walk. The most direct way, which follows the lift stations, takes between 2 and 3 hours on well-defined paths marked by signposts. If you plan to continue directly to Schynige Platte and Mürren, you should consider staying overnight at the Faulhorn mountain inn, but we advise that you phone ahead for reservations (tel. 036 53 27 13). If you are going to descend to Grindelwald, and if the weather is good, we suggest that you continue to the Bachalpsee to see the view, as the weather can change abruptly in the Bernese Oberland.

5. FIRST TO MÜRREN, VIA SCHYNIGE PLATTE

Rating: strenuous
Distance one way: 15 km
High point: 2681 m
Ascent/descent: 700 m/800 m
Time: 6 hours
Recommended transportation: lift and railway
Map: page 191; also Wanderkarte Berner Oberland Ost 1:50000, Kummerly + Frey; Grindelwald Wanderkarte 1:25000; or Landeskarte der Schweiz 1:25000, Grindelwald—1229

From the First lift station, above Grindelwald, follow the signs to Bachalpsee and Faulhorn. Reach the little lake in 1 hour and then, following red and white blazes painted on rocks, climb a steep slope above the lake to a saddle. At the saddle (2620 meters) you can continue to the Faulhorn inn (tel. 036 53 27 13), a 15-minute climb up the little peak of the Faulhorn. To walk to Schynige Platte, however, continue straight ahead (westward). The trail has a short, narrow section, after which it becomes less exposed.

After another hour of walking you'll reach the little hut at Mandlenen (2344 meters), where you can purchase refreshments. Past the hut, the trail turns right (north), then swings left into a long, wild valley. The route is blazed "S.P." for Schynige Platte. Continue down this valley and cross over at the end to the right, proceeding westward. Then turn south and west again into another valley. The trail is always unmistakable. At

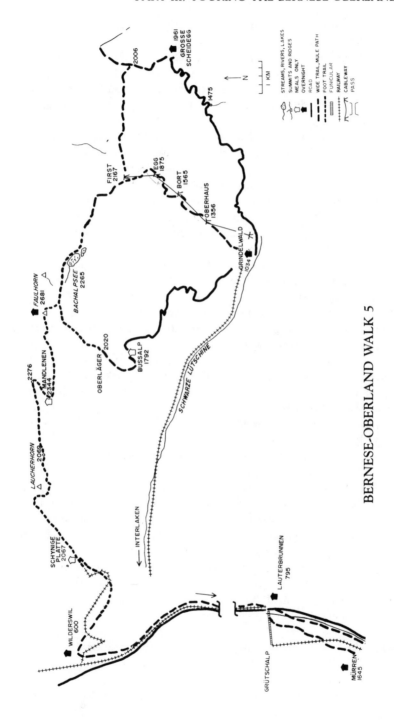

GROSSE
SCHEIDEGG
1961

2006

1475

N
1 KM

STREAMS, RIVERS, LAKES
SUMMITS AND RIDGES
MEALS ONLY
OVERNIGHT
ROAD
WIDE TRAIL, MULE PATH
FOOT TRAIL
FUNICULAR
RAILWAY
CABLEWAY
PASS

FIRST
2167

EGG
1875

BORT
1565

OBERHAUS
1356

GRINDELWALD
1034

FAULHORN
2681

BACHALPSEE
2265

MANDLENEN
2344

2276

OBERLÄGER
2020

BUSSALP
1792

LAUCHERHORN
2069

SCHWARZE LÜTSCHINE

INTERLAKEN

BERNESE-OBERLAND WALK 5

SCHYNIGE
PLATTE
2067

LAUTERBRUNNEN
795

WILDERSWIL
600

GRÜTSCHALP

MÜRREN
1645

191

the end, a short uphill climb leads you to the tiny Schynige Platte station, where we recommend that you catch a ride on an old-fashioned cog railway, which makes the long descent (1466 meters) to the Wilderswil rail station in 1 hour. (See Chapter 8.) If you decide to walk down to Wilderswil, there's a wide, well-graded trail that descends on switchbacks, occasionally crossing the tracks. The trail is 4.5 kilometers long, and it will take approximately 2 hours to descend.

The trail between Wilderswil and Lauterbrunnen runs through a narrow valley, parallel to a busy road with high-speed traffic and close to the rail line. For that reason we strongly recommend that you take the train to Lauterbrunnen, although you can walk this leg of the route if you prefer. It is 8 kilometers long, ascends 200 meters, and will take about 2 hours 30 minutes to walk. (If you choose to walk the entire route past Schynige Platte to Mürren, you will need to break it up with an overnight stop, probably at Wilderswil or Lauterbrunnen.)

To continue the pass route to Mürren you can take the well-marked trail that starts from the Lauterbrunnen station and climbs 800 meters in 5 kilometers up to Mürren. This route will take about 2 hours 30 minutes to walk. At first the trail climbs through forest, then it runs parallel to the Grütschalp-Mürren cog railway. There are fine views from the trail past Grütschalp. The fastest way to cover the distance between Lauterbrunnen and Mürren is to take the funicular from Lauterbrunnen up to Grütschalp, where a cog railway connects to Mürren—the trip takes 30 minutes.

Wilderswil has inexpensive, moderate, and expensive accommodations; Lauterbrunnen has moderate accommodations. Mürren has expensive accommodations between July 12th and August 17th (approximately); during the remainder of the summer, prices drop so that some accommodations enter the moderate range. Inexpensive accommodations are available at Blumental above Mürren.

If you want to take the side trip to Stechelberg and Obersteinberg (see following), proceed from Lauterbrunnen to Stechelberg. You can do this by PTT bus in 20 minutes or take a well-marked trail through fields and woods, reaching Stechelberg by crossing a bridge over the river. The trail is fairly level—the ascent to Stechelberg is about 100 meters. The distance measures 7.5 kilometers, and the walk takes about 2 hours 30 minutes. This trail parallels the road for much of the way, but is well shielded from it. Moreover, this road has much less traffic than the one between Wilderswil and Lauterbrunnen.

Side Trip: Stechelberg, Obersteinberg to Schmadrihütte

Rating: strenuous
Distance round trip: 20 km

High point: 2263 m

Total climb: 1400 m

Time: 2 hours 30 minutes up to Obersteinberg, 3 hours 45 minutes up to Oberhornsee, 2 hours 45 minutes down, 6 hours up to Schmadrihütte, 4 hours 30 minutes down

Map: pages 198–99; also Wanderkarte Berner Oberland Ost 1:50000, Kummerly + Frey or Lauterbrunnental Jungfrau-Region Wanderkarte 1:33333

The Lauterbrunnental is a very striking valley, cut like a narrow trench from north to south between long cliffs of sheer rock: the Jungfrau wall rises to the east and the Schilthorn massif to the west. Numerous waterfalls plunge down these cliffs to the valley floor. The road ends at Stechelberg (910 meters), after which the valley rises sharply to the south, ending in a cirque of glaciers and mountains. To continue past Stechelberg you can travel only on foot, and as relatively few hikers come here the valley remains unspoiled. There are two pleasant mountain inns toward the end of the valley: Hotel Tschingelhorn (tel. 036 55 13 43) and the Hotel Obersteinberg (tel. 036 55 20 33). Farther on are the little turquoise Oberhornsee and the Schmadrihütte, both set amid magnificent scenery. If you decide to stay overnight in the area, you can drop your pack at one of the inns and spend the afternoon wandering.

At Lauterbrunnen, between Schynige Platte and Mürren, take the PTT bus to Stechelberg. The bus leaves from a stop just behind the Lauterbrunnen train station and as it connects with the train, you should head directly for the bus as soon as your train arrives.

At Stechelberg, the road ends at a point just a few steps from the bus stop; there you'll find the trailhead and several signposts. Head south on the route to Obersteinberg, the Oberhornsee, and the Schmadrihütte. The trail begins to the left of the stream, then crosses to the right, up a gentle grade through fields and then woods. Pass Trachsellauenen, where there's a mountain inn. At a fork marked by a signpost, bear right.

At the next junction, you will find both ways signposted for Hotel Obersteinberg and the Schmadrihütte. The trail to the left proceeds along the west side of the stream, then crosses farther south and climbs up to Hotel Obersteinberg; the one to the right continues along the west of the stream. Do not take the trail to the left—it often gets washed out. The trail to the right climbs steadily and rather steeply through the woods. Reach Hotel Tschingelhorn (1685 meters) in 2 hours 15 minutes, after a 775-meter ascent. The trail levels out, and Hotel Obersteinberg (1774 meters) is 15 minutes farther up the trail.

From here, continue southwest toward the Oberhornsee. The trail climbs gradually, then descends to cross the stream, and climbs the oppo-

Late afternoon at the mountain inn at Obersteinberg

site slope. The final uphill section of the route is quite steep. The Oberhornsee (2065 meters) is a small, extremely cold, glacier-fed turquoise lake, surrounded by massive rock walls and glaciers. Resist the temptation for a dip, even on a warm day, for the water is extremely cold.

From the lake you can continue to Schmadrihütte, which takes at least twice the time indicated on the signpost (1 hour). From the end of the lake, walk down to the river, where you turn left. Walk along the river bank until you come to a very simple bridge—two parallel planks, placed over a small gorge. Old and young hikers make this crossing, but if it worries you, head back up the river bank until the waterway becomes shallow and broad and then cross over on the rocks. Make your way along the other bank, keeping inland from the stream and passing above a short band of rock, until you see the trail coming up from the bridge.

The blazed trail then climbs steeply up a mound, at the top of which is a splendid view of the mountains and glaciers at the upper end of the valley. Pause here and drink in the views—you'll be facing an astonishingly close, huge wall of black rock, hung with ferocious glaciers on which menacing seracs are piled. To the right, the valley ends at the foot of a big glacier, with ice visible under the moraine. Above the moraine is a pile of ice and, above that, a great snow-capped peak. To your left is the south wall of the Jungfrau (4158 meters). If you wish to continue to the hut, you must descend from this mound to a second river and plank bridge. On the other side, the trail swings up to the left, then climbs steeply through meadows and onto a moraine to reach the hut.

To return to Stechelberg, follow the route by which you came. The scenery is equally worth seeing in reverse.

The next portion of the Bernese Oberland walking tour—from Mürren to Kandersteg—is a grand but very strenuous route over two high passes, Sefinenfurke and Hohtürli, though you can hike only one, if you prefer. Both are long and taxing, though Hohtürli is a little more difficult—in fact, this is the most strenuous pass route for hikers in the Bernese Oberland. (If you decide to walk across the Oberland from west to east, do not attempt these passes until you are well conditioned.) This route should by no means be attempted in bad weather or after recent snow, and you should inquire locally about conditions before starting out, especially if you come early in the season or if the summer has been snowy.

The route starts at Mürren, crosses the Sefinenfurke to Griesalp, and then crosses Hohtürli to Kandersteg. You can walk over the two passes in two days, stopping overnight at or near Griesalp. If you want to do only one pass, you can exit from the route by PTT bus at Griesalp. You can also break the route down into shorter segments by staying at various huts, simple guesthouses, or farms along the two segments of the route.

6. MÜRREN TO GRIESALP

Rating: very strenuous
Distance one way: 16 km
High point: 2612 m
Ascent/descent: 1000 m/1300 m
Time: 7 hours 30 minutes
Map: pages 198–99; also Berner Oberland Ost 1:50000, Kummerly +
    Frey, or Wanderkarte Lauterbrunnental Jungfrau-Region 1:33333,
    Verkehrsvereine Lauterbrunnen-Mürren-Wengen

Start the route at Mürren, a very attractive small resort perched on a rather high shelf (1645 meters) above the Lauterbrunnental and below the Schilthorn. Mürren has a glorious position, facing the Mönch and the Jungfrau across the valley. No automobile traffic is permitted in Mürren, making it even more attractive.

Mürren's only drawback is that it's rather expensive, but pleasant and inexpensive accommodations are available at a couple of mountain inns just above the village in a place called Mürrenberg on maps, Blumental on local signs. Blumental (1836 meters) is a 30 minute walk from Mürren. From the train station at Mürren, walk east to the sports center (Sportzentrum), then follow the signs to Pensions Sonnenberg (tel. 036 55 11 27) and Suppenalp (tel. 036 55 17 26). Turn right at the bakery, where a signpost indicates paths to Allmendhubel, Schilthorn, and Blumental. You'll walk up past farms to a grassy shelf with magnificent views of the Jungfrau, Mönch, and Eiger. The profusion and beauty of the wildflowers at this little alp are unforgettable.

If you start this route from Blumental (Mürrenberg), walk from Pension Sonnenberg to Pension Suppenalp. At Suppenalp ascend on the trail to your left, which is signposted for Schiltalp. Walk to the farm at Schiltalp (1951 meters) and follow the route to Sefinenfurke and Rotstockhütte. The next sign points you left (south) to Spielbodenalp and Wasenegg. Cross the Schiltbach on the rocks (not a difficult crossing; a bridge is under construction) and take the trail to your left, which rises steeply to Wasenegg (2155 meters), a superb viewpoint. At Wasenegg a signpost to your left marks the trail for Boganggen and Sefinenfurgge (a variant spelling). The trail descends to Oberlager, where you join the trail from Mürren.

To begin the Sefinenfurke route from the Mürren train station, walk left (southwest) on a carriage road in the direction of Schönegg, Gimmeln, and Sefinenfurke. Pass under the Schilthorn lift line and proceed southwest. Shortly afterward the paved road ends. Continue on the broad track, climbing gradually, through a brief stretch of woods and then into

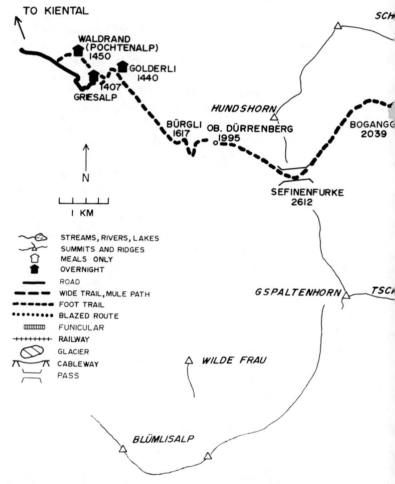

SCHMADRIHÜTTE SIDE TRIP AND BERNESE-OBERLAND WALK 6

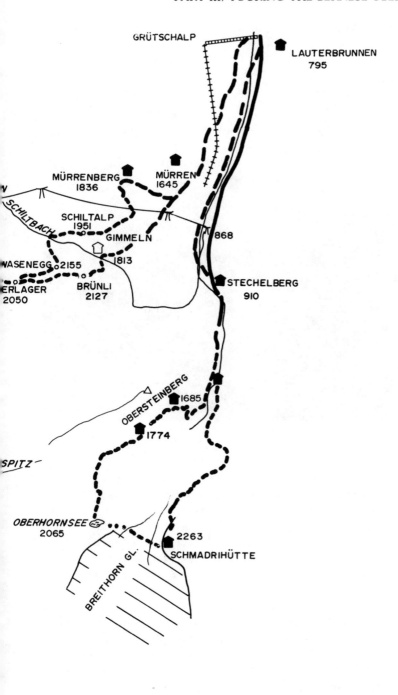

Near Mürren, with the Mönch in background

open pastures. Superb views of the Jungfrau chain to your left; grim walls of rock with tier upon tier of glaciers tower over the green meadows. You'll pass a mountain restaurant shortly after Gimmeln (1813 meters), where the path turns left (south) and crosses the Schiltbach. The path then narrows and rises, ascending in switchbacks to Brünli (2127 meters), 1 hour 30 minutes from Mürren. Continue toward the west, at first descending slightly, to Oberlager (2050 meters), where the trail from Mürrenberg (Blumental) joins the route.

After another hour, you'll reach Boganggen (2039 meters), where you find the Rotstockhütte (meals, Matratzenlager), owned by the Stechelberg Ski Club but open to the public. Cross the stream on rocks, then ascend gradually on the right (north) side of the valley. Follow the blazes. The country is wild and open, with magnificent long views of the Lauterbrunnen wall. You are heading for the saddle (or notch) above a wall of black

Haying near Mürren, with the Mönch in background

rock. The final ascent (150 meters) is very steep, up this wall of dark scree, where you may find snow. There are only traces of a trail, in tiny switchbacks, up to the notch above—the Sefinenfurke (2612 meters): 4 hours 30 minutes from Mürren, 4 hours from Blumental.

From the pass, descend carefully on your right; the trail is extremely steep for the first hundred meters and remains very steep after that, with scree and loose shale for the first three hundred meters. The trail follows the right slope of the narrow, V-shaped valley. One hour below the pass you reach the little farm at Ober Dürrenberg (1995 meters). Here you can buy fresh goat cheese and soft drinks and spend the night (Nachtlager).

The trail continues through beautiful meadows, with superb views to your left (south) of the Wilde Frau and Blümlisalp peaks. Cross the stream, continuing down to the farm at Bürgli (1617 meters) and Steinenberg (1463 meters). The trail becomes a narrow, surfaced road as it reaches the cluster of houses near Griesalp (1407 meters). There is a minuscule general store at Golderli and there are mountain inns at Golderli (tel. 033 76 12 42) and Griesalp (tel. 033 76 12 31). Another 10 minutes brings you to pleasant Pochtenalp, within earshot of the rushing mountain torrent, and Hotel Waldrand (tel. 033 76 12 08). More hotels at Kiental, a short bus ride from Griesalp.

The PTT bus from Griesalp descends through the Kiental to the rail station at Reichenbach, and there are several buses a day. The trip is a remarkable one, initially through a steep gorge. Watch the driver take these hairpin turns on a road cut through the cliff, with only an inch of clearance between bus and rock.

7. GRIESALP TO KANDERSTEG

Rating: very strenuous
Distance one way: 14 km
High point: 2778 m
Ascent/descent: 1400 m/1620 m
Time: 9 hours
Optional transportation: lift
Map: page 203; also Berner Oberland Ost 1:50000, Kummerly + Frey, or Wanderkarte Reichenbach–Kiental–Griesalp 1:33333, Verkehrsvereine

Glorious, but the highest and most demanding pass route in this book. Never to be attempted if conditions are poor, in threatening weather, or if you are not in top condition. There may be snow at the pass even in dry, hot summers, but if there is heavy snow the hike becomes something of a technical climb, and an ice ax and a knowledge of self-arrest are advisable. We have seen parties of ill-equipped hikers ascending

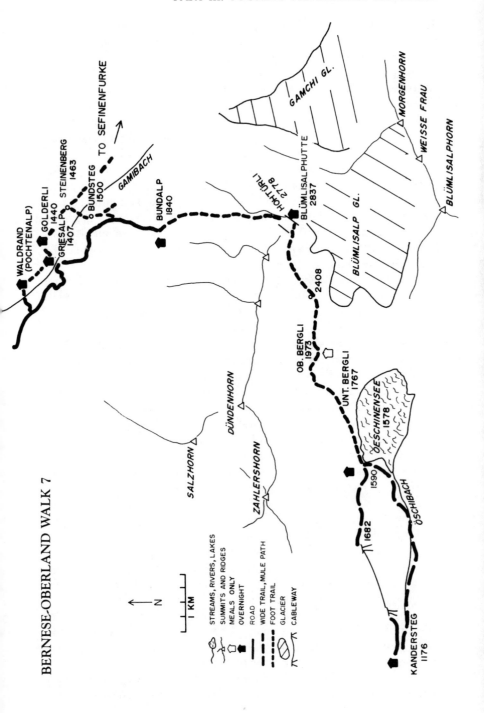

BERNESE-OBERLAND WALK 7

TO SEFINENFURKE

GAMIBACH

WALDRAND (POCHTENALP)

GOLDERLI 1440

GRIESALP 1407

STEINENBERG 1463

BUNDSTEG 1500

BUNDALP 1840

GAMCHI GL.

MORGENHORN

WEISSE FRAU

HOHTÜRLI 2778

BLÜMLISALPHUTTE 2837

BLÜMLISALP GL.

BLÜMLISALPHORN

2408

DÜNDENHORN

SALZHORN

ZAHLERSHORN

OB. BERGLI 1973

UNT. BERGLI 1767

OESCHINENSEE 1578

1590

ÖSCHIBACH

1682

KANDERSTEG 1176

N
I KM

STREAMS, RIVERS, LAKES
SUMMITS AND RIDGES
MEALS ONLY
OVERNIGHT
ROAD
WIDE TRAIL, MULE PATH
FOOT TRAIL
GLACIER
CABLEWAY

the northern slope just below the pass on their hands and knees, plunging their arms into the snow to maintain balance. But we have also climbed this route when there was no trace of snow.

If you have any doubts, telephone the hutkeeper at the Blümlisalp-hütte (tel. 033 76 14 37), which is atop the Hohtürli pass, and ask about conditions. There are telephones at the inns at Griesalp, Golderli, and Pochtenalp; ask around and you'll probably find someone who speaks English and can translate the call for you. At Mürren and Kandersteg you can also purchase an ice ax—you can't buy one at Griesalp.

The leg between Griesalp and Hohtürli is more difficult than the one between Hohtürli and Kandersteg—it's steeper, with a more exposed, eroded trail. Less experienced hikers who want to see Hohtürli can proceed by train to Kandersteg, climb up to the pass, and then return again to Kandersteg. Families with small children should not attempt to cross Hohtürli, although children who are 10 or 12 can probably complete the walk if they're fit and have had some experience.

If you start from Griesalp (1407 meters), the signpost in front of Hotel Griesalp directs you to Bundalp, Hohtürli, and Kandersteg. The path heads south through forest and pastures up to Bundalp. Recently, the paved road was extended from Griesalp to Bundalp, and the footpath climbs steeply up, crossing the broad loops of the paved road. At Bundsteg there is a signposted fork—the trail to the left heads for Steinenberg and Golderli across the Gamchibach. Continue on the right (south) fork to Bundalp (1840 meters), where there's an inn with Matratzenlager, about 1 hour 15 minutes from Griesalp.

If you start from Pochtenalp, walk to Golderli (1440 meters) and follow the sign to Bundalp and Hohtürli. Five minutes past Golderli, at Steinenberg, turn right (south) at a signposted junction. Walk up through the woods on a gravel path, then cross a small stream on a stone bridge. Cross a very pretty meadow, surrounded by snow-capped mountains, then come to another signposted junction. The fork to the left leads up to Sefinenfurke; the one to the right, to Hohtürli. Turn right here, crossing the Gamchibach on a bridge. On the other side, the path is steeper. At the next fork, continue straight ahead (keeping to the right) and reach Bundsteg, at 1500 meters. Continue straight (southwest), up through meadows. There's an unsigned junction at a fence with a gate, but there are blazed rocks to guide you. Turn left, following the blazes. Climb through the woods, then emerge into high meadows and reach the Griesalp-Bundalp road. (The footpath is steeper but shorter than the road.) Continue straight up, reaching Unter Bundalp at 1690 meters and the Obere Bundalp restaurant at 1840 meters.

Bundalp is on a big, level green shelf. From there, the trail climbs up a very steep, black spiny ridge, in the center of the massif. The path is very poor, sometimes climbing straight up this shaly dark slope, sometimes traversing a little or ascending in switchbacks on loose scree, which may be covered with snow. The route becomes very steep; the trail on scree is often badly eroded. Watch closely to make sure you stay on the track. There are long exposed traverses on ridges and along narrow sections that were cut out of the rock. Reach the pass at 2778 meters after at least 4 hours. The Blümlisalphütte is perched on the pass about 150 meters southeast of the point where the trail reaches the height of the pass. Phenomenal views of mountains rolling away for vast distances: a sea of snowy Alps. And there are superb close views of the summits of the Blümlisalphorn and the Weisse Frau, with glaciers spilling down their flanks. The hut tends to be crowded on weekends but it's a magnificent place to stay for the evening.

To descend to Kandersteg, continue westward on the trail. It descends 300 meters down a steep wall of scree (though this is not as steep as on the other side), then proceeds along narrow, rocky ledges and through alpine tundra into high pastures where cows graze. Descend to a narrow, high meadow, enfolded between cliffs to your right and hanging glaciers and mountains to your left: a magnificent setting. The transition from ice, snow and rock into the living zone of grass and cattle is one of the delights of the pass route.

After crossing a bridge you arrive at the alp at Ober Bergli (1973 meters), which has Matratzenlager and sells milk, cheese, hot chocolate, and simple food. Here the trail jogs to the left. Cross a small stream on stones, and then descend a short, steep rock face: the trail is cut in steps into the rock. Below this is the alp at Unter Bergli (1767 meters). Here you reach the edge of the beautiful, turquoise Oeschinensee. Above the lake tower walls of rock streaked with waterfalls, and snow-capped mountains.

The trail proceeds high above the lake, which remains to your left. At 1590 meters (Oeschinensee/Kuhmatti), a sign points you right for the chairlift (Sesselbahn). Follow the signs to the chairlift, which operates in high season from 7:30 to 18:30. If you wish to walk down to Kandersteg, take the trail to the left. This intersects a wide jeep road at the lakeshore, where you'll find several restaurants and hotels. The trail to Kandersteg descends steeply, crosses the Oschibach, and leads you down to the main street of the town (1176 meters).

Kandersteg is a very attractive village with a wide range of hotels. The tourist information offices on the main street and at the railroad station are very helpful about finding rooms for visitors and will phone hotels for you if you arrive without a reservation. From Kandersteg you can travel to the Valais by direct train through the Goppenstein tunnel, or to any other point in Switzerland.

12

TOURING THE VALAIS

The map of Switzerland shows a big square wedge protruding southward into Italy; this is the Valais, where the Swiss–Italian border runs along the peaks of the highest mountains in Switzerland, including the Matterhorn. Watercourses pour northward from the Valaisian Alps to the broad, flat Rhône valley, creating a row of nearly parallel valleys west to east across the region. The classic image of an alp—a high, pointed, snowclad mountain—is found more often in the Valais than in any other region of Switzerland. Such giants as the Dom, Täschhorn, Weisshorn, and Dent Blanche have sharply pointed summits and flanks that look as if they'd been planed by hand.

Despite the elevation of these mountains, the Valaisian climate is the driest and sunniest in the Swiss Alps; because of the elevation of these mountains, the region was once geographically and socially isolated. This was the last canton to join the Swiss Federation. Some curious dialects are heard in the villages high in the mountains: no outsider will understand the local tongue in Zermatt, for example, and few visitors, listening to a conversation between natives of Evolène, realize they're hearing French. Yet the natives also speak standard French or German. The western part of the canton (le Valais) is French-speaking, the eastern part (das Wallis) is German-speaking, and the line of demarcation between the two is very sharp: in the mountains, it's literally the rock wall that separates the Val d'Anniviers from the Turtmanntal.

You can traverse much of the Valais, crossing from one valley to the next over the pass routes. Some people enjoy the challenge of crossing a

On the trail between Hotel Weisshorn and Zinal

OVERVIEW OF VALAIS TOUR

pass every day for a week, but others will prefer to break it up by stopping en route. You could spend a couple of days in one of the Val d'Hérens villages, at St. Luc, or anywhere else that strikes your fancy. Then you can rest or take day hikes, seeing local sights you would miss if you walked straight through.

Should rain set in or should you want a change, there are interesting towns to visit in the Valais. Sion, the capital of the Valais, has a splendid medieval castle, the Chateau de Valère, which contains a museum and a marvelous church with Romanesque frescoes and the world's oldest playable organ (there's a music festival every summer and organ concerts on Saturday afternoons). Sion also has a ruined fortress, the Chateau de Tourbillon, and other interesting sights. You can visit Martigny 25 kilometers west of Sion, the home of the Fondation Pierre Gianadda, which mounts major art exhibitions. The Fondation, a striking contemporary building, also contains a Gallo-Roman museum.

You can begin your Valaisian tour in the Val d'Hérémence (take a PTT bus from Sion to Vex, change there to a private bus for Le Chargeur) and walk over the Col de Riedmatten to Arolla, in the Val d'Hérens. Or you can begin in the Val d'Hérens (PTT bus from Sion), cross the Col de Torrent to Grimentz, continue by PTT bus to St. Luc, walk the Meidpass to Gruben (also called Meiden), and then cross the Augstbordpass to St. Niklaus. From St. Niklaus you can proceed by bus to Grächen, then walk the high route (the Höhenweg) to Saas-Fee. From St. Niklaus you can also proceed by train to Saas-Fee or to Zermatt. As the Mischabel range intervenes between Zermatt and Saas-Fee, only climbers equipped for glacier travel can cross between those two valleys. You can of course traverse the Valais in reverse order (from east to west), and you can choose to do only a few segments of the route. You can exit easily by PTT bus from any of the Valaisian valleys, except the Turtmanntal.

1. LE CHARGEUR TO AROLLA

Rating: strenuous
Distance one way: 17 km
High point: 2919 m
Ascent/descent: 810 m/970 m
Time: 8 hours 45 minutes
Optional transportation: lift
Map: page 210; also Arolla 1:50000, Carte pédestre; or Carte touristique de la région Evolène 1:40000

This is a somewhat adventurous long walk with varied and magnificent views, enabling you to cross from the Val d'Hérémence into the

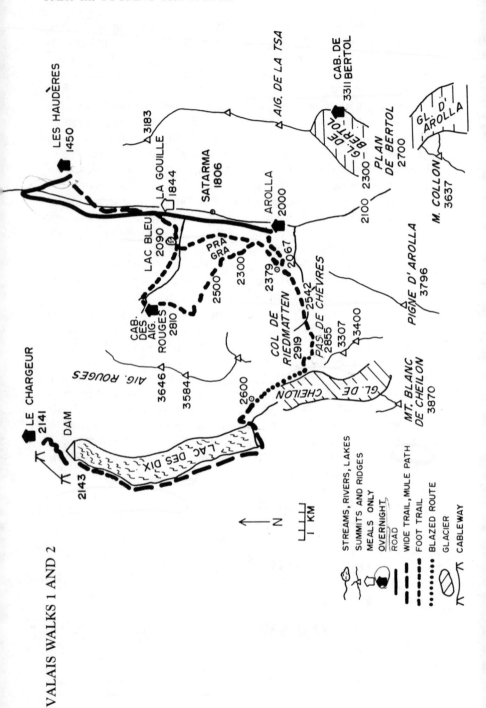

VALAIS WALKS 1 AND 2

PART III/TOURING THE VALAIS

LES HAUDÈRES
1450

3183

LA GOUILLE
1844

SATARMA
1806

LAC BLEU
2090

PRA GRA

2300

2500

2379

2067

 AROLLA
2000

AIG. DE LA TSA

CAB. DE
BERTOL 3311

PLAN
DE BERTOL
2700

2300

2100

GL. D'
AROLLA

M. COLLON
3637

PIGNE D'AROLLA
3796

3400

3307

PAS. DE CHÈVRES
2855

COL DE
RIEDMATTEN
2919

2542

2600

GL. DE
CHEILON

MT. BLANC
DE CHEILON
3870

CAB.
DES
AIG.
ROUGES
2810

AIG. ROUGES

3646

3584

LAC DES DIX

DAM

2143

LE CHARGEUR
2141

N

1 KM

STREAMS, RIVERS, LAKES
SUMMITS AND RIDGES
MEALS ONLY
OVERNIGHT
ROAD
WIDE TRAIL, MULE PATH
FOOT TRAIL
BLAZED ROUTE
GLACIER
CABLEWAY

Val d'Hérens without going onto the Glacier de Cheilon. The route begins at the top of the huge Grande Dixence dam and proceeds along the Lac des Dix, the huge artificial lake for which the Grande Dixence power system is named. Beyond the lake is the Glacier de Cheilon, in the midst of which rises the Mont Blanc de Cheilon, a massive pyramid of black rock topped with snow. Beyond the lake, the trail climbs steeply to the Col de Riedmatten and then descends to Arolla.

From Sion, take the PTT bus to Vex, then change for the bus to Le Chargeur; this is a private line where the Holiday Card is not valid. Le Chargeur, below the huge wall of the Grande Dixence dam, consists of the bus stop and a large hotel, nothing more. From here, take a small cable car (télépherique) up to the top of the wall.

Walk southward along the west bank of the Lac des Dix, which is very long: 6.5 kilometers. The route, however, is almost level. At first you walk through several dark tunnels; the first of these has electric lights (as you enter, press a button, which will keep the light on for 5 minutes). After 1 hour 30 minutes to 2 hours, reach the south end of the lake, and turn left. Cross a metal suspension bridge that spans the inlet to the lake, then climb a fixed steel staircase. From here, the trail first climbs steeply to the left (north) but then it bends to the right (southeast). Ascend through meadows, then hike up to the moraine above the Glacier de Cheilon. Continue up over boulders and make a final, very steep climb on tiny switchbacks up a wall of scree, shale, and dirt, to the Col de Riedmatten.

The descent is steep at first, then joins the trail down from the Pas de Chèvres. The trail descends eastward; cross the stream on your right on an old plank bridge. The footpath descends through meadows, crossing over a dirt road. At 2379 meters, the trail leads out onto a gravel road, where you go right (northeast). Then follow the footpath with yellow diamond blazes past the Grand Hotel & Kurhaus, and down to Arolla, where you can find both inexpensive and moderate accommodations.

(This walk is described in greater detail in Chapter 7, page 120, in which the route is given in the reverse direction.)

2. AROLLA TO LES HAUDÈRES

Rating: strenuous
Distance one way: 13 km
High point: 2844 m
Ascent/descent: 900 m/1400 m
Time: 6 hours
Optional transportation: bus

Map: page 210; also Arolla 1:50000, Carte pédestre; or Carte touristique de la région Evolène 1:40000

If you're interested in saving time, you can reach Les Haudères much more directly by the footpaths that parallel the road between Arolla and Les Haudères. But this walk is a very fine excursion, leading to some beautiful meadows above Arolla, from which there are stunning views of Mont Collon and its glacier. The trail then proceeds up to an SAC hut, in a glorious location, with more superb views.

From the square in Arolla, walk up the paved road toward the group of chalets above the village. Turn right (northeast) at the yellow sign and climb northwestward up to the pastures of Pra Gra. There, a yellow sign points you right (north) toward the Cabane des Aiguilles Rouges; the trail has red blazes. Turn left past a rocky shoulder and continue northwest, reaching the SAC hut in 3 hours.

Pick up the trail behind (west of) the cabane for the descent southeast to Lac Bleu. From this little lake, continue down to La Gouille, where you can pick up the bus to Les Haudères (the bus trip takes about 15 minutes); the last bus leaves La Gouille at 17:35 hours. A signpost at the bus stop at La Gouille indicates the walking route to Les Haudères, which descends from the paved highway and follows an old cart road through the woods to Les Haudères. The walking route from La Gouille to Les Haudères is a gradual 400-meter descent in 3.5 kilometers and takes 1 hour. Inexpensive and moderate accommodations are available in Les Haudères.

(This walk is described in greater detail in Chapter 7, page 122.)

3. LES HAUDÈRES TO ST. LUC

Rating: strenuous
Distance one way: 18 km
High point: 2918 m
Ascent/descent: 1200 m/1400 m
Time: 6 hours 30 minutes
Recommended transportation: bus
Map: page 213; also Carte touristique de la région Evolène 1:40000 and Carte d'excursions aux vals d'anniviers 1:50000, or Carte Nationale de la Suisse, Montana 1:50000, No. 273

This walk leads up the long, sloping meadows of the east side of the Val d'Hérens to a notch in the rocky crest above and then descends to the Val de Moiry.

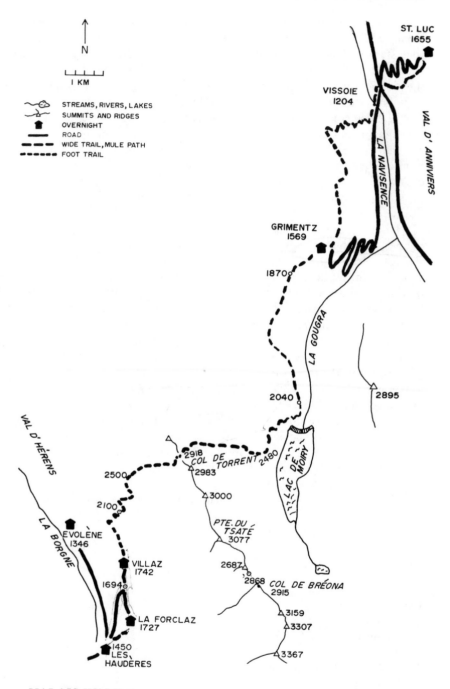

N

1 KM

STREAMS, RIVERS, LAKES
SUMMITS AND RIDGES
OVERNIGHT
ROAD
WIDE TRAIL, MULE PATH
FOOT TRAIL

ST. LUC
1655

VISSOIE
1204

VAL D' ANNIVIERS

LA NAVISENCE

GRIMENTZ
1569

1870

LA GOUGRA

2040

2895

VAL D' HÉRENS

2918
COL DE TORRENT 2480
2983

2500

3000

LAC DE MOIRY

2100

PTE. DU TSATÉ
3077

EVOLÈNE
1346

LA BORGNE

VILLAZ
1742

2687
2868   COL DE BRÉONA
2915

1694

LA FORCLAZ
1727

3159
3307

1450
LES HAUDÈRES

3367

VALAIS WALK 3

213

Take the bus from Les Haudères to Villaz (which is also called Villa). From the Café Col de Torrent, walk back down the road for 50 meters; the trail starts to your left, heading northeast, then turning sharply left (north). Follow the red and white blazes, up through the meadows. Near the Col de Torrent the path turns east and climbs steeply to the summit ridge line. Reach the Col in 3 hours 30 minutes.

The descent on the other side is steep at first. Pass a little lake and continue straight eastward to the large, artificial Lac de Moiry. Turn left at the dam wall and head north for Grimentz, which you reach in 3 hours from the Col. You can stay in Grimentz, a charming village that is full of flowers, or take a bus for St. Luc via Vissoie (a 40-minute trip). Inexpensive and moderate accommodations are available in Grimentz and St. Luc.

If you prefer to walk from Les Haudères to Villaz, follow the signposted path that starts at the grocery store at the southeast corner of the village (near the small square where the PTT buses stop). The path climbs 250 meters and intersects the paved automobile road to La Forclaz, then leaves the road and continues up to La Forclaz. From that little village, follow the signposted path to Villaz. Walking this section of the route will add 4 kilometers and 1 hour 30 minutes to the trip.

From Grimentz you can follow the signposted route to St. Luc. Signposts will be found at the PTT office and at the northeast end of the village. Follow the route for St. Luc, which descends 500 meters through woods and fields to the village of Vissoie (1204 meters). The distance is 10 kilometers and it will take you at least 3 hours. Vissoie has an old chapel, a medieval tower, and a house dating from 1576. The path to St. Luc follows an old cart road and ascends 450 meters through open fields. The distance from Vissoie to St. Luc is another 3 kilometers; the added time, 1 hour 30 minutes. (If you intend to walk this section, it would be best to spend the night in Grimentz.)

(This walk is described in greater detail in Chapter 7, on page 136.)

Side Trip: St. Luc to Bella Tola

Rating: strenuous
Distance round trip: 9.5 km
High point: 3025 m
Total climb: 900 m
Time: 3 hours 30 minutes up, 2 hours down
Optional transportation: lift

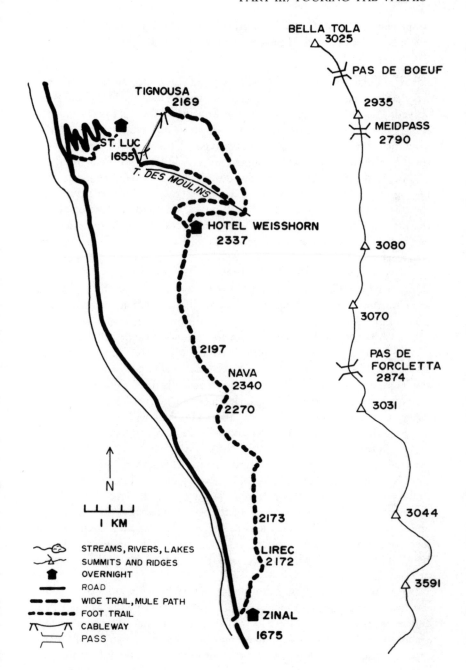

BELLA TOLA
3025

PAS DE BOEUF

2935

MEIDPASS
2790

TIGNOUSA
2169

ST. LUC
1655

T. DES MOULINS

HOTEL WEISSHORN
2337

3080

3070

2197

PAS DE
FORCLETTA
2874

NAVA
2340

3031

2270

N

1 KM

2173

3044

LIREC
2172

STREAMS, RIVERS, LAKES
SUMMITS AND RIDGES
OVERNIGHT
ROAD
WIDE TRAIL, MULE PATH
FOOT TRAIL
CABLEWAY
PASS

ZINAL

1675

3591

ST. LUC TO ZINAL SIDE TRIP

215

PART III/TOURING THE VALAIS

Map: page 219; also Carte d'excursions aux vals d'anniviers 1:50000, or Carte Nationale de la Suisse, Montana 1:50000, No. 273

The Bella Tola is one of those peaks that the Victorians loved: there's a perfectly circular view from the summit, and no technical climbing is involved. As with Piz Languard in the Engadine, the Victorians made a ritual of climbing the Bella Tola before dawn so they could see the sunrise from the summit. One can still see engraved Victorian panoramas showing the 250 mountains that they claimed are visible from the Bella Tola.

Begin this route by walking east down the main street of St. Luc, following the signs for the chairlift (télésiège) Tignousa, which is just past the east end of the village. The chairlift takes you up to 2169 meters. From the lift, walk northward straight up the slope, continuing in the direction of the lift. In 20 minutes you'll reach the Cabane de Bella Tola (Matratzenlager) at 2346 meters.

If you prefer to avoid the lift from St. Luc and want to walk up the slope, head for the northeast end of the village and follow the signposted route for the Pierre des Sauvages (a rock with ancient Celtic runic inscriptions chiseled into it). The path will lead under the Tignousa chairlift cables. After about 30 minutes take the signposted path to the left for Chalet Blanc (2170 meters), a farmhouse marked on the topographic map. At Chalet Blanc you reach a broad jeep road; a sign points to the left for the Tignousa lift station and the Cabane de Bella Tola. Follow the broad jeep road, which is almost level, to the upper Tignousa lift station and join the route to the summit of the Bella Tola. This walk will add about 3 kilometers and 550 meters to the climb and will take an additional 2 hours.

From the Cabane de Bella Tola, the route continues straight up; soon, the trail turns in a more northeasterly direction. Follow the blue arrows or the blue and white blaze marks; also, some rocks are blazed "B. T." for Bella Tola. Don't take the jeep road leading to your right (east). In 10 minutes the trail intersects a loop of the jeep road, but continue straight ahead on the footpath. After another 5 minutes, the trail intersects the jeep road again. (Do not follow the trail that climbs under the ski lift here.) The footpath cuts across loops of the jeep road, always heading east or northeast.

At 2520 meters, 1 hour from the cabane, reach a junction. Stay to the left (north and northeast) for the Bella Tola; a trail to the Meiden Pass (blazes read "M. P.") diverges to your right (southeast). Ascend a narrow gravel mule path, moderately steep and blazed with red arrows. Pass another junction to the Meiden Pass to your right; the Bella Tola route is to your left.

At 2900 meters the trail forks again. The path to the left proceeds to the Rothorn, the peak northwest of the Bella Tola. You can distinguish the Bella Tola because it looks silvery-gray from a distance. Take the path to the right (southeast). Just above this point there are two flat-topped outcrops of rock with one gendarme (a high finger of rock) to their left. To your right are two more gendarmes—tall, erect slabs.

The trail to the Bella Tola traverses the ridge that runs between the Rothorn and the Bella Tola. Because the trail is very exposed, do not attempt this final section of the route in snow or fog. Use caution—there are no handholds. When you see the summit cone or mound before you, just past the two gendarmes at 2910 meters, take the trail to your left (northeast). This trail ascends the center of the cone on tiny switchbacks to the summit. (A second trail, to your right at 2190 meters, looks better at first but is not the best route. It ascends steeply and is quite exposed.) Three hours 30 minutes after setting out, arrive at the summit (3025 meters).

Side Trip: St. Luc to Zinal

Rating: moderate
Distance one way: 16 km (return by bus)
High point: 2420 m
Ascent/descent: 900 m/900 m
Time: 6 hours
Recommended transportation: bus; **optional transportation:** lift
Map: page 215; also Carte d'excursions aux vals d'anniviers 1:50000

This is a second side trip that can be taken from St. Luc. It's an interesting route, with good views of the Valaisian Alps above Zinal. At the conclusion of the hike, you could stay in Zinal, but we recommend returning by bus to St. Luc—Zinal is in a valley between low ridges and doesn't offer much of a view.

The Hotel Weisshorn is an odd sight: a tall, square white building standing alone above treeline on a high shoulder, about 700 meters above the valley. You can see it from everywhere in the area, including St. Luc. The hotel was built in 1884, burnt in 1913, and then partially rebuilt. Once elaborately furnished, it's now a very simple inn. Throughout the St. Luc-Zinal area, "H. W." blazed on rocks refers to the hotel; a yellow "Z" refers to Zinal.

You can walk from St. Luc to the Hotel Weisshorn or take the Tignousa chairlift to gain most of the altitude. From Tignousa, the walking route is almost level, making a semicircular traverse to the hotel around the open slopes below the peak of Le Touno. From the lift, walk southeastward toward Chalet Blanc and "H. W." Pass by a farm with a blaze for "H. C. W." Cross a stream, then come to a signposted junction. The left fork leads to the Meidpass, the Bella Tola, and Pas de Boeuf. Turn right, however, and head for the Hotel Weisshorn. Turn left at the point where the footpath joins a jeep road (there's a signpost). About 50 minutes from Tignousa, the trail from St. Luc joins the road on your right. Continue climbing up a slight grade. At 2170 meters reach another junction; a sign points left for the Meidpass, right for "H. W." Another sign, about 2 minutes past the junction, indicates a route down to St. Luc. Reach the Hotel Weisshorn (2337 meters) 1 hour 30 minutes after leaving the lift.

To walk up from St. Luc, head eastward out of the village past the chairlift to Le Prilet, where there's a campground, 20 minutes from St. Luc. A signpost indicates the route to the hotel. The trail heads to the east; ascend up switchbacks and reach Hotel Weisshorn in about 2 hours 30 minutes.

To continue to Zinal, walk behind the hotel (on the side away from St. Luc) and a little to the left, to a junction (2337 meters), where a signpost points you southwest to Zinal. A narrow trail proceeds below the ridge; to your right, you can see Grimentz in the valley far below. Pass some snow dikes and areas bulldozed for avalanche protection. As you walk almost due south, a distant wall of snow-covered peaks and high glaciers comes into view: the Grand Cornier, Besso, the tip of the Zinal Rothorn, and other mountains in the chain of Valaisian Alps that separates the Zinal and Zermatt valleys. For this reason, it's good to walk this route in this direction rather than the reverse.

There are long slopes and meadows above and on your left, and the countryside is empty except for one farm. One hour 15 minutes past Hotel Weisshorn, you reach Alpe Nava at 2340 meters; a large sign points left to Pas de Forcletta and Gruben. The path to Zinal continues south, winding around a ridge and presenting views of the end of the Zinal valley. The route begins to descend after Alpe Lirec (2172 meters), and after a final steep descent, you arrive in Zinal, 3 hours 30 minutes after leaving the Hotel Weisshorn. To return to St. Luc, take the PTT bus to Vissoie, then change for St. Luc. The bus trip takes about 45 minutes.

4. ST. LUC TO GRUBEN

Rating: strenuous
Distance one way: 12 km
High point: 2790 m
Ascent/descent: 700 m/1000 m
Time: 5 hours 30 minutes
Optional transportation: lift

ST. LUC TO BELLA TOLA SIDE TRIP AND VALAIS WALK 4

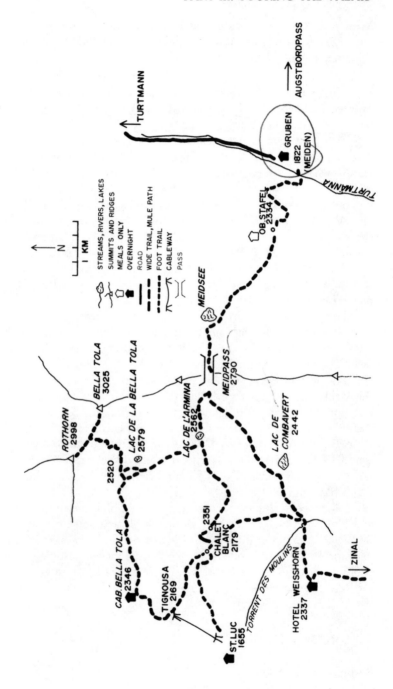

N

1 KM

STREAMS, RIVERS, LAKES
SUMMITS AND RIDGES
MEALS ONLY
OVERNIGHT
ROAD
WIDE TRAIL, MULE PATH
FOOT TRAIL
CABLEWAY
PASS

TURTMANN

AUGSTBORDPASS

GRUBEN
1822
(MEIDEN)

TURTMANNA

OB STAFEL
2334

MEIDSEE

MEIDPASS
2790

BELLA TOLA
3025

ROTHORN
2998

LAC DE LA BELLA TOLA
2579

2520

LAC DE L'ARMINA
2562

LAC DE
COMBAVERT
2442

CAB. BELLA TOLA
2346

TIGNOUSA
2169

2351

CHALET
BLANC
2179

ST. LUC
1655

TORRENT DES MOULINS

HOTEL WEISSHORN
2337

ZINAL

Map: page 219; also Carte d'excursions aux vals d'anniviers 1:50000, or Wanderkarte Turtmanntal Augstbordregion 1:25000, Buchdruck Offset Mengis, Visp

The route from the Val d'Anniviers east to the Turtmanntal takes you over the Meidpass. The Meidpass trail is well marked, but like most of the pass routes, it should not be attempted in fog or snow.

From St. Luc, follow the main street eastward; just outside the village, take the chairlift (télésiège) to Tignousa. The lift takes you up to 2169 meters, where a sign points you to the right (southeast) to the Meiden Pass and the Lac de Combavert. Proceed to the farm at Chalet Blanc and a junction: the fork on the right leads to Hotel Weisshorn, blazed as "H. W." Take the fork to the left and follow the trail that climbs generally eastward on a few broad switchbacks. "M. P." blazed on rocks means Meidpass. Pass the Lac de l'Armina (2562 meters) and arrive at the junction with the trail from the Hotel Weisshorn. The trail continues to the east for a final steep climb up switchbacks and you reach the pass (2790 meters) in 3 hours.

The pass is a notch in a long, jagged, rocky ridge, with a panoramic view that is similar to that from the Bella Tola. You can see dozens of summits. The eastern side of the ridge is hollowed into a cirque, and the barren rocky terrain is sprinkled with little lakes.

The descent toward Gruben is steep at first, then more gradual. Pass the Meidsee to your left (north) and descend past some farm buildings and through pine woods to meadows below. Gruben and Meiden are essentially the same place, a tiny hamlet. The only accommodations are at the Hotel Schwarzhorn (tel. 028 42 14 14) so you should phone ahead. There is no PTT bus in this valley, but the hotel sends a van to Turtmann, at the head of the valley, every day at 7:15 and 20:45 hours, or on request. Turtmann has a rail station.

(The topographic map shows an apparent link between the Bella Tola and Meiden, which might lead you to think that you can combine the Bella Tola climb and the hike to Meiden on the same day. This route, over the Pas de Boeuf and the Borter Pass, is indeed possible but is very poorly marked; in fog, or if the blazes were covered with snow, you could get lost. Therefore the better course is to climb the Bella Tola and cross the Meidpass separately.)

5. GRUBEN TO GRÄCHEN

Rating: very strenuous
Distance one way: 12 km

High point: 2894 m
Ascent/descent: 1100 m/1000 m
Time: 6 hours
Recommended transportation: lift and bus
Map: page 222; also Wanderkarte Turtmanntal Augstbordregion 1:25000,
    Buchdruck Offset Mengis, Visp

The trail across the Augstbordpass takes you through a region that's unpopulated from almost the moment that you leave the Hotel Schwarzhorn—parts of the route would be very difficult to follow in conditions of low visibility, so don't take this route in bad weather. If the weather closes in for an extended period, you can leave the valley by walking out or by taking the hotel van to Turtmann, which is on the Rhône valley rail line.

The trail starts at the signpost next to the Hotel Schwarzhorn in Gruben. It rises almost due east on switchbacks through woods, crossing a stream. Another trail enters from the right at 2151 meters. Turn left (north), following the signpost; then, at a second junction shortly afterward, turn right (east). The trail climbs on broad switchbacks up grassy slopes past the last buildings of the alp at Oberstaffel (2369 meters) and continues almost due east to the Augstbordpass.

Arrive at a big shelf, with two long barrows on either side and boggy ground between them. The trail jogs to the right a little, but stays between the two barrows, at first to the left and then to the right of the stream. Watch carefully for the red and white blazes on rocks, because the trail is not very distinct. (Binoculars can be useful in picking up the route if you lose it.) The stream is a useful reference because the trail, for the most part, keeps to the left (north) bank. This section of the route is totally wild and desolate. The trail gradually rises to the foot of the pass, then climbs a final sharp, steep slope of scree. The climb to the pass takes about 3 hours 15 minutes. The Augstbordpass (2894 meters) is a narrow stony crest that offers long views into the Turtmanntal and Mattertal. The best scenery is not at the top of the pass, but farther down to the east, where the Valaisian Alps come into view. You will usually find more people at the top of the pass because the valley on the other side has two lifts.

The trail descends at first on steep scree, but soon levels off. The well-marked route keeps north of the Embdbach, which is on your right. Two lifts are available below: the Embd and the Jungen (Jungu on maps). The Embd lift descends to Kalpetran, the Jungen lift to St. Niklaus, a little farther south. (You'll pass signs advertising the Embd lift as the most direct way down to the valley. St. Niklaus, however, has more frequent trains

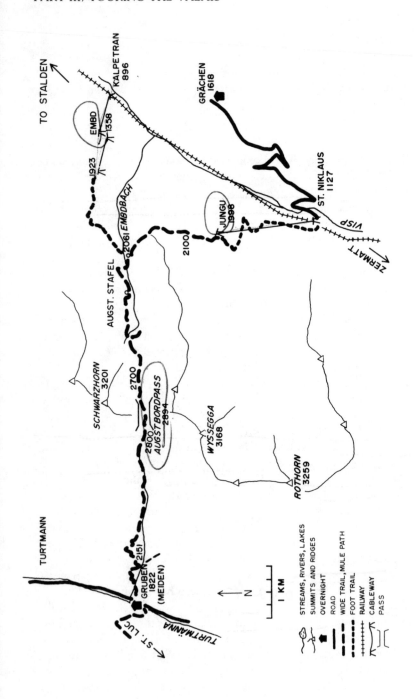

TO STALDEN

KALPETRAN
896

GRÄCHEN
1618

EMBD
1358

1923

ST. NIKLAUS
1127

2061 EMBDBACH

JUNGU
1998

2100

VISP

ZERMATT

AUGST. STAFEL

SCHWARZHORN
3201

2700

AUGSTBORDPASS
2894

2800

WYSSEGGA
3168

ROTHORN
3259

TURTMANN

2151

GRUBEN
1822
(MEIDEN)

ST. LUC

TURTMÄNNA

STREAMS, RIVERS, LAKES
SUMMITS AND RIDGES
OVERNIGHT
ROAD
WIDE TRAIL, MULE PATH
FOOT TRAIL
RAILWAY
CABLEWAY
PASS

N
1 KM

VALAIS WALK 5

and better connections than Kalpetran. Moreover, you get better views walking to Jungen.) Continue straight ahead, rather than turning right (southeast) at the first junction below the pass, even though this turn to the right is marked for Jungen. You will shortly arrive at a second junction with a new high route or Höhenweg that's been laid out to connect the Embd and Jungen lifts. Continue straight ahead on the left bank of the stream, following the yellow blazes. The trail passes a barn at Augstbordstafel, crosses the stream and descends to a junction (2061 meters), where you can turn left for the Embd lift.

For the Jungen lift, take the right turn (south), following the high route that skirts the rocky edge of the valley, with spectacular views of the Valaisian Alps. The trail proceeds south, rising and falling to negotiate the cliffs through which it's carved, and gradually descends to the Jungen lift (1998 meters), 1 hour past the 2061-meter point. The lift descends steeply to St. Niklaus (1127 meters). The trail from Jungen to St. Niklaus, also steep, is easy to follow; allow another 2 hours if you decide to walk down.

The trail to Embd is a little shorter and more level. If you choose to take the Embd lift, go left at the junction at the 2061-meter point. Continue northeast, then turn east, crossing a rocky section, and arrive at the upper part of the two-stage lift at 1923 meters.

St. Niklaus is a small village—the bus stop is at the rail station. There are frequent PTT buses, at approximately half-hour intervals, from St. Niklaus to Grächen, and the trip takes 30 minutes.

You can also walk from St. Niklaus to Grächen, though we recommend that you take the bus. The signposted trail from St. Niklaus to Grächen follows the automobile road, cutting across its graded switchbacks. The route is 5 kilometers long, with an ascent of 500 meters, and will take about 2 hours. Accommodations in Grächen range from inexpensive to expensive.

6. GRÄCHEN TO SAAS-FEE (HÖHENWEG BALFRIN)

Rating: very strenuous
Distance one way: 14.5 km
High point: 2364 m   7 0 9 2 ft
Ascent/descent: 600 m/1000 m
Time: 6 hours 30 minutes to 7 hours
Recommended transportation: lift
Map: page 224; also Saas-Fee 1:25000 Wanderkarte Saastal, or Landeskarte der Schweiz 1:25000 Saas, Blatt 1329, and St. Niklaus, Blatt 1308

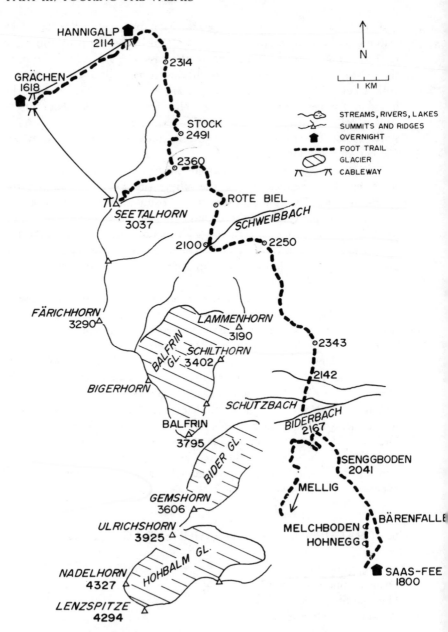

HANNIGALP
2114

GRÄCHEN
1618

⊙2314

STOCK
2491

⊙2360

ROTE BIEL

SEETALHORN
3037

SCHWEIBBACH

2100⊙   ⊙2250

FÄRICHHORN
3290

LAMMENHORN
3190

BALFRIN GL.

SCHILTHORN
3402

⊙2343

2142

BIGERHORN

SCHUTZBACH

BIDERBACH
2167

BALFRIN
3795

BIDER GL.

SENGGBODEN
2041

GEMSHORN
3606

MELLIG

BÄRENFALLE

ULRICHSHORN
3925

MELCHBODEN
HOHNEGG

NADELHORN
4327

HOHBALM GL.

SAAS-FEE
1800

LENZSPITZE
4294

N

1 KM

STREAMS, RIVERS, LAKES
SUMMITS AND RIDGES
OVERNIGHT
FOOT TRAIL
GLACIER
CABLEWAY

VALAIS WALK 6

This is one of the best-known high routes in Switzerland. As you walk toward Saas-Fee, you have good views of the Balfrin and its glaciers on your right and of the Weissmies group across the valley. Looking north, you can see across the Rhône valley to the Bernese Oberland in the distance. And as you approach Saas-Fee, you'll see fine views of the upper end of the Saas valley, where the Mischabel range comes into view.

The route is a long one and requires a whole day—it's also fairly strenuous, continually dipping up and down, so that the accumulated ascent is considerable. The trail is fairly exposed in places, with an abrupt drop to the valley floor below, so this route is not advisable for those suffering from vertigo. However, the trail is well marked and this is a very popular excursion. On a fine day you will see a number of other hikers on the route. There are no farms, huts, or mountain restaurants on the route, and there's no way off the trail once you're underway, so do not undertake this route in snow or bad weather or if you do not feel fresh and in good condition.

In Grächen, take the Hannigbahn lift if you want to save 500 meters of ascent. If you decide to walk instead of taking the lift, the path from Grächen to Hannigalp is easy to find. Signposts in Grächen indicate the route, which ascends 500 meters in 2.5 kilometers, through woods. This walk adds about 1 hour 45 minutes to the trip to Saas-Fee. At Hannigalp you emerge at the lift station.

A signpost at Hannigalp, outside the lift station, points you toward the southeast. The trail continually climbs, descends and climbs again, and swings in and out, following the contours of the slope. Continue southeast and south. As you approach Saas-Fee, the trail forks: left toward Bärenfalle, right toward Hohnegg and Melchboden. Either will take you to Saas-Fee, which has accommodations that range from inexpensive to expensive.

(This route is described in greater detail in Chapter 6, page 107.)

225

13

Touring the Upper Engadine

The grandest feature of the Upper Engadine is its broad glaciers. The mountains here, though high, are lower than those in the Valais or the Bernese Oberland, being for the most part under 4000 meters. The highest mountains, which form the Bernina group, are strung in a tight chain on or near the Italian border: Piz Bernina, Piz Palü, Piz Roseg, and others. There are SAC huts on each "bank" of the two main glaciers that pour down from the Bernina group, so that it's possible for a hiker to tour the region and visit the huts without stepping onto the glaciers; moreover, the walks to the huts are short and quite easy. The hiking route around the Roseg and Tschierva glaciers leads you to two SAC huts (Coaz and Tschierva) that have magnificent glacier views. This route requires much less exertion than you usually need to get to an SAC hut or so close to big glaciers.

You can make several other interesting excursions in this region as well, notably a climb up the Piz Languard and hikes down the valleys south of the lake ("lej" in Romansch) of Sils (Segl).

The Upper Engadine is popular among the Swiss and other Europeans because it enjoys good weather and because of several famous resorts: St. Moritz (large, expensive and ostentatious) and Pontresina, much smaller and unpretentious but still rather expensive.

There are two main glacier areas in the Upper Engadine: one in the broad Val Roseg (where the Roseg, Sella, and Tschierva glaciers meet), and the other in the next valley to the east (which contains the Morteratsch and Pers glaciers). We would recommend that you start with

Lac da Cavloc from the north, above Maloja

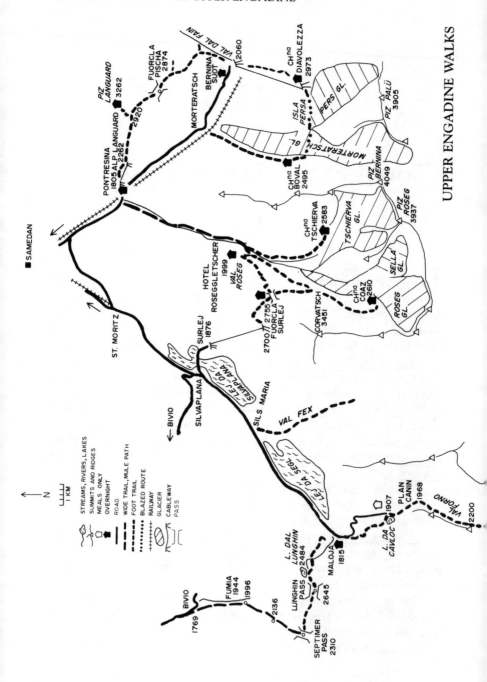

UPPER ENGADINE WALKS

the Val Roseg, which you can tour in two or three days; if you have time, continue to the next valley.

There are several ways to organize a walking tour of the Val Roseg, which you can approach from Pontresina or from the En valley to the west (in which St. Moritz, Silvaplana, Sils, and Maloja are located). From Silvaplana, you can take the Corvatsch lift up to Fuorcla Surlej (or walk up) and then walk down into the Val Roseg.

The approach from Pontresina, however, is more direct. From Pontresina, you walk to the Hotel Roseggletscher, a country hotel that's fancier than an ordinary mountain inn (higher meal prices, more elegant dining room), but that has Matratzenlager available. The walk to the Hotel Roseggletscher is a short hike but because it can take 4 to 5 hours to reach the Upper Engadine from other parts of Switzerland and you might arrive at Pontresina in the midafternoon, Roseggletscher would be a convenient stop for the first night. You can then take a side trip to the Tschierva hut, which is popular and can be very crowded, especially on weekends in good weather. Consider staying there if there's space—otherwise, return to the hotel. (An advantage to making this a side trip is that you can leave most of your gear at the hotel and hike with a light pack.)

On the third day, you can walk from Roseggletscher up to Fuorcla Surlej and then to the Coaz hut. Spend the night at the hut. The next day, walk back past Roseggletscher to Pontresina.

From Pontresina, you can continue up to Piz Languard, then descend to Bernina Suot, a railway stop in the Val Bernina. You can make this excursion in one day or break it up with an overnight stop at the Georgyhütte, which is just below the summit of the Piz Languard.

From Bernina Suot, you can continue up to the Diavolezza and Boval huts. Alternately, if your time is short, you can return to Pontresina and travel directly to Maloja (take the train to St. Moritz, then the PTT bus to Maloja). From Maloja you can take a side trip to Lac da Cavloc in the Val Forno. And you can leave the Engadine from Maloja by hiking across the Lunghin and Septimer passes, a route that takes you north to Bivio, which has good connections to Chur and other points.

If you have to choose between a trip to the Coaz and the Tschierva huts, the difference is this. The Coaz hut sits below a cirque, with a grand sweep of glaciers over a very wide area, so that it appears that you are at the edge of a sea of glacier. The peaks above the wall of ice, however, are foreshortened and don't appear to rise very high. From the Coaz hut, you also have a long view down the Roseg valley to the lake, the Ova da Roseg river, and even Pontresina very far away. From the Tschierva hut, the great cirque of glaciers at the end of the valley is cut off from view. But you're closer to the high mountains, and the Tschierva glacier is right before you. Moreover, the glacier looks wild and tumultuous, almost alive: wild seracs stand above the ice like giant pyramids—a more dramatic sight than the calmer though larger expanse you see from Coaz.

The recommended topographic maps for all Upper Engadine walks are Landeskarte der Schweiz 1:50000, Julierpass No 268 and Berninapass No 269.

1. PONTRESINA TO HOTEL ROSEGGLETSCHER

Rating: easy
Distance one way: 6 km
High point: 2000 m
Ascent/descent: 200 m/0 m
Time: 2 hours
Map: page 228

A horse-drawn carriage (Pferde Omnibus) runs regularly between Pontresina and Hotel Roseggletscher, taking people out for lunch. You can walk either on the broad cart road, which is in the open, or on a footpath (Fussweg), which proceeds through woods for a good part of the way.

The cart road begins behind the Pontresina rail station, which is across the river and southwest from the town. It follows the Roseg stream southwest to the hotel. You can pick up the footpath either from the road that connects the rail station with Pontresina or from the southeastern end of the town, after crossing the river on the smaller of the town's two bridges. Shortly before you reach the hotel, the cart road and the footpath merge. You'll arrive at Hotel Roseggletscher (1999 meters) 2 hours after leaving Pontresina. Fine views from the hotel of the cirque of glaciers to the south.

Side Trip: Hotel Roseggletscher to Chamanna da Tschierva

Rating: moderate
Distance round trip: 11 km
High point: 2583 m
Total climb: 600 m
Time: 2 hours up, 1 hour 15 minutes down
Map: page 228

The trail to the Tschierva hut is on the other side of the braided Roseg stream. Leave the Hotel Roseggletscher and follow the cart road for a few minutes toward Pontresina; just past the bridge there's a junction. Turn sharp right (south) for the Tschierva hut. The well-marked and easy trail proceeds southward along the river bank, with a fine glacier view before you. Then you climb through a little pine wood and up to the left, parallel to a ridge of moraine on your right. The route follows the shoulder of the Piz Tschierva, curving slightly to the east, and as you ascend the gentle grade, the Piz Roseg is to your right and the Piz Bernina before you. A final short but steep section brings you up to the hut. Above you are the peaks of Morteratsch, Bernina, and Roseg, and a big, wild, tumbling glacier running down to the river below.

There are some popular climbs from here, and the Tschierva hut can be very crowded on weekends in good weather. The hut was built to hold 100 people but when we were there, 140 had already telephoned for places, and more people were arriving all the time. In contrast, the smaller Coaz hut is less crowded.

2. HOTEL ROSEGGLETSCHER TO CHAMANNA DA COAZ

Rating: moderate
Distance one way: 8 km
High point: 2755 m
Ascent/descent: 800 m/0 m
Time: 5 hours
Map: page 228

Between the Val Roseg and the chain of lakes in the En valley is a long, mountainous wall, of which the highest peak is the Piz Corvatsch (3451 meters). Fuorcla Surlej is a notch in this wall, at which there's a mountain inn, Berghaus Fuorcla Surlej (tel. 082 06 63 03). You can walk up to this spot from the Val Roseg (or walk or take the Corvatsch lift from Surlej in the En valley).

To climb up to the notch from Hotel Roseggletscher, find the trail behind the hotel. It ascends through trees at first, then, after a few switchbacks, heads steeply up to the southwest. The trail soon rises above treeline. Reach Fuorcla Surlej (2755 meters) in about 2 hours 30 minutes. From Fuorcla Surlej you can see a panoramic view across the Val Roseg to the Piz Roseg and Piz Bernina, and from the notch itself there is a breathtaking view of the peaks across the En valley to the west.

To reach the Coaz hut, follow the trail southeast (signpost) from the inn. Walk to a junction, where a trail bears left (northeast) for Val Roseg, right (southwest) for Coaz. As you walk to the south, you can see the Tschierva hut to your left (east), across the glacier valley. The trail to the Coaz hut, which is almost level, traverses the slope above the Roseg glacier. At the end, the roof of the hut comes into view, and there's a very short ascent to the hut (2610 meters). Reach the hut in 2 hours 15 minutes from Fuorcla Surlej. From here, a sweeping view of glaciers both above and below you—the effect is of an ocean of glacier. The Roseg glacier climbs in great steps behind the hut to a wall of rocky peaks.

3. CHAMANNA DA COAZ TO PONTRESINA

Rating: moderate
Distance one way: 14 km
High point: 2610 m
Descent: 830 m
Time: 4 hours 15 minutes
Map: page 228

To return to Pontresina, retrace your steps, now heading northeast. After an hour, you come to the junction where you can turn left (northwest) for Fuorcla Surlej. Follow the trail straight ahead for Hotel Roseg-gletscher, then continue to Pontresina.

4. PONTRESINA TO BERNINA SUOT, VIA PIZ LANGUARD

Rating: strenuous
Distance one way: 13 km
High point: 3262 m
Ascent/descent: 1500 m/1500 m
Time: 7 hours 30 minutes
Optional transportation: lift
Map: page 228

Piz Languard is a solitary peak with a magnificent, 360-degree view and was a favorite excursion for Victorian travelers. You can climb it in a day (a lift goes part way up) with an optional overnight stay at the little

Georgyhütte, perched on a bit of ledge just below the summit. Then descend to Bernina Suot, from which you can continue up to the Diavolezza and Boval huts.

From the railroad station, walk up to Pontresina and turn right at the square in the center of town. Bear left at the fork just past the tourist office. Continue down the street for a short distance; the lift to Alp Languard is to your left. If you want to take the path up from Pontresina, walk to the lift station but continue straight ahead instead of turning left to the lift. You're on the Via Cruscheda. Pass the Santa Maria chapel to the Spagniola tower, then walk up a steep but shaded path to the square (the Röntgenplatz). Continue on the trail to Alp Languard, which is 1 hour 15 minutes from Pontresina.

At Alp Languard (2262 meters) a signpost indicates the path to Piz Languard. Head almost due east, crossing the entrance of the lovely Val Languard, a deep, wild valley down which the stream Ovel da Languard runs. The trail traverses the northern slope above this valley and climbs steeply. At a junction (2920 meters) just below the final ridge, take the left fork for the hut and the summit. The final section is very steep and takes about 45 minutes to climb.

The trail ascends on tiny switchbacks through loose pebbles and scree. Three hours from the Alp Languard lift station, you reach the little Georgyhütte (3176 meters), which has Matratzenlager places for about 20 people. Phone ahead for reservations (tel. 082 3 65 65). You'll find tremendous views of the Piz Palü– Piz Bernina group, and range upon range of other peaks. A 20-minute scramble takes you to the summit (3262 meters), which has sweeping views of the Bernina group and the Italian Dolomites.

To continue on to Bernina Suot, descend to the base of the steep ridge of scree and take the left fork (southeast) instead of the right one, which would take you back to Pontresina. The trail descends, traversing southeastward below the long ridge of Crasta Languard. Cross over the notch, Fuorcla Pischa (2874 meters), and come to a junction, where you bear right. Here you come into a very barren, stony, high basin, impressively wild and arctic. Follow cairns and blazes for this part of the route. After heading southeast across this basin, the trail descends steeply on switchbacks and then down a rather steep, grassy slope, heading southeast. As you reach the valley floor, turn right (southwest) at a junction for Bernina Suot and the main road. Proceed south down this valley, the Val dal Fain, and cross the Ova da Bernina on the bridge. A dirt road then leads you down to the highway and the tiny railroad station of Bernina Suot (2060 meters), 3 hours from the Georgyhütte. The Gasthaus Bernina Suot has Matratzenlager accommodations (or you can cross the highway and take the lift up to the Diavolezza hut).

5. BERNINA SUOT TO MALOJA, VIA CHAMANNAS DIAVOLEZZA AND BOVAL

Rating: strenuous, guide necessary
Distance one way: 14 km
High point: 2973 m
Ascent/descent: 920 m/1100 m
Time: 7 hours
Recommended transportation: railroad, bus; **optional transportation:** lift
Map: page 228

The big Morteratsch glacier merges with the Pers glacier and flows north from the Piz Bernina and Piz Palü to the Val Bernina. There are very grand views from its high banks; the Boval hut is on the Morteratsch's west bank, the Diavolezza hut on the north bank of the Pers. But you can't cross this valley to see both huts unless you hire a guide for the glacier crossing.

On our first trip to the Upper Engadine, a native of the region who was attempting to tell us about the Diavolezza hut could not think of the word he wanted in English. "It's a *kermesse,*" he said finally: the French word means a fair, with the connotation of a zoo. The lift from the highway (a main route between Italy and Switzerland), just east of Bernina Suot, transports large numbers of people up to Diavolezza, so you'll find crowds milling around the Diavolezza "hut," which is in fact a hotel with a big cafeteria and sun terrace. Yet the views are superb—so fine that it's hard to say that you shouldn't go.

If you decide to walk up, the trail to Diavolezza begins from the highway, slightly to the east of the Bernina Suot rail station. After an initial steep section, the trail moves toward the lift line, crossing under it a couple of times. The route passes to the left (east) of a tiny lake, then turns southwest through a snowfield, and up to Diavolezza.

To cross from the Diavolezza to the Boval hut, you must have a guide. Every day, from mid-June to October, a licensed guide leads an excursion across the glacier. The 4-hour route crosses the Pers glacier to Isla Persa, the island in the middle of the glacier, then across the Morteratsch glacier to the Boval hut, then down the west bank to the railway station of Morteratsch. If you wish to go, sign up for the trip at the little wooden booth behind the topmost Diavolezza lift station between 10 and 11:45 a.m. (A minimum of eight persons must sign up.) The excursion starts at noon or at 11 a.m. after September 25, and the cost is low. A protective sunblock cream and dark glasses (preferably glacier glasses) are absolutely essential.

The crossing is made on a fairly level section of the glacier. Unless there has been a recent storm, this glacier is likely to be "open"; that is, not covered by snow, and crevasses will be visible.

After the glacier crossing, which takes about 2 hours 30 minutes, walk up a stretch of moraine for about 1 kilometer and then up a steep final section to the Boval hut. The Boval hut can be very crowded so it's best not to count on an overnight stop. The trail down from the Boval hut to Morteratsch is steep at first but then levels out before a final descent through woods. The best views of the valley with the snowy mountains in the background are farther down the trail, where the moraine does not obscure the view. Follow the signposts to the Morteratsch railway station, from which you can continue to Maloja. The last train leaves at about 19 hours; change at St. Moritz for the PTT bus to Maloja. The total rail and bus trip will take 1 hour 30 minutes.

Maloja is located on the shore at the end of the Lake of Sils, and is the starting point for the Lunghin-Septimer pass route, by which you can leave the Upper Engadine. If you spend an extra day here you can take a side trip up to the Val Forno, which offers a stunning contrast between the forest and the stony, narrow valley beyond it.

Side Trip: Maloja to Val Forno

Rating: moderate
Distance round trip: 17 km
High point: 2200 m
Total climb: 400 m
Time: 2 hours 45 minutes up, 1 hour 30 minutes down
Map: page 228

The Lac da Cavloc is justifiably considered a beauty spot. The route to the lake begins at the southern end of Maloja, past the Hotel Maloja Kulm and the viewpoint for the Maloja Pass. Walk to the start of the first of the hairpin turns of the automobile road that descends the pass. Stay on the left (east) side of the road and watch for the signpost and path to Lac da Cavloc and Val Forno.

The path heads due south at first but loops to the east, where it intersects a farm road and passes the hamlet of Orden. Turn right at the next signposted intersection and cross the bridge over the Orlegna stream, continuing on a dirt road. After another 10 minutes, just after the road begins to climb, a signpost to the right indicates the shortcut (Abkurzung) trail. This route ascends fairly steeply through the forest to the northern shore of

Lac da Cavloc (1907 meters). The trail is rough at points, with mossy, slippery logs underfoot, but the advantage of the shortcut is that the view of the lake when you emerge from the forest is superb. The peaks of the Upper Engadine mountains are reflected in the dark blue water, which is so clear that you can see the fish in it. It takes 1 hour 15 minutes to walk to the lake.

The trail to the left (east) takes you around the lake, with more fine views. The route then joins a dirt road, the main route from Maloja on the eastern shore of the lake, where there's a simple restaurant, benches for picnickers, and a barn. Continue to the southeast on the signposted trail to the Val Forno, Chamanna da Forno, and the Passo del Muretto.

The scenery continues to be soft and lovely, with woods and meadows, until you emerge into a stone-strewn valley with very steep walls. You don't see the Val Forno (some signs call it the Fornotal) until you pass the concrete waterworks building at Plan Canin (1968 meters) and reach the junction for the Val Muretto and the Val Forno. Take the trail to the right (southwest) as you enter the Val Forno, a narrow, wild, rocky valley with a blue-gray glacial stream. The walls are great rock slabs. The well-blazed trail ends at the terminal moraine of the Vadrec (glacier) del Forno, which you would have to ascend and traverse to get to the Forno hut (2574 meters). Turn back before the ascent up the glacier and retrace the route back to Lac da Cavloc.

At the lake, you can take the road to the right, which descends on graded switchbacks to Maloja. This road is pleasant, more open than the shortcut and has lovely views of meadows. The shortcut path through the forest is slippery in places for descent.

6. MALOJA TO BIVIO

Rating: strenuous
Distance one way: 13 km
High point: 2645 m
Ascent/descent: 900 m/870 m
Time: 6 hours
Map: page 228

The ancient Septimer Pass (Pass da Sett), used by both the Romans and Germanic tribes, was once one of the major routes across the Alps. In the late nineteenth century the roads leading up to the Maloja Pass were improved, and the Septimer Pass fell into disuse. Today, only hikers frequent the former imperial route to the north, which is now a cart road at its broadest point. This is a pass route by which you can walk out of the Engadine.

The route starts from the main road at the northern edge of Maloja, 50 meters west of the vast old hotel (now a Belgian children's summer camp) overlooking the lake. (If you're coming by PTT bus from St. Moritz or Sils, get off at Restaurant Longhin, the stop just before Maloja.) The trail starts on the west side of the road. It climbs up 30 meters to the houses at Pila, then turns right at the signposted junction; at a second junction soon after, bear left (west).

The trail ascends through meadows and past a tumbling stream with a waterfall. Climb on fairly steep switchbacks up a small wall. As the trail levels out, you arrive at the deep blue Lac dal Lunghin (2484 meters), a quite spectacular lake that sits before an almost sheer rock wall. It's about 2 hours from Maloja to the lake, from which you can see the Lunghin Pass. A short climb (30 minutes) up rubble and scree takes you to the pass at 2645 meters. This geographical point is the watershed for three seas: from here, the En flows into the Black Sea, the Maira (Mera) into the Adriatic Sea, and the Julia Wasser into the North Sea. The Piz Lunghin to the left (south) of the pass is only 135 meters higher than the pass.

You then descend through meadows to the Septimer Pass (4 hours from Maloja), which, at 2310 meters, is lower than the Lunghin Pass. The view from here is of the Bernina group. You can also see the broad track ascending from the south past the old buildings that once housed travelers to and from Italy. From here, turn right (north) into a wide green valley. The path becomes a broad, even track that descends gradually for 3 kilometers until you reach the first farms at 2000 meters. Two hours from the Septimer Pass you reach Bivio (1769 meters), where you can take a PTT bus to Chur (the capital of the canton) and make train connections to Lucerne, Zurich, and Bern.

14

TOURING THE TICINO

Traveling south through the St. Gotthard Pass, you emerge at Airolo in the Valle Levantina, the central valley of the canton of Ticino. Abruptly, the language switches from German to Italian. Once part of Lombardy, the region was fiercely contested for control of this crucial alpine pass; later it became a Swiss colony. During the Napoleonic period, it became an independent Swiss canton.

The Ticino is Italian Switzerland, politically Swiss and culturally Italian. The canton is shaped like an inverted triangle, with its base set in the southern slope of the Bernese Oberland. Surrounded on two sides by Italian territory, the canton narrows to the south, its tip resting on the northern Italian lakes of Maggiore and Lugano.

Two of the loveliest Swiss cities are here, Lugano and Locarno, each on a beautiful lakefront; and one of the pleasant features of walking in the Ticino is that you can also easily visit these cities. Lugano is larger, with a splendid vista of green, mountainous islands and slopes rising from the lake; Locarno has more of the aspect of a resort. In both, many buildings are Italian in appearance, with plaster facades in joyful colors: peach, pink, and pale green, and numerous Italian features of architecture and design. The restaurants serve pasta, polenta, and risotto.

Lugano is the home of an important museum, the Villa Favorita, which houses the collection of Baron Thyssen-Bornemisza, including paintings by Piero della Francesca, Raphael, Holbein, Velasquez, and Goya, among other masters. The Villa is open only on Friday, Saturday, and Sunday, from Easter to mid-October. Locarno has a splendid old

Anzonico villagers on their balcony, on the Strada Alta Leventina

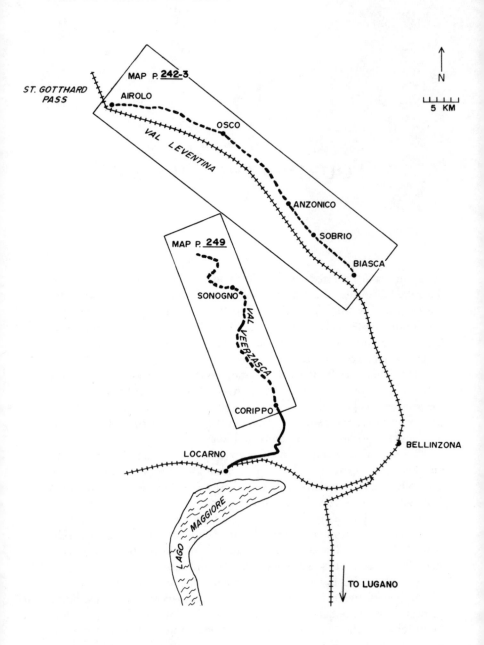

OVERVIEW OF TICINO TOUR

castle with interesting artifacts and a collection of modern art donated by Jean Arp, long a resident of Locarno, which includes works by himself, Max Ernst, and others of their circle. There is also an interesting display commemorating the Treaty of Locarno.

Lugano and Locarno look Mediterranean, with palm trees and camellias in their gardens. But within a few kilometers of the lakes are 2000-meter mountains, and most of the peaks in the Ticino are between 2300 and 3000 meters. The charm of hiking here is the blend of rugged country and the Ticinese villages. One of the celebrated Swiss high routes, the Strada Alta Leventina, is a very old route that connects a string of villages on the slopes above the Valle Leventina. The Val Verzasca hiking route passes through one of the Ticino's finest valleys.

The charm of the Strada Alta Leventina is that you walk from village to village, through fields and woods, as people once did here to see or trade with their neighbors. Now of course it's only the hikers who do the walking; the local residents drive. But nearly all the Strada Alta consists of footpaths apart from the paved roads. The villages are small and charming, with an Italian flavor—there are stone as well as wood houses and stone campaniles on the churches. The scenery is gentle: close at hand are farms and fields and views of the next villages; farther, you can see down the long valley and across to the mountains on the other side.

The Strada Alta runs from Airolo to Biasca, following the Ticino river as it curves in a long, gentle arc to the southeast. From Airolo in the valley, on the river's north bank, the route climbs several hundred meters and then traverses the long slope above the river, descending to the valley again at Biasca. To walk the whole route requires three days but you can see the most scenic part—between Lurengo and Sobrio—in two days.

The villages on the valley floor are on the railway, and there are footpaths linking some of these villages with the Strada Alta above. Between Airolo and Biasca, the intermediate access points are at Ambi-Piotta, Faido, Lavorgo, and Giornico. And hikers can walk down to make train connections to Lugano or Locarno. Most of the footpaths between the railway and the Strada Alta take about an hour to walk.

Once you are up on the Strada Alta, the route continues at a fairly steady altitude, though you jog up and down a good deal, gaining and losing one or two hundred meters between one village and another. But the only substantial ascent or descent is between the valley floor and the Strada Alta. The route is well-blazed, with frequent signs—even when these are absent, the route is generally unmistakable. At the Airolo and Faido rail stations, you can get simple maps and brochures listing all the accommodations and their telephone numbers.

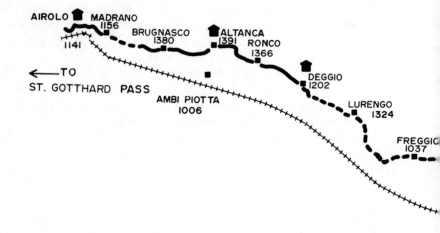

TICINO WALKS 1 THROUGH 3

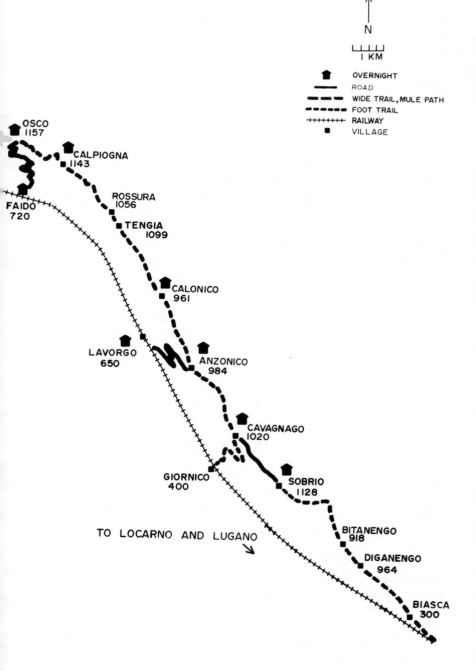

N

1 KM

⬠ OVERNIGHT
▬ ROAD
▬ ▬ WIDE TRAIL, MULE PATH
▪ ▪ ▪ FOOT TRAIL
+++++ RAILWAY
■ VILLAGE

OSCO
1157

CALPIOGNA
1143

ROSSURA
1056

FAIDO
720

TENGIA
1099

CALONICO
961

LAVORGO
650

ANZONICO
984

CAVAGNAGO
1020

GIORNICO
400

SOBRIO
1128

BITANENGO
918

TO LOCARNO AND LUGANO

DIGANENGO
964

BIASCA
300

1. STRADA ALTA LEVENTINA: AIROLO TO OSCO

Rating: moderate
Distance one way: 17 km
High point: 1391 m
Ascent/descent: 550 m/500 m
Time: 5 hours
Map: pages 242–43; also Carta nazionale della svizzera 1:50000, Valle
   Leventina 266

From the Airolo station (1141 meters) with the railway behind you, walk to your right, then head up a ramp-like street to the main street above. Turn right on the main street (signposts), and proceed to the village of Madrano. Past Madrano you climb a steep section of trail to a road above. This section of the route takes 1 hour. Follow the road to the next village, Brugnasco (1380 meters). On this stretch you can hear the traffic noise from the new super highway in the valley below.

The walk becomes more attractive as you reach Altanca (1391 meters), Ronco (1366 meters), Deggio (1202 meters), Lurengo (1324 meters), and Freggio (1037 meters). Continue to Osco (1157 meters), where you can spend the night at Ristorante Marti (tel. 094 38 11 89). If they have no room, the next village, Calpiogna (1143 meters), has accommodations at Ristorante La Baita (tel. 094 38 10 84) and Ostello Strada Alta (tel. 094 38 22 06).

2. STRADA ALTA LEVENTINA: OSCO TO ANZONICO

Rating: moderate
Distance one way: 12 km
High point: 1388 m
Ascent/descent: 400 m/600 m
Time: 3 hours 30 minutes
Map: pages 242–43; also Carta nazionale della svizzera 1:50000, Valle
   Leventina 266

The walk from Osco to Calpiogna takes 40 minutes. From Calpiogna there are lovely views of the valley and the mountains behind. Continue through fields and small villages—Rossura (1056 meters), Tengia (1099 meters)—then descend slightly to Calonico (961 meters), where you come upon a church perched on top of a great exposed cliff towering over the valley. You can stop for the night in pretty Anzonico (984 meters), which is full of old stone and wood houses (some are many hundreds of years old) surrounded by fruit trees. There's one hotel in the village, Albergo Bella-vista (tel. 094 39 11 10). Though it's in a tiny village, the hotel is rather like a mountain inn: old-fashioned, neat, and unassuming. The dining room is decorated with a large old photograph of the great San Francisco fire.

Anzonico is 5 hours from Calpiogna, which will allow you ample time for eating lunch, looking at the villages, and taking photographs.

3. STRADA ALTA LEVENTINA: ANZONICO TO SOBRIO TO LOCARNO

Rating: moderate
Distance one way: 17 km
High point: 1128 m
Ascent/descent: 250 m/950 m
Time: 5 hours, 2 hours 30 minutes with bus
Recommended transportation: train; **optional transportation:** bus
Map: pages 242–43; also Carta nazionale della svizzera 1:50000, Valle Leventina 266

From Anzonico you can walk to Cavagnago (1020 meters) in 45 minutes, then to Sobrio (1128 meters). From Sobrio you can catch a PTT bus departing at about 17 hours for the railroad station at Lavorgo. Although the Strada Alta continues to Biasca—about 3 hours distant—we recommend that you leave the route at Sobrio, as after this it deteriorates, occasionally becoming very narrow and passing through areas of ferns and rough, low vegetation. If you do continue on the Strada Alta, eventually you descend through woods to Biasca, about 5 hours from Anzonico. To continue to Locarno, take the train from the Biasca station toward Lugano, changing at Bellinzona for the train to Locarno. If you arrive at Biasca by 14:30 you can reach Locarno at 17:30 (or Lugano at 15:15).

4. LOCARNO TO VAL VERZASCA: CORIPPO BUS STOP TO SONOGNO

Rating: moderate
Distance one way: 16 km
High point: 919 m
Ascent/descent: 450 m/90 m
Time: 5 hours
Recommended transportation: bus

Abandoned houses in the hamlet of Puscen Negro

Map: page 249; also Tenero e Valle Verzasca, Carta delle escursioni 1:50000, or Carta nazionale della svizzera 1:50000, Valle Verzasca 276

You can easily travel to this attractive valley from Locarno. In the Val Verzasca, you can see the typical Ticinese farm houses, constructed of dry stone, the walls and roofs made of stone slabs laid horizontally. The stone is often gray but sometimes golden, giving a rich visual texture. Many houses are now abandoned and the area is thinly populated. During hard times at the end of the nineteenth century, many Ticinese emigrated to California, where they established "Italian Swiss colonies" and became vintners. On the fountain at Frasca are inscribed the words, "Benefatori Californiesi," and the date 1901.

The route north through the Val Verzasca is a footpath up the valley that leads through a string of picturesque Ticinese villages and hamlets. To begin, take the PTT bus from Locarno (the bus stop is next to the rail station) to the Val Verzasca. You can get off at the Corippo bus stop (a 15 kilometer trip that takes 35 minutes), or at Lavertezzo, and walk up the valley toward the mountains, to the charming village of Sonogno, from which buses return to Locarno at 15:05 and 16:30 hours.

Sonogno, the tourist center of the valley, is very small and unspoiled, with lovely old stone houses, flowers blooming on the balconies, and fine views of the rock walls that rise behind the village and along its sides. The village has a little folk museum and an "artigianato" selling local handicrafts. Yet Sonogno has only one hotel, Ristorante Alpino: (tel. 093 90 11 63) and you must reserve accommodations well ahead. If you find that Sonogno has no overnight vacancies, there are also hotels in Frasco, the Albergo Efra (tel. 093 90 11 72), Gerra, Ristorante Froda (tel. 093 90 14 52), and at several other points in the valley.

The walking route up the valley is carefully signposted. You can start at the PTT bus stop for Corippo, which is the first stop at the north end of the lake of Vogorno. (A very short side trip to Corippo, a village classified by the Swiss Federal Commission for the protection of historical sites, is worthwhile if you have an hour to spare.) The walking route from the bus stop (485 meters) follows the Verzasca, at this point a fair-sized river, along its west bank, opposite the automobile road. The route gradually climbs to the hamlet of Oviga (545 meters), which is connected to the village of Lavertezzo on the opposite bank by a lovely arched medieval bridge. The PTT bus from Locarno stops at Lavertezzo and all the other villages of the Val Verzasca.

The route from Oviga continues along the west bank of the Verzasca, crossing to the east bank at the hamlet of Gana (spelled Ganne on some maps). The walking route is always on the bank of the river opposite the automobile road. You can make a short side trip to the village of Brione

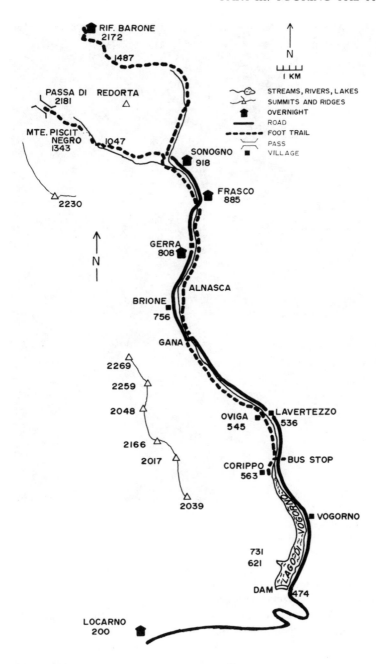

**TICINO WALK 4 AND SONOGNO TO
PASSO DI REDORTA SIDE TRIP**

In the village of Sonogno

(756 meters) at the footbridge that you'll reach about 20 minutes after you cross to the east bank of the Verzasca. Brione has a church with thirteenth-century frescoes and other interesting old buildings.

The walking route continues on the east bank through the farm houses at Alnasca, where fresh fruit and soft drinks are sometimes sold, past the village of Gerra (808 meters), which is on the west bank. A footbridge across the Verzasca connects the walking route with the village. The trail crosses the river to its west bank about 30 minutes past Gerra, and you reach Sonogno (918 meters) 45 minutes past this point.

Side Trip: **Sonogno to Passo di Redorta**

Rating: strenuous
Distance round trip: 12 km
High point: 2181 m
Total climb: 1350 m
Time: 4 hours 30 minutes up, 3 hours down
Map: page 249; also Tenero e Valle Verzasca, Carta delle escursioni
1:50000, or Carta nazionale della Svizzera 1:50000, Valle Verzasca
276

Sonogno is so charming that you might well wish to linger and enjoy
the setting and the flavor of rural Ticino a little longer. This route is one
of the hikes that you can take from Sonogno. The trail runs next to a
beautiful stream through open pine woods, then climbs over rocks and up
through meadows, providing lovely views of the narrow valley hemmed in
by rock walls and steep green slopes. On the way you pass a nearly deserted
farm hamlet with the characteristic, attractive Ticinese stone houses and
barns.

Walk westward out of Sonogno on a paved road, with the stream to
your left. In a few minutes, you pass the Grotto Efra, a restaurant in the
woods. Continue on a broad path above the stream, and in 45 minutes you
reach Fraced, a cluster of abandoned stone houses. The path begins to
climb, then forks. Bear right for Passo di Redorta. Ascend a rocky, slabby
section, with the stream tumbling down to your left. After 1 hour 30
minutes, arrive at the hamlet of Puscen Negro (1343 meters), which is
now almost abandoned.

Cross the stream on a bridge. The path continues northwest up
through steep meadows, with fine views. There are occasional easy stream
crossings on rocks. The path gradually bears west, then climbs to a final
green shelf (1900 meters), where a waterfall spills over the edge; the path
then turns to the right (northwest) and climbs steeply to the pass, which
you can see on your right. From Sonogno it's 4 hours 30 minutes to the
pass at 2181 meters. (Allow more time for this walk in hot weather.) Fine
views across the valley, which is enclosed by mountains of about 2800
meters. (From the pass you can descend to the west and north to Prato in
the Val Lavizzara, 7 hours 30 minutes from Sonogno.)

From Sonogno you can head north for the long hike up to Alpe
Barone, where there is a hut (rifugio), and continue to Lago Barone (a 5-
hour walk) in the Val Vegorness. Signposts in the parking lot at the
entrance to Sonogno show this and other possibilities.

15

TOURING THE EMMENTAL

The Emmental is a region essentially unknown outside of Switzerland, though many people know that "Emmental" is the proper name for what we Americans call Swiss cheese. The name means the valley (tal) around the river Emme, which lies east of Bern.

It's a countryside of small hills. Numerous streams from the glaciers and mountains to the south have cut the land into deep valleys; no other region in Switzerland has such a configuration of valleys sharply divided by streams. The land is partially wooded but most of it is open, used for grazing or growing winter hay. This is the landscape of children's picture books: soft, round hills, little curving roads, farmhouses surrounded by fruit trees.

Two things make this gentle, lovely country extraordinary: the handsome Emmental farmhouses, unique in architecture and design, and the network of walking trails that take you not only through woods and fields but right through farmyards and past the magnificent old farmhouses. Hikers are welcome here. Imagine a place where you don't drive past farmland (barbed wire on each side of the highway), with only an occasional distant glimpse of a farmhouse, but where you can walk on trails that wind through the farms and take you up to the farmhouse door.

Each Emmental farm is a little independent domain, with land for pasture and crops, woods for winter fuel, a fruit orchard, and vegetable garden. In the farmhouse cellar is a year's supply of apple cider, fruit preserves, pickles, and relish, all made from home-grown produce. The potatoes, vegetables, and even the ham and sausage served at meals come

Grandfather Ramsei at his Mörisegg farm

from the farmer's garden and livestock. Yet these farms are small by American standards. The famous cheeses are made in small cheese factories (Käserei) that employ two or three people. These little dairies are scattered throughout the Emmental; there's one in nearly every village, and they can generally be visited.

The traditional Emmental farm consists of three buildings. The Bauernhaus, the largest structure, contains farmhouse, stables, and a huge hayloft, united under an enormous, magnificent roof that folds over the gabled ends and dips almost to the ground over the sides of the house. Across the house facade, tiers of balconies are hung with flowers; on one side wall is a cavernous door, large enough to admit a fully loaded hay wagon.

Behind the big house is a little one, the Stockli, or dower house. In the Emmental, the farms are passed on to the youngest son. When the parents turn the farm over to the next generation, they move into this smaller house, near enough to help, but under another roof. Next to the farmhouse is a smaller Speicher, or storehouse. This may contain herbs, preserves, and family heirlooms, and the facade is often beautifully carved and painted. Surrounding the farmhouses are flower gardens, kitchen gardens and fruit trees. Beyond are the pastures and fields, and every farm has a small wood.

The whole region is laced with walking trails. Though Emmental walking routes go up and down over the soft, undulating hills, they are never strenuous: they're rambles rather than challenging hikes. They typically include some stretches of paved road (though traffic is scant), trails through woods, farm lanes across fields and through pastures, and paths through farmyards, past farmhouses and through home orchards. You can walk beneath rows of trees bearing cherries and apples, and the path below you strewn with dropped fruit.

The Emmental region is full of charming and unspoiled towns and villages with old inns, so that you can walk from village to village and stay at inns along your route. Some of these villages are so pretty that you'd expect them to be buzzing with tourists and full of quaint tea rooms. But that's not the case—these are working agricultural communities, not showcase villages, fashionable retirement spots, or bases for upscale city commuters. Or perhaps it's that the crush of tourists is drawn to the Alps rather than here.

At the Tourism Information window at the railroad station in Bern or Langnau, or at the Langnau tourist office (Verkehrsverband), you can get a pamphlet listing the Emmental inns. Note that most are closed one day a week: "Rühetag" means day of rest, or closed. The day of closure varies.

The Emmental is quite unlike the high alpine areas in which we've recommended other walking tours. For this reason, we're presenting a

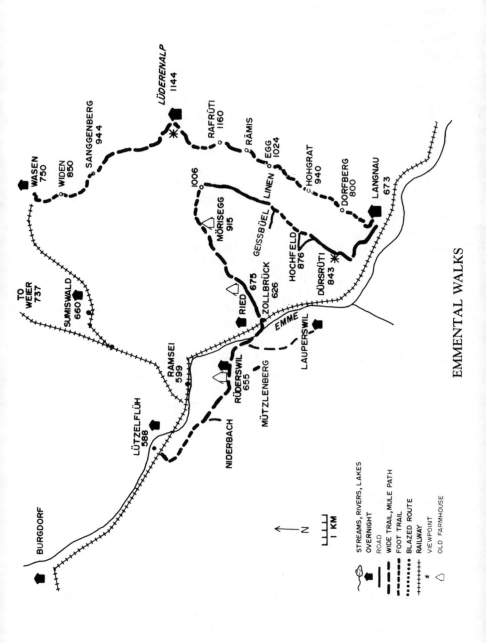

EMMENTAL WALKS

LÜDERENALP 1144

RAFRÜTI 1160

RÄMIS

EGG 1024

HOHGRAT 940

DORFBERG 800

LANGNAU 673

SANGGENBERG 944

WIDEN 850

WASEN 750

1006

MÖRISEGG 915

LINEN

GEISSBÜEL

HOCHFELD 876

DÜRSRÜTI 843

SUMISWALD 660

TO WEIER 737

RIED

ZOLLBRÜCK 626

675

EMME

LAUPERSWIL

RAMSEI 599

RÜDERSWIL 655

MÜTZLENBERG

NIDERBACH

LÜTZELFLÜH 588

BURGDORF

← N

1 KM

STREAMS, RIVERS, LAKES
OVERNIGHT
ROAD
WIDE TRAIL, MULE PATH
FOOT TRAIL
BLAZED ROUTE
RAILWAY
VIEWPOINT
OLD FARMHOUSE

255

walking tour but, at the same time, we suggest that the Emmental is a good region in which you can establish a base and take day hikes. Langnau, a delightful little town in the heart of the Emmental, makes a good base; you can also use the city of Bern. In fact, if you go to Bern during a spell of bad weather in the high mountains, you may find that the weather will allow a walk in the Emmental. It is also possible to arrange to spend a weekend on an Emmental farm. Some English-speaking farm hosts are available, but you will have to write the tourist office or telephone at least a month in advance. If you can speak German, arrangements sometimes can be made in a week or two.

The Emmental is liberally supplied with signposts, placed at each trail and road junction and noting where each intersecting path or road goes and how long it takes to get there. It is impossible to become stranded in the wilderness here because there is no wilderness; you're always near a farm, village, or town. There are no gorges, cliffs, glaciers, or similar hazards. If you decide to change your route and go off in another direction at some signpost, there is no risk. You only have to keep the end point in mind so you can return to an inn, a PTT bus stop, or a railroad station. There are no restaurants outside the villages, so take lunch and beverages with you.

In this section, we present three typical walks and list several other possibilities, but with a map of the region you can easily make your own routes as you ramble through the Emmental. You can buy maps of the region at larger train stations, such as those of Langnau and Burgdorf.

The recommended topographic map for all Emmental walks is Wanderkarte Emmental 1:50000, Schad + Frey, Bern, or Wanderkarte Emmental, Napf, Entlebuch 1:50000, Kummerly + Frey.

1. LÜTZELFLUH TO ZOLLBRÜCK

Rating: easy
Distance one way: 9 km
High point: 776 m
Ascent/descent: 200 m/170 m
Time: 2 hours
Map: page 255

This simple walk takes you through the little village of Rüderswil, one of the prettiest in the Emmental. There are marvelous old houses with superb carvings and painted doors and a handsome old inn, all set amid rolling hills.

Take a train from Bern (change at Burgdorf) or from Langnau to Lützelfluh. From the station there, follow the signposts to Rüderswil. The route initially follows the road to the southeast, away from the river Emme. Almost immediately, the route turns left (east) onto a path that, after 1 kilometer, joins a small road that you follow past an intersection to Niderbach (which is to your right). Continue straight ahead, toward Mützlenberg. At 776 meters you come to a junction and make a sharp turn left (north) for Rüderswil. In Rüderswil be sure to walk along the main street to the west (left) of the church so that you can see the houses. From Rüderswil follow the signposts to the railroad station at Zollbrück. (Lauperswil, just south of Zollbrück, is also pretty and worth a visit.) Both Rüderswil and Zollbrück have inns that range in price from inexpensive to moderate in which you can spend the night.

2. ZOLLBRÜCK TO LANGNAU

Rating: easy
Distance one way: 14 km
High point: 1006 m
Ascent/descent: 450 m/480 m
Time: 3 hours 30 minutes
Map: page 255

Although the following instructions may seem complex, the route is not complicated and every turn is signposted.

From Zollbrück station (626 meters) follow the signposted route up to Ried (675 meters), where you'll find a farm with a superb old Speicher, or storehouse. Continue following the signs and road up to Mörisegg (915 meters). Just above Mörisegg, the route intersects a road that leads to an old Bauernhaus. (Take a short detour to look at the farm.) The trail then ascends to the right (east); follow the signposts to Tällihüttli. At 1006 meters you'll reach an intersection where the trail joins a road to the right (south). Turn right onto the road, following the signs for Hulleren and Äugstmatt.

The road descends to the farms at Hulleren and Äugstmatt—at Äugstmatt you can make a detour to the right to look at one of the older farms at Geissbüel. To keep on the main route, return to Äugstmatt and follow the signposts for Hochfeld and Dürsrüti. Here the route leaves the road, which goes to the houses at Linen (to the left), and becomes a trail. At the intersection for Hochfeld, take the left fork (which is signposted) toward Dürsrüti. A few minutes past this intersection you'll come to a second intersection for Hochfeld, where the route again continues to the left on the road to Dürsrüti. The road continues to descend, and you'll have a good open view of the rolling fields of the Emmental. The road turns almost 90 degrees to the left (southeast) just above the farm buildings of

Typical Emmental haystacks

Dürsrüti and then makes a second 90-degree turn to the left (east). Go through the gate and follow the signs to Langnau. The trail descends as it goes through a stand of trees and emerges onto the streets of Langnau. Follow the signs to the Langnau Bahnhof (railway station). Some of the signs simply show a picture of a railroad locomotive to indicate the station. The inns in Langnau are all within a few streets of the station, and accommodations range from inexpensive to moderate.

3. LANGNAU TO WASEN

Rating: moderate
Distance one way: 18 km
High point: 1160 m
Ascent/descent: 550 m/400 m
Time: 5 hours
Map: page 255

As you walk down the main street of Langnau toward the station, you will pass the signpost, indicating the route to Lüderenalp, near the Migros supermarket. Follow the sign pointing to Dürsrüti. Don't worry about these seemingly complex instructions—every turn is signposted.

At the intersection where you turned left for Dürsrüti, you'll see the route for Lüderenalp, which continues straight ahead to the northeast. The intermediate placemarks that you should look for on the signposts are Dorfberg, Hohgrat, Egg, Rämis, and Rafrüti. About half of the route follows roads, the other half is on trails. A particularly beautiful stretch of trail occurs between Ramis and Rafrüti (1160 meters), and there are splendid views of the Emmental as you walk between Rafrüti and Lüderenalp (1144 meters). At Lüderenalp there's a modern inn with moderate prices.

The pastures around Lüderenalp are the summer pastures of the Emmental, and you will be close to the grazing herds that yield the milk for the famous cheese. The walking time from Langnau to Lüderenalp is about 2 hours 30 minutes to 3 hours.

From Lüderenalp follow the signposted route to Sänggenberg, Widen, and Wasen. The footpath follows the road descending northwest to Sänggenberg (944 meters), then branches off from the road (to the left) about 1 kilometer before Sänggenberg. Wasen, which has inexpensive to moderate accommodations, is at the end of a small train line from which you can ride to either Bern or Langnau by means of connecting trains. The ticket clerk will work out the train change for you, if you so desire.

Woman in traditional costume in the doorway of her house,
built in 1509 in Les Haudères in the Val d'Hérens

Appendices

1. USEFUL ADDRESSES

In Switzerland, the zip code precedes rather than follows the name of the town. The abbreviation "CH" is the European code for Switzerland.

Arolla: Société de Développement, CH-1961 Arolla. (Tel. 027 83 10 83)

Emmental: Verkehrsverband Emmental, Hirschenplatz, CH-3550 Langnau. (Tel. 035 2 34 34)

Evolène: Office de Tourisme, CH-1968 Evolène. (Tel. 027 83 12 35)

Grindelwald: Verkehrsbüro, CH-3818 Grindelwald. (Tel. 036 53 12 12)

Les Haudères: Office de Tourisme, CH-1961 Les Haudères. (Tel. 027 83 10 15)

National Park: Schweizerischer Nationalpark, Nationalparkhaus Zernez, CH-7530 Zernez. (Tel. 082 8 13 78)

Saas-Fee: Verkehrsbüro, CH-3906 Saas-Fee. (Tel. 028 57 14 57)

Scuol (Bad Scuol): Verkehrsverein, CH-7550 Scuol. (Tel. 084 9 94 94)

Swiss National Tourist Offices:
  150 New Michigan Avenue, Chicago, IL 60601, (312) 630-5840.
  608 Fifth Avenue, New York, NY 10020, (212) 757-5944.
  260 Stockton Street, San Francisco, CA 94108, (415) 362-2260.
  P.O. Box 215, Commerce Court West, Toronto, Ontario, M5L 1E8, (416) 868-0584.
  Swiss Centre, New Coventry Street, London, (01) 734 1921.

Zermatt: Verkehrsbüro, CH-3920 Zermatt. (Tel. 028 66 11 81)

2. GLOSSARY

German	French	English

(All nouns are capitalized in German)

Accommodations

German	French	English
Ferienwohnung	appartement de vacances	vacation apartment
Berghotel, Bergasthaus	hotel de montagne	mountain inn
Gasthaus, Gasthof	auberge	inn, hotel*
Garni		hotel with no restaurant, or where meals are optional
Pension	pension	simple hotel
Kurhaus	spa	spa hotel or sanatorium
Hütte	cabane, refuge	hut**
Matratzenlager, Massenlager, Touristenlager	dortoir	dormitory
Bett	lit	bed
Zimmer	chambre	room
Gaststube	salon	public room
W. C.	toilette	toilet
Besetzt	occupé (toilet) complet (hotel)	occupied (full)
Frei	libre	free (available)

*The Italian word for hotel is *albergo*.
**The Romansch word for hut is *chamanna*; the Italian word for hut is *rifugio*.

Equipment

German	French	English
Rucksack	sac à dos	backpack
Steigeisen	crampons	crampons
Seil	corde	rope
Pickel	piolet	ice ax

Food

Lebensmittel	épicerie	grocery store
Supermarkt	supermarché	supermarket
Bäckerei	boulangerie	bakery
Speisekarte	menu	menu

Hiking, Climbing

Wanderweg	chemin pédestre	trail
Pfad, Fussweg	sentier, chemin	footpath
Bergweg	chemin de montagne	more difficult trail
Höhenweg	haute route	high trail
Steinmann	cairn	cairn
Landeskarte, Wanderkarte	carte	map
Blatt	feuille	sheet of map
Höhe	altitude	elevation
M.Ü.M.		meters above sea level
Links	à gauche	left
Rechts	à droite	right
Ober		over
Unter		under
Geradeaus	tout droit	straight ahead
Nord	nord	north
Ost	est	east
West	ouest	west
Sud	sud	south
Stunde, Minuten	heures, minutes	hours, minutes
Gondelbahn	télécabine	gondola lift
Seilbahn	télépherique	cable car
Sesselbahn, Sessellift	télésiège	chairlift
—bahn (suffix)		road or way
Letzte Tahlfahrt	dernière descente	last departure (for the day)

Bergführer	guide de montagne	mountain guide
Bergsteiger	alpiniste	climber
Grüezi, Grüesach	Bonjour	Hello, Hi!

Hazards

Steinschlag	chute de pierres	falling rock
Lawine	avalanche	avalanche
Hilfe	secours	help
Achtung	attention	attention, warning
Gefährlich	dangereux	dangerous
Verboten	défense de...	forbidden (to)

Geographical Features

Wald	forêt, bois	forest, woods
—see (suffix)	lac	lake
—tal (suffix)	val, vallée	valley
Hügel	colline	hill
Horn, Spitze, Berg	mont, pic	mountain, peak
Gipfel	sommet, cime	summit, peak
Kumme		narrow valley, enclosed on three sides
Joch, Sattel	col, selle	saddle, pass,
Furgg, Furka		notch
Bach	ruisseau	stream
Brücke	pont	bridge
Gletscher	glacier	glacier
Firn	névé	field of old snow
Grat	arête	ridge
Geröllhalde	éboulis	scree, talus
Stausee	réservoir	reservoir
Staudamm	barrage	dam

Travel

Zug	train	train
Bahnhof	gare	railroad station
Postauto	car postale	post office bus
Auskunft	renseignement	information
Gepäck	bagages	sending luggage ahead
Handegepäck	bagages à main	small luggage
Annahme	expédition	sending luggage off
Ausgabe	livraison	picking up luggage
Abfahrt	Départ	departures
Ankunft	Arrivée	arrivals
Kursbuch	Indicateur Officiel	Official timetable
Regionalfahrplan	Horaire régional	Regional timetable
Verkehrsbüro, Verkehrsverband, Verkehrsverein	bureau de tourisme	tourist office

Weather

Wetter Prognose, Bericht	météo, prévision de temps	weather forecast
Warm	chaud	warm, hot
Kühl	frais, froid	cool, cold
Sonnig	beau temps, du soleil	sunny
bedeckt, bewölkt	nuageux	cloudy
Stark bewölkt	très nuageux	totally overcast
Nebel	brouillard	fog, mist
Wind	vent	wind
Mässiger Wind	vent modéré	light or moderate wind
Schauer, Regenschauer	pluie	showers, rain
Niederschläge	pluie à verse	heavy rain
Gewitter	orage	thunderstorm

Wechselhaft	temps variable	changing, changeable weather
Föhn	fohn	warm, dry wind
Schnee	neige	snow
Null grad grenze		altitude at which it's 0° Centigrade

3. METRIC CONVERSIONS

Meters	Feet
100	328
300	984
500	1640
1000	3280
1500	4920
2000	6560
2500	8200
3000	9840
3500	11,480
4000	13,120

kilometers	miles
0.5	0.3
1.0	0.6
1.6	1.0
2.0	1.3
5.0	3.1
8.0	5.0

Centigrade	Fahrenheit
0	32
10	50
20	68
30	84

	Meters	Feet
Matterhorn	4478	14,691
Jungfrau	4158	13,642
Eiger	3970	13,025
Monte Rosa	4634	15,203
Dom	4545	14,911
Täschhorn	4490	14,731
Zinalrothorn	4221	13,848

Index

INDEX